DIGITAL SENSE

THE **COMMON SENSE APPROACH** TO **EFFECTIVELY BLENDING SOCIAL BUSINESS STRATEGY, MARKETING TECHNOLOGY,** AND **CUSTOMER EXPERIENCE**

TRAVIS **WRIGHT** | CHRIS J. **SNOOK**

WILEY

"To both of my true loves, Brianne and Beckett. You ground me and inspire me daily to be more than I was yesterday, and you patiently share me with the business world, which is my other true love. I dedicate this book, and all the blood and sweat that I put into it, to you."

—Chris J. Snook

"To my two not-so-little ones, Jharek and Liliana. All that I do is because of both of you. Much love to you and your mom, Mari. Thanks for allowing me to be a business dude who travels around and works on all of these crazy projects. Hopefully I've taught you a strong work ethic, a true curious love of learning, and a kind, helpful approach to human interaction; and hopefully you always keep your playful nature. Keep smiling, laughing, and loving. I'll love you forever, throughout all space and time. May God and the Universe bless you, always."

—Travis Wright

CONTENTS

ACKNOWLEDGMENTS

We owe so many wise and loving people thanks for the completion of this project and wish to acknowledge them below.

Thanks to Brian Solis for your friendship and your willingness to support our efforts with your amazing foreword.

Thanks to our awesome team at Wiley Business, which begins with our editors, Lia Ottaviano, Lauren Freestone, and Pete Gaughan, and the entire design and development team, who helped us come up with the awesome cover and clean layout.

Thanks to all of our peers, fellow thought leaders, and mentors (alive and dead) who have influenced us and the content of this book with your wisdom. You all inspire us to be lifelong learners and ever-more curious with each waking day. Love you all! Napoleon Hill, W. Clement Stone, Joseph Murphy, Charles Haanel, Maxwell Maltz, Elon Musk, Sinan Kanatsiz and the entire Internet Marketing Association family, Danny DeMichele, Charlene Li, Brian Solis, Gerd Leonhard, Peter Diamandis, Tony Robbins, John Lennon, George Carlin, Nikola Tesla, Eckhart Tolle, Steve Jobs, Woz, Elon Musk, Mark Zuckerberg, John Battelle, Michael Arrington, Bob Proctor, Adam Yauch, Peter Drucker, Steven Levy, Marc Andreessen, Jay Adelson, Randi Zuckerberg, Biz Stone, Jeff Clavier, Chris Pulley, Adrienne Goss, Dan Loiacano, Josh Eliseuson, Mia Dand, Kare Anderson, Bill Murray, Jonathan Shaun, Dirk Hacker, Joel Comm, Lori Ruff, Peter Kay, Wendy Sweetmore-Hinton, Bryan Kramer, Bernie Borges, Julio Viskovich, Roland Smart, Tristan Bishop, Zoya Fallah, Allen Kelly, Mike O'Neil, Mohit Maheshwari, Jason Ary, Dave Fluegge, Ramsey Mohsen, Zena Weist, Koka Sexton, Jon Ferrara, Jason Miller, Danny Sullivan, Michelle Robbins, Elisabeth Osmeloski, Chris Sherman, Vala Afshar, Matt Heinz, Didier Bonnet, Chris Elwell, Sean Moriarty, Matt McGee, Brett Tabke, Paul Graham, Kelsey Jones, Brent Csutoras, Kevin Rose, Anil Dash, Arnold Aranez, Kinmun "Mr. Brown" Lee, Hillel Fudd, Walter H. Jennings & Ren

Zhengfei of Huawei, Jeremiah Owyang, Pamela Parker, AJ Wilcox, Jason Falls, Kevin Mullett, Kristi Hagen, Casey Markee, Stephen Mahaney, Alan Bleiweiss, Rand Fishkin, Tim Ash, Bryan Eisenberg, Jeffrey Eisenberg, Shelly Kramer, John Jantsch, Blake Miller, Brian Clark, Liz Strauss, Dan Zarrella, Michelle D'Attilio, Shawn Elledge, Stewart Rogers, Robert Scoble, Jennifer Wong, Jeffrey Hazlett, John Swartz, Andre Bourque, John Rampton, Dave McClure, Sarah Austin, Bill Hicks, Dennis Yu, Tiffany DiPanni, Mike 'Bubbles' Smith, Gary Langston, Carol Rydell, Toby Evans, Terence McKenna, Tim Ferriss, Maria Lucent, Alister Ku, Antonia Silas, Chris Kovac, Mother Earth, God, the Universe, Kyle Moody and Lisa Bowman of Bowman PR, Rick Astley, Mike Ramsey, Jean Grey, Alex Grey, Alex Scoble, Alex Petrides, Dr. Gary Jones, Joey Knight, Steve Moser, Dave Kinison, Keith Leff, Mitch Hedberg, Nicole Schreiber, Lazlo, Randy "Macho Man" Savage, Bruce Lee, Chuck Norris, Tim Curtis, Rhonda Shantz, Anabella Watson, Hugh MacLeod, Ian McCleary, Zeina Khodr, Melina Gouveia, Jeremy Knibbs, Yen Japney, Pam Kozelka, Leslie Carruthers, Drew Hendricks, Inspector Gadget, Doc Brown, Carrie Royce, Pam Hedger, Alan Mundey, Larry Binggeli, Mari Smith, Reid Hoffman, Joe Chernov, Sarah Lacey, Kara Swisher, Chris Heuer, Peter Kim, Seth Godin, Malcolm Gladwell, Scott Brinker, Anita Brearton & Sheryl Schultz of CabinetM, Lisa Qualls, Simon Kuo, Kristi Colvin, Allen Gannett, Brett Glass, Jill Rosen, Waldo, Dominique O'Hara, Karl Geisler, Mayur Gupta, Mike 'Jortsy' Gelphman, Gary Vaynerchuk, Eric Mitchell, Corey Ganzman, Tamar Weinberg, James Hanusa, Alison Raby, Allison Paige Presley, Soren Gordhamer, David Berkowitz, David Armano, Jasmin Brand, Avinash Kaushik, Chris Brogan, Jeff Scult, Akhil Anumolu, Imran Khan, Mary Meeker, Jason Calacanis, George Lucas, Danuska Bartak, Aaron Swartz, Alexis Ohanian, Sarah Evans, Chris Penn, Scott Stratten, Mark Abay, Mathew Sweezey, Shawn Goodin, Marty McDonald, Eric Granell, Phil Kloster, Clay Wendler, Clark Hunt, Andrew & Elizabeth Davis, Jill Rowley, Joe Cox, Jason Elm, Evel Knievel, Alex Ortiz, Joe Pulizzi, Jay Baer, Robert Rose, Ted Rubin, Ann Handley, David Meerman Scott, Marshall Kirkpatrick, Bruce Clay, Virginia Nussey, Akvile Harlow, Jeff Jarvis, Mitch Joel, Lee Odden, Steve Rubel, Pete Cashmore, Dharmesh Shah, Sujan Patel, Neil Patel, Ryan Lefebvre, Focus Seminars of KC, Fauna Solomon, Aseem Badshah, Steve Rayson, Tim O'Reilly, Jack Dorsey, Ewing Kauffman, Lance Sargent, Bryan Smith, Richard Sargent, Brian Ryerson, Todd Nutter, Jeffrey Pruitt, Tony Quiroz, Anna Hrach, Oliver Tani, Mike Barbeau, Jen Walsh,

Dayton Moore, Jeff Gibbard, Keisha Malivert, Sean Rice, Alyssa Yatabe, Greg Poinar, Gavin Francis, Oprah Winfrey, Robert Wallace, Jeremy Hudgens, Jeanniey Mullen, Whitney Parker Mitchell, Chris Zakharoff, Robert Moseley IV, Dan Brady, Josh Goodwin, Josh Manion, Dan Dal Degan, Jessica Tyner, Chris Wojcik, Jeanne Bliss, Shawn Barrieau, Josh Denne, Jessica Alba, and all of our friends, coworkers, fans, and social media followers. Much love and respect to every one of you. Thank you for inspiring us!

Big thanks to Wright/Hayden/Beshore/Brower family peoples. Thanks for helping Travis to become the inquisitive solution finder he is today. His love of learning, experimenting, and laughing came directly from interactions with you, Cathy Wright, Elmer Wright, Ken Brower, Rebecca Brower, Barbara Wright, Gene Hayden, Jeff Hayden, Mark Hayden, Mabel Beshore, Michael Beshore, Rachel Gamble, Jamie Gamble, Hank and Olivia Lamlech, Sarah Brower, and William Wright.

As for those in the Snook/Sorg clan, thank you for allowing Chris to be the abnormally curious and brave risk taker that he is. It is because of your solid foundation and knowing that he will be loved through failure and success alike that he has been able to repeatedly bloom where planted. Chet Snook, Ginny Snook, Palook and Sarge Snook, Gus and Barb Leconte, Corrie Snook Albrecht, Bob Albrecht, Mike Sorg, Karen Sorg, Melisa Gleason, Joe Gleason. *"Hard work defines us, character separates us, and love is our legacy!"*

And a special thanks to Hai Chen, as Travis and Chris never would have met if it wasn't for you, buddy!

FOREWORD

You are not a digital marketer . . . at least not yet.

I want to use this foreword to officially warn you. You're in for a delightful experience. Normally books that teach you so much aren't supposed to be this fun to read. But that's Travis and Chris for you. They not only share their real-world experiences in shaping the future of digital, they do so in an engaging and entertaining way that keeps you laughing *and* learning.

Now, with that said, let's get to work.

We live in an era of digital Darwinism, a time when technology and society evolve. The question is, how are you—or how are you not—evolving to keep up with change? It's not an easy question to answer.

There's an illusion that makes us believe that just because we are investing in new technologies and strategies, that we are ahead of the curve . . . that we're leading the way to the future of digital transformation because we use the same networks or apps as customers. But that doesn't make you a digital marketer. A digital marketer is someone who understands that, to engage someone digitally, it must be done in a meaningful, personalized and contextually + culturally relevant manner. Digital marketers understand the dynamics of online sites, communities, and apps individually, not in the aggregate; and more so, they understand the human on the other side of the screen based on preferences, behaviors, values, intents, lifestyles, aspirations, and so on. As such, digital is a means to reach a different breed of customers, one who's connected, informed, empowered, demanding, elusive, a bit narcissistic, and definitely in control of their online experiences.

Digital marketers, in the very least, are digitally literate and also empathetic, appreciating the extent of how people have changed and continue to do so. Only then can they design strategies, messages, content, and such that break the old chains and confines of traditional marketing and abolish the dated checklist and metric system many so-called digital, social, and mobile marketers rely upon today.

There's a reason you are reading this. It might be the same reason I wrote this. We're ready to sharpen our digital sense so we learn and, more important, unlearn, to grow and lead. In its purest form, that's digital "sense." It's our ability to perceive outside inputs and assess new horizons and states that are driving the digital economy better than we do now. But it's also more than that. All of this is designed to help you be more in tune than your peers in grasping the gravity of change and do the things that put you ahead of your competition. And more so, you're learning how to step outside of what you think your role is in marketing to actually lead your organization into a digital-first era. This is a story that's equally about changing the future of marketing as it is a story of personal transformation.

The other reason I believe you're reading this is because you possess something that others in your organization do not . . . the ability to see what others can't; and as such, you're then willing to do what others won't. We can't do any of this alone. And, this is why you are part of a special group of people who share your passion for knowledge, who look for support from one another to blaze new trails, and who reassure one another in times of need.

One of the greatest challenges we all face is the difficulty in getting others to recognize the importance of digital when they don't personally live a digital lifestyle. As such, it's impossible to feel the importance of digital in the future of brand and customer experience. Without empathy and belief, you will never have the support you need.

And, that's really the heart of the matter. Most executives don't live the brand the way customers do, yet they're responsible for driving business objectives and managing resources to achieve them. If you're waiting for someone to tell you what to do next, you're on the wrong side of innovation. That's why we are here together right now. We're not waiting . . . we're leading the way.

Read the book. Make a plan. Let's go . . .

Observe: See the world differently without your personal filters. See people for their differences and let it all inspire you.

Visualize: Define where it is you need to go versus where you are and what success looks like both now and over time.

Act: Start learning and unlearning the things necessary to achieve your milestones and also help bring others on the path to transformation.

Earn: You are more than a marketer, you are a change maker; and as such, you will write the future of marketing as you evolve and earn the support and accolades you deserve.

Your partner in change,
Brian Solis, provocateur, futurist, believer in new possibilities
@briansolis
www.briansolis.com

PREFACE
A TALE OF TWO "TWEETIES"

On September 9, 2012, the Kansas City Chiefs lost to the Atlanta Falcons by a score of 40 to 24. The next evening, Travis was chatting with his buddy since fifth grade, Bryan, and they were complaining about how the Chiefs were approximately $30 million under the salary cap for the fifth year in a row.

Travis said, "You mean to tell me the Kansas City Chiefs have been approximately $100–$130 million dollars under the salary cap in the last five years? OMG, I'm sooo tweeting that."

So he sent this one tweet: "I'm not much of a @KCChiefs fan anymore. Clark Hunt's yearly [$]30m under the [salary] cap is bullshit. Greedy bastard owners can F.O. cc @nfl"[1]

Figure P.1 "The Tweet Heard 'Round the World"

This was not a friendly tweet, Travis understands that. He was angry, as a fan, and decided to tweet about it. It was one glorious tweet from one gloriously disgruntled fan. It was only one rude tweet, not a barrage of tweets.

As you'll soon find out from this book, both Travis and Chris tackle the consequential and inconsequential, in life and in business, with strong opinions and tremendous fervor, with a balance of hilarity and humility, that comes from an insatiable thirst for continued learning and teaching.

After Travis complained about the salary cap on Twitter, he was over it. He sent that one tweet and went on his merry way. It wasn't until the next day at lunch that he looked through his Twitter direct messages. It was only then that he noticed the tweet from the Chiefs. He nearly choked on his delicious Chipotle burrito! Travis thought about it for a few minutes, and then took a screencap of the direct message, as shown in Figure P.2. It said, "Would help if you had your facts straight. Your choice to be a fan. cc get a clue."

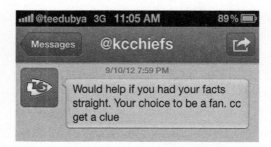

Figure P.2   The Tweet Response with No Digital Sense

The Chiefs had sent this tweet just three minutes after Travis sent his rude, disgruntled tweet. Somebody from the Chiefs' social media team immediately tweeted to Travis, while in an emotional state, from the Chiefs' official Twitter handle, @kcchiefs. Note: the Chiefs switched their official Twitter handle to @chiefs in 2016.

The Chiefs' social media manager didn't seem to have much "digital sense." That person clearly gave zero f's at that time. It was not a good common sense approach to attack Travis. In fact, Travis wasn't even that angry. He was just sending out a bit of a rant regarding his displeasure with how the Chiefs were being cheap and spending significantly less than the salary cap.

Jay Baer recently published a great book on this subject called *Hug Your Haters.*[2] The Chiefs' social media team should have tried to defuse the situation, not fuel the flame. The first indicator that it would be wise to hug their hater was that at the time, Travis's account had more Twitter followers than the Chiefs'.

 Digital Bit: This is one reason why organizations should have a social media governance policy in place for how to respond (or prioritize) tweets such as his.

(Look for more Digital Bits, free templates, and resource downloads throughout the book.)

After seeing the emotionally charged response to his tweet, Travis did what any social media savvy person would do, who has just had a crummy customer experience; he took the screencap of the Chief's' message and tweeted it out to his followers.

This is where the social s#%t-storm started.

 Digital Bit: If you send a private message via Twitter or Snapchat, it's not necessarily private. Anyone can screenshot anything.

Travis replied to the private, direct message by sending out this tweet: "It's good to know the @kcchiefs social media is ran [sic] by immature teen-agers. Fact. Hunt hoards salary cap $$$. #KC" (Figure P.3).

Whoever responded to Travis's tweet from the Chiefs' Twitter handle lacked both common sense and digital sense. He made a hasty assumption that it was appropriate to defend the Chiefs in private via direct message, indicating the absence of a social media governance policy. He lacked or ignored any protocol that would enable him to respond in real-time, pro-actively, to Travis' public complaint in a way that allowed for a productive dialogue. He also failed to acknowledge that in a world of noise, Travis's

Figure P.3

initial tweet was far less damaging to the Chiefs' image than was the tweet storm that followed.

Look at the data: the first tweet had 15 retweets; the follow-up had more than 3,200!

The Chiefs' staffer didn't have, or ignored, any protocol that would enable responding in real time to this public fan rant in a way that could allow for a proactive dialogue. They also forgot that in a world of noise, his initial tweet was far less damaging than the tweet storm that followed. They had no social media governance policy in place to make a decision as to whether to respond at all, and it had big consequences.

What did the social media manager have to gain by being rude back to a rude fan? Nothing except the brief satisfaction of telling someone off. You can do that, all day long, on a personal account. However, if you do that on a corporate branded account, get ready for some backlash.

Keep in mind, in the beginning, Travis was just complaining. People bitch about their sports teams ALL. THE. TIME. This was nothing out of the ordinary. Immediately after Travis publicly replied to the Chiefs' tweet, all hell broke loose. He received a bunch of responses (Figure P.4).

Figure P.4 This Is One of the First Recorded Selfies by Travis Wright in 2012

"TW, did the Chiefs actually send you that?" —name removed
"Are you serious, bro? The Chiefs said that?" —name removed

Tweets started flying back and forth asking him questions about the situation. Many of them had the @KCChiefs twitter handle included. Even some local Kansas City sportscasters started asking him, "Hey @teedubya, is this real? Did the Chiefs really tweet that to you?" The response: yes. And then the Chiefs blocked @teedubya on Twitter.

When they blocked Travis, he could no longer see their public tweets, and any private tweets they had between them disappeared. Now that made him angry.

 DIGITAL BIT: You don't want to add fuel to the fire on social media without a clear understanding of the unintended consequences that may ensue. Try to de-escalate or do nothing at all.

After being blocked from his beloved team on Twitter, Travis decided to teach them a lesson for their lack of digital sense. The first thing that Travis did was go to Reddit.com, and to the NFL subreddit, Reddit.com/r/nfl, and he posted his rant.

*@KCChiefs Twitter Account, tells fan (Me) to Get a
Clue and stop being a fan. Submitted September 11,
2012 * by teedubya*

"The KC Chiefs just blocked me on Twitter @teedubya. Last night,
I tweeted that for the 4th year in a row, the Chiefs are at the bottom
of salary cap spending and that the owner, Clark Hunt, is hoarding
cap dollars. The Chiefs commitment to mediocrity has made me not
care much about being a fan . . .

1. My first tweet to them (see Figure P.2).

2. They responded with this DM (see Figure P.3).

3. I responded that it is good to know that the KC Chiefs have an
   immature teenager running their social media.

4. Then they blocked my account.

   I, as a fan for my whole life of nearly 40 years, who has never
   seen the Chiefs in a Superbowl; nor have I seen a playoff win in
   nearly 20 years; nor have I seen a QB drafted [EDIT: in the first
   round] in the last 27 years. Chiefs fans have a right to be pissed.

   The Kansas City Chiefs have no right to be pissy toward the
   fans. We are the ones paying for their salaries. Shame on you,
   Chiefs. Oh, and congrats on 50 years of being in KC. 10 years
   of greatness, followed by 40 years of pathetic profiteering. Clark
   Hunt sits in Dallas siphoning Kansas City dollars."

Keep in mind the customer's (fan) perspective as context for this situation. The Chiefs had not drafted a quarterback since 1983, and it was 2012!
The Chiefs hadn't won a playoff game since 1993. They were in the middle
of a nearly 20-year playoff-win-drought. The Chiefs lost seven playoff games
in a row, and they were spending millions below the salary cap.

Early in the 2012 season, when Travis sent the tweet, the announced
amount under the cap was $26.6 million; it was later adjusted to $16.1
million. In 2011, when there was no salary cap or salary floor, the Chiefs

spent the least in player salaries. Beginning in 2013, teams had to spend at least 89 percent of the cap or be subject to penalties.[3,4]

The NFL football is serious business to paying fans in America. And being under the salary cap for multiple years in a row had angered many Kansas City Chiefs fans.

The rant made the front page of Reddit. Some readers were mad at the Chiefs. Some were mad at Travis, calling him many different colorful terms. The story began to go viral because of this activity.

Once it made the front page of Reddit, the social media shit-storm gained strength and started being referenced on big news sites and the local media.

One local disc jockey in Kansas City named Lazlo started going off about the situation on his broadcast that day.

Lazlo has a show called *The Church of Lazlo* in the afternoon in the Kansas City market. He was yelling about how people behind their computer screens are keyboard warriors. How weak and ridiculous they are! Lazlo (on air) said, (paraphrasing)

> "The Internet trolls would never talk like that in public, like they do on the Internet! That ASSCLOWN on Reddit, who was talking about the Kansas City Chiefs rude tweet today, Oh! they told him to get a clue? Boo hoo! Big freaking deal!"

One of TW's buddies called him up and said, "Hey Travis, Lazlo's talking about you and your Reddit post and the Chiefs deal. You should call into the station and chat with him."

So, Travis did. He couldn't get through the phone line, so he sent a text to the *Church of Lazlo* show saying, "Hey this is Travis Wright @teedubya, the guy who got the tweet from the Chiefs, and if you want to have a conversation, let's do it."

Lazlo called Travis, and immediately they were on air. In the digital world of media today, it is all about attention and trust, and Lazlo couldn't pass up the chance to hype the story for his show's gain. Lazlo was chomping at the bit to destroy an Internet troll, live and on air. At first, he was echoing some comments from some Redditors, trying to make Travis look like a whiny idiot. It was clear that he had an angsty attitude about keyboard warriors and disdain for Internet trolls, who are always louder and braver behind a keyboard. Little did Lazlo know that Travis is that loud in real life, too.

On air, Travis stated many of the reasons why KC Chiefs fans should be fed up with the Kansas City Chiefs at that point. He mentioned a litany of strategic, management, and cultural errors that the organization had made, and while they were having this conversation, he actually started converting Lazlo to his line of thinking.

Lazlo recanted, acknowledging how Travis was right, how it had been since 1983 that the Chiefs have drafted a first-round quarterback! The Chiefs hadn't won a playoff game since Joe Montana was the Chiefs QB. Maybe the Chiefs were bad because they weren't spending enough on salaries? Why do the Chiefs not let the former players and alumni come to Arrowhead? Why are they hoarding salary cap dollars?"

Nobody changes Lazlo's opinion, yet on that day, Travis did with his own well-informed and impassioned one.

After Reddit and Lazlo, Travis was contacted by local TV stations to do interviews about the scenario. It made Yahoo!'s front page. *USA Today* talked about it. Mashable wrote about it. There was even a segment on it on ESPN .com.[5]

When you have digital sense, you realize that page views are an economic driver that has forever bastardized traditional and nontraditional journalism and media, in potentially irreparable ways. The 2016 election debacle in the United States proved this more than any other single event in recent history.

Travis never expected the Chiefs to respond to him and tell him to get a clue. If you look at the comments of any YouTube video on the Web, you see people saying way more rude, and sometimes disrespectful or disgusting, things about artists or brands than TW was saying to the Chiefs. And most of these comments are never replied to by the brand.

As a fan, Travis had been to more than 100 games at Arrowhead Stadium. He was a loyal paying customer (100 games ain't cheap). A passionate advocate for Kansas City sports teams, he had been to every crushing home playoff loss the Chiefs had had since 1986. Them telling him that "it's his choice to be a fan and get a clue" just wasn't good digital sense. Of course it was his choice. It was also his choice and his right to vent his displeasure, as any customer can, when the product they support fails to deliver.

Shortly after the 2012 NFL season, Travis spoke at the SMX Social Media Conference in Las Vegas. After he shared the story about the Chiefs, a half dozen other social media directors and managers of other sports teams approached him. They all stated that the day after the Chiefs told him to get a clue, every one of those six sports teams had a meeting. The all told their social media managers to not be rude to their fans and they began to institute formal governance around their branded accounts on social media channels.

 Digital Bit: Don't feed the trolls. (Also don't feed the Zombies, which you will read about in Chapter 2.)

The "Save Our Chiefs" Movement

The situation with the Chiefs continued to gain momentum. The wave of public disgruntlement grew toward the Chiefs almost daily, and the compounding losses in future weeks did nothing to quell the rage. A couple of more losses into the season and people from all over began to reach out to TW about doing something bigger.

ChiefsPlanet.com had been around since 2000, before Internet 2.0, and was one of the few remaining independent message boards about the Chiefs. It was founded in August 2000 after a group of core users were fed up with the Kansas City Star message board moderators. After a negative experience with moderators at the KC Star happened in 2000, they started their own private community to commiserate with fellow Chiefs fans. Travis has been a card carrying member since 2003.

Message forums are a form of social media organized around communities of common interests. As a participant, you can really get to know people, over time, through the medium. There had been several ChiefsPlanet in-person bashes and tailgating events at Arrowhead with members of this forum over many seasons. It remains a great community, that commiserates over the 16 years of Chiefs futility. ChiefsPlanet is still going strong today.

A couple of weeks after the initial tweet shit-storm, Travis was perusing ChiefsPlanet and one of its users, Eric Granell, created a thread that said "Hey we're thinking about flying banners over Arrowhead Stadium before each Chiefs game. What do you think of this idea?" In another thread, Marty McDonald was setting up a Facebook page and a Twitter page for something he coined *Save Our Chiefs.*[6] As they were all talking virtually on the thread, it was decided to merge efforts. Save Our Chiefs was born after the fourth game of the 2012 season.

With Travis being the disgruntled Twitter "cc get a clue" guy, he wasn't about to be on the forefront of this movement. However, he was able to give key strategic advice and help grow their social media channels rapidly. A fundraiser was created on ChiefsPlanet for airplane banners to fly over Arrowhead. When it was all said and done, they had crowdfunded almost $6,500 to have airplanes fly a banner over the home stadium and parking lot before each game. Once the banner was funded, Travis reached out to his local media contacts, who had interviewed him for the Chiefs Twitter story. He relayed the news back to the members at ChiefsPlanet.

> Okay, I talked with Fox 4 and told them "ChiefsPlanet is a 12-year-old forum (at the time) for Chiefs fans from all over the world . . . and the banner idea got funded and organized here. Other groups of Chiefs fans are voicing their displeasure with sites popping up like SaveOurChiefs.com and many other Facebook groups. People are becoming very, very vocal in this social age, and expressing their choice to be a fan or not. LOL. They said they are doing a video news story on it, probably the 10 PM tonight or tomorrow night . . . and most likely an accompanying story on their web-site, that will have the video on it."

WE DESERVE BETTER! FIRE PIOLI! BENCH CASSEL! the first banner said.

The local KC news outlets feasted on that development. Within two weeks, @SaveOurChiefs had almost 80,000 followers on their Twitter account. For perspective, that was more than the seating capacity (76,416) of Arrowhead Stadium where the Chiefs play. The perception of having nearly 100,000 followers on Twitter freaked out the Kansas City media. It was

2012. New stations were still struggling to figure out how to leverage Twitter. They ate it up. They were like, "Oh My God! The Save Our Chiefs movement (Figure P.5) already has 100,000 followers and over 20,000 Facebook fans!

Figure P.5 The Save Our Chiefs Facebook Page

The media freak-out enabled greater visibility. Eric and Marty were being interviewed on sports radio stations all over the nation, talking about what's going on with *Save Our Chiefs*.

Travis penned a letter and sent it to the CEO of the Chiefs, Clark Hunt, and the general manager, Scott Pioli, stating what the plan was and that the intended outcome was to see Pioli get his walking papers. Using e-mail technology called Yesware, he was able to track all opens for that e-mail. His e-mail never got a response from the Chiefs; however, it was opened up 49 times on 27 devices in 13 different cities. The movement definitely had the Chiefs' attention.

The group even worked out a deal with a local sporting goods company, Sports Nutz, and created custom black hoodies that said, "Save Our Chiefs Blackout-Arrowhead November 18th, 2012. (Figure P.6)"

On November 18, 2012, roughly 50 percent of the fans were wearing black on that game vs. the Bengals. *Save Our Chiefs* literally blacked out the *Guinness Book of World Records* for "Loudest Stadium in the World."[7]

The group had other, more positive community events planned as well, like a food drive. They were partnering with a local food bank on a canned-food donation campaign called "Can Pioli." Phil Kloster, CEO of Edgewood

Figure P.6 Arrowhead Stadium, November 18, 2012, During the #blackout

Construction in KC with the username "Phobia" on the ChiefsPlanet forum, came up with that one.

However, in a parallel narrative, that was the week that a linebacker of the Chiefs, Jovan Belcher, committed a double homicide-suicide. Which was absolutely tragic and brought everyone back to reality about what really mattered in life. Out of respect for all parties involved, the entire group ceased all of the Save Our Chiefs activities until the last two weeks of the season.

The overall statistics from the movement were impressive: 41,545 mentions of Save Our Chiefs, with 359 news articles written about it, 160 blog posts about the movement, and 113 mentions (Figure P.7) on various message forums.

At the end of the 2012 season, the Chiefs ended up with two wins and 14 losses. On the Monday following the last game of the season, Clark Hunt, the owner of the Kansas City Chiefs, went after the best candidate possible and hired Andy Reid as coach. He also hired John Dorsey from the Green

Figure P.7 The Social Media Mentions of #saveourchiefs after the @teedubya @kcchiefs Firestorm

Bay Packers front office as his new general manager. Former GM Scott Pioli and the Chiefs' head coach, Romeo Crennel, and the coaching staff were fired and a new regime began. The Chiefs were saved! For fans, it was long overdue justice. Travis immediately sent Clark Hunt, the CEO of the Chiefs, a note of thanks.

> Mr. Hunt,
>
> Thank you. You've proven yourself to be extremely tenacious in getting your man, Andy Reid. I'll never call you cheap again. You've displayed balls of steel, went above and beyond, and as a result KC fans are rejoicing, today, at your awesomeness. I put on a Chiefs jersey for the first time since preseason, just now. It feels good to have our Chiefs back from Pioli and in the hands of Andy Reid and John Dorsey.
>
> I love the Chiefs and am grateful that we have an owner who cares. Could I be unblocked from the @kcchiefs twitter now? Thanks again for saving our Chiefs, Mr. Hunt. You're a badass. Sincerely, Travis Wright @teedubya

The day that Scott Pioli was fired, the Chiefs unblocked @teedubya and the Chiefs ticket department connected with Travis and offered him half-price season tickets for the 2013 season. He gladly accepted them, and has continued to be a die-hard fan.

What started, earlier in the year, with a disgruntled guy tweeting a forgettable tweet to the Chiefs after a loss had snowballed into this major movement all because one individual on the Chiefs' social media team did not use digital sense. Save Our Chiefs was a brilliant social media experience in that it showed how people can impact change when they handle it right. The idea was born from frustration: Create a social media experience to allow fans with similar thoughts a place to engage and interact with. Our movement became a cornerstone of daily life for Chiefs fans: we were talked about on multiple radio stations and local TV, and it drew national attention from NFL.com, ESPN.com, even the *New York Times*.

The fallout from this effort was amazing: the Chiefs' organization had a digital transformation. They listened to their biggest customer, the fan base. Sure, they fired their GM and head coach, and they cut ties with an over-priced sloth of a quarterback (we still relish in helping accomplish that), but that wasn't the amazing thing. The Kansas City Chiefs' organization physically and mentally shifted into a fan-friendly culture.

They rolled out "Chiefs Kingdom," which serves as a universal rally cry to bring all fans back together. They were more positive in social interactions. They stopped banning people and started to listen, engage, and learn. In short form, it proved brands are capable of change.

From a digital media perspective, the main takeaway here should be this: by creating experiences and publishing content that is engaging as well as entertaining, brands and marketers will build relationships with prospects and cement foundational relationships with brand loyalists.

"As someone who has been involved in digital media and marketing since the late '90s, I don't think people set out to be marketed at in the social channel. Rather, you have to apply some 'marketing psychology' to your message through various types of engagement," says Marty McDonald, coconspirator of Save Our Chiefs and senior director of Strategic Development and Sales at G/O Digital. "Simply stated, your prospects and customers simply want to be a great guest at the dinner table of your brand. Treat them that way and they'll embrace your brand."

Fast forward to January 2016, the Chiefs 23-year playoff futility ended, when they won their first playoff game since 1993. Saved indeed.

Optus in Australia

In November 2014, Travis was traveling to Australia for the first time to speak at Ashton Media's conference, the Data Strategy Symposium, north of Sydney in an area known for its wine, Hunter's Valley. It's a great conference put on by Mark Abay and his Ashton team.[8]

Before travelling, Travis sent out a tweet to his friend @ChrisBrinkworth asking if T-Mobile had service there, as he was feeling a bit unprepared for

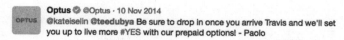

Figure P.8

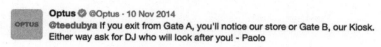

Figure P.9

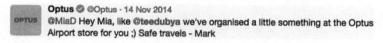

Figure P.10

international travel and need to figure out his SIM card situation. The local phone carrier, Optus, was doing some social listening and tuned into the conversation. Paolo from @optus (Figures P.8, P.9, and P.10) sent a couple of tweets to Travis, instructing him to drop by once he arrived in Sydney and they could set him up with their prepaid options.[9]

"Sweet," Travis replied. "Nicely done. Consider this a conversion, Paolo." He then recommended that Optus connect with @MiaD, my former boss at Symantec, who was also speaking at the same conference.

Well, when Travis arrived in Sydney, he saw the Optus store and was ready to buy a SIM card for the trip. However, when Travis walked up to the store, an Optus employee, Jordan Zac, said, "Hello, Travis. Welcome to Australia. We've been waiting for you."

"What?!" Travis was blown away (Figure P.11) by the customer service already. But wait, it gets better. Jordan handed Travis a huge Optus bag, and inside it were some Australian items, such as a six-pack of Victorian Bitter Beer, some flip-flops, some delicious Tim-Tam cookies, some Vegemite so he could make a sandwich, some other gadgets and gizmos and, best of all, a free 4G hotspot with 10 GB of free data for the trip.

In case you were wondering if they had a system in place to serve others this way, they gave Mia Dand a similar experience (Figure P.12).

78 Travis Wright ✔ @teedubya · 14 Nov 2014
Wow. @Optus is the coolest carrier ever. Damn they gave me the hookup.
Australia is the friendliest country ever.

Figure P.11 Optus Australia

 61 Mia Dand @MiaD · 10 Nov 2014
These socially savvy Aussie biz are blowing me away :-) @teedubya @Optus cc:
@daveando

Figure P.12

Optus gave Travis the free hotspot since Apple and T-Mobile wouldn't unlock his iPhone 5S, so they went the extra, extra mile and hooked him up. Talk about digital sense. Travis has been back to Australia twice since then, and guess which phone carrier he uses?

The moral of these two stories is that digital sense goes both ways. It can infuriate a customer or inspire them. It is also possible to gain real momentum out of a major commitment to redeem your organization when you have failed to have digital sense in the past.

The Genesis of This Book

What you have in your hands right now is a book that will teach you how to keep up with the pace of change, keep your customer at the center of your decision processes, and inspire the people inside your organization to lead from wherever they are with more honed *Digital Sense.*

Soon after the Chiefs incident in 2012, Travis and Chris were speaking on the same panel at the 2013 *Denver Startup Week* festival in Colorado. Chris, a serial entrepreneur, was on a personal sabbatical in Colorado, mired in ethnographic research around the Fourth Industrial Revolution and customer experience, following a venture exit. Chris and Travis immediately hit it off.

In Summer 2015, they reconnected and the concept of this book was born. Chris was back in build mode with Ethology (a customer experience performance media agency) and Travis had become one of the most sought after thought leaders in marketing technology. Travis was working on building his agency, CCP Digital, was a paid columnist at *Inc.* magazine, and had a new podcast on VentureBeat, called VB Engage, with the incomparable Stewart Rogers. We had originally decided to write the book and self-publish it, when serendipitously a few weeks later, Lia Ottaviano, from John Wiley & Sons, Inc. in Hoboken, NJ, reached out, and a deal for *Digital Sense* was born with the country's oldest and most prolific business book publisher.

In this book, you will learn how to blend customer experience, social business strategy, and marketing technologies using the Experience Marketing Framework.™ This book will teach you how to amplify that content correctly, and give you some different hacks and tricks on how to look at digital. It will help teach your organization how to be more digitally savvy at an individual and collective level.

We want digital sense to permeate your whole organization and the world at large.

With over 3 billion more humans coming into the commercial cycle globally in the coming years, as mobile web and smartphone access proliferates in the Third World, we no longer live in the information age, instead residing firmly in the age of opportunity.

You have an unprecedented chance to capitalize and thrive (not just survive) through what Klaus Schwab, the founder and executive chairman of the World Economic Forum, has called the Fourth Industrial Revolution.[10]

Having a model to cultivate a continually increasing digital sense will be an imperative. In the coming decade, the road ahead will not merely be a prolongation of the Third Industrial Revolution, which used electronics and information technology to automate production. It will be a complete and distinctly different revolution wherein everything exists as bits centered around velocity, scope, and impact as humanity enters a time of scale where technology has no historical precedent.

Our hope with this book is to share some of the wisdom we have picked up during our collective 40-plus years of marketing and technology startup experience. We have unified our sharp tongues and quick wits into one voice for the narrative to make your reading experience fluid.

You've heard the quote from Wayne Gretzky that says, "I skate to where the puck is headed, not where it is." That's been one of the guiding lights and principles of Travis's whole existence. Chris's personal tagline for those who have seen him speak, mentor, or invest, is "The real risk is doing nothing." Strap yourself in and let's begin.

Section I
Overview

1 The Game at Speed

Every second of every day the rate of change is accelerating and we all fall further behind. Welcome to your new reality. You will realize this reality slowly at first and then suddenly in the coming years. As an executive, a marketer, and/or a founder/entrepreneur, you are no longer dealing with the convenience of saying outwardly that the customer is always right while staying with legacy processes and metrics internally as you march toward your next quarterly earnings call or round of funding.

We now live in a world where the customer is always right and enabled by technology, platforms, and channels to provide unparalleled support for the brands they love in any given moment and to enact massive justice/vengeance in real time on the brands that violate their trust or abuse/take for granted their attention.

We are already four compounding—exponential—years from the dates in Travis's personal *Save Our Chiefs* story and two years from the Optus story, and we have just watched the most interesting/disruptive political race in the history of the United States unfold. We are in the crosshairs of a dying traditional media universe and the rise of the earned media era, where every individual is both empowered and feeling helplessly lost by the digital power and complexity at their fingertips. Time moves fast in the digital world.

Why Your Organization Needs a Digital Sense DNA Layer

No industry is immune to the new rules of social business, the increasing demands, and the need to make customer experience the one metric that matters. World renowned futurist Gerd Leonhard has gone on record to say that the exponential speed and evolution of technology has created a digital-first world in which "humanity will change more in the next 20 years than the previous 300."

Think about that for a minute. Imagine it is the year 1717 (300 years ago from the release of this book) and that you are hanging out with us over your favorite adult beverage in a candlelit tavern on Manhattan Island in New York. Imagine that as we all fill up our bladders and make our way to the outhouse (or side of the building) to relieve ourselves, we notice a small hot spring on the ground. We decide in our stupors to take off our sweet powdered wigs and take a relaxing bath for the first time in a few weeks, while continuing our imbibition.

As we begin to relax, Travis tells some joke about the British soldiers, making you laugh so hard that you spill what is left of your beverage into the sulfur-infused bubbling water and it transforms our hot spring into the *Hot Tub Time Machine*! Immediately we are transported to present-day New York City 300 years into the future! (It could happen.) Talk about feeling overwhelmed. We would have a real challenge (Colonial skivvies aside) assimilating into the 2017 world with our 1717 understanding of how society is organized, information is proliferated, and commerce is done.

Well friends, whether Gerd is 100 percent correct or not, the reality is that all humans alive today will experience the same level of change by the year 2037 as our fictitious Colonial counterparts would experience if they were transported to present day. In the next 20 years, with 5G Internet, AI, AR, VR, chatbots, and the Internet of EVERYF#%KINGTHING, the world as we know it is certainly going to change (Figure 1.1). Welcome to the *Fourth Industrial Revolution*! Nothing before has ever prepared us for what is going to happen. As *Wired Magazine*'s founding executive editor, famed futurist Kevin Kelly, also states, "It's Inevitable."

Are you ready?

The Game Has Forever Been Changed

Your reality today is that your customer doesn't care about your internal battles, political hurdles, or legacy technologies' lack of integration into your newer cloud-based ones. She doesn't care about your struggle to retain top talent, or your troubles creating a culture unified around core values, while

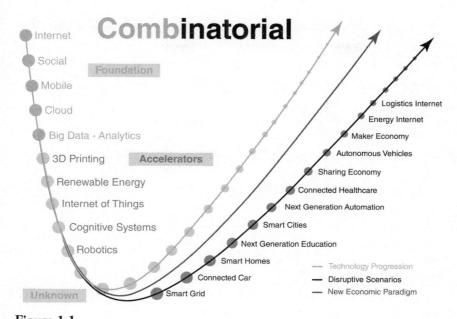

Figure 1.1

Source: Gerd Leonhard, "Exponential and Combinatorial Futures: All Depends on Ethics (Futurist Gerd at Tedx)," https://vimeo.com/117335574.

continuing to hit the quarterly earnings numbers. Nor does she care why, at different touch points along the journey, you can't seem to deliver the same brand promise she bought into on the front end. She could give two craps about your issues and is—like all of us—no longer loyal to a brand as much as she is loyal to the need for a solution to the problem she has in that moment. She grades you only on how you deliver against it and how consistently you can meet her evolving needs over time.

Just because you have satisfied customers doesn't mean you have happy ones. Satisfied customers are best defined as those customers who continue to pay for the service you provide, because they have not yet found another way to live without you.

Think about that for a minute.

It makes sense but it is hardly aspirational as an offensive strategy. It merely serves as a temporary defensive one that can fool you into complacency, because it doesn't currently violate the universal Law of

Compensation. There is a universal Law of Compensation you ask? Yes, there is. There are only three rules to earning the majority of the market share at any given time, and for those who haven't read any of our earlier stuff, the Law of Compensation is defined below as follows:

1. the need for what you do,

2. your ability to fulfill that need consistently, and

3. how difficult or easy it is to replace you.

Satisfied customers are not secure customers in tomorrow's marketplace, and you are vulnerable because of the false sense of security you feel as it relates to number three in this law. The reason is simple. If your customer is merely continuing to pay you because you fulfill their need consistently (taxi cabs fill the need of rented individual transport) and you are difficult to replace (2007), then once Uber/Lyft and so on get to scale (2010), your satisfied customer becomes your disruptive competitor's happy one. Then the cycle starts all over again.

Satisfied customers of Uber are now just as vulnerable to leave if it becomes easier and more exciting to replace Uber with some other option for timely, affordable, easy transport. In the same way, happy lessees or owners of (insert your favorite automaker here) cars and trucks are a vulnerable asset the minute they decide ridesharing is more economically viable and convenient than paying for a vehicle they only use on average 5 percent of their week.

Companies like GetAround, Turo, and Skurt are renting people cars and disrupting the car rental business now. If you're driving your car only 5 percent of the time, why not rent it out to someone who needs it? The sharing/trusting economy is in full effect, and some simulations *show that in the coming years taxibots could replace 90 percent of all cars on the road*, drop commute times 10 percent, and open up acres of land for parks and public use, completely transforming cities with a marriage of mass carpooling and UPS delivery intelligence.[1]

The cycles of innovation around your customer experience, business model, and solution set as a differentiator must continue to speed up without sacrificing the reliability of that delivery. Your organizational DNA and leadership teams must make immediate shifts in prioritization around the following new ideals.

- The Customer is the Number One Asset. (We suggest you follow fellow Wiley author Jeanne Bliss at CustomerBliss.com. immediately, read *Chief Customer Officer 2.0*, and commit to implementing her five core competencies to your corporate list of Key Performance Indicators [KPIs].)
- There is no online/offline world in which we exist. It is now an always-on world.
- There may be multiple budgets within the org chart, but there is only one bank account.
- Every decision must be measured against how it impacts the customer experience.
- The internal customer (employee) is as important as the external customer you seek to serve.
- You can't keep up with it all, so focus on improving the areas with the least friction and highest ROI first, and then gain momentum daily, monthly, and yearly to tackle more.
- Empathy (EQ) is the number one skill to cultivate in your organization.
- Design thinking is not just for creatives and should be rooted in your professional development plan for all departments.
- In a software-is-everything world, your product is your focus group, as sensors connect everything, availing data-fed iterations in real time for those who build the proper technology stack.
- Your organization needs digital sense.

As you read this book, please understand that we are both pragmatists at our core, more than we are anything else. We are both insatiable learners and fearless doers, but at our mutual hearts, we are pragmatic problem solvers and dot connectors before we are anything else. Each of us has been blessed with the gift of gab, and our intention with this book is to use our ability to assimilate a multitude of inputs into succinct and focused outputs that inspire you to action that causes massive impact. We have endeavored to make this book a pragmatically powerful perspective and reference resource for you, the reader. Our goal is that *Digital Sense* will help provide you the context and configuration to build a custom solution for your business that achieves a focused social business strategy, powered by the proper technology, to deliver your customers (internal and external) a world-class experience, day in and day out.

This book is not going to read like a marketing or operations textbook or technology manual. Instead, it will be infused with cross-functional exercises, a framework, a mental model for optimizing communication, case studies statistics, data, a few emojis, and jokes. We will discuss some of the research and provide assessments at your fingertips that are cutting edge, but we did not run any double-blind experiments on a group of test subjects in a lab.

We are not those authors. We are not in an ivory tower. We are warrior generals in the field running full speed into success and failure, licking our wounds while researching, thinking, and DOING in real time. We know that a large percentage of the tactical advice in this book won't work exactly the same in the near future and will face obsolescence, but the framework and thinking that created those efforts will be foundational for your ability to stay ahead of the game and solve the problems you face in the future.

The book is designed to build, more than anything else, a common set of language, visual tools of communication, and an active community of fellow field generals. Join the community and stay up on trends with our newsletter at DigitalSen.se and help each other as we iterate this work in the future.

We will provide references to several of the extremely valuable ivory-tower authors and *sense-making* organizations throughout this book, since we consume content voraciously from them, but we are writing this book primarily to deliver on its subtitle and provide you with *"The Common Sense Approach to Effectively Blending Social Business Strategy, Marketing Technology, and Customer Experience."*

Our recommended approach within this book is completely customizable. It is simple, but won't be easy. We have provided Chapter 2 and Chapter 5 to ensure that you are armed with the proper mental awareness and leadership ammo to take the ideas in this book and put them into use in any organization regardless of where you sit in the hierarchy.

Bits of Knowledge

Throughout the chapters, we will have several *Digital Bits* of knowledge that we call out or link to for your further discovery or deeper diving into key topics. We also will utilize these links and assets to continually update the supplemental and supportive content of this book as the months and years pass and exponential shifts change the truth around some of the strategies and tactics we are sharing in this version. Please consider this a reference point and check back often with our *Digital Bits* as we provide updates and changes to the ideas and recommendations we discuss herein.

Who Is This Book For?

Our goal for *Digital Sense* is to empower all executives, marketers, internal change agents, and entrepreneurs with a framework and structure to build an amazing work culture that aligns the customer needs to the major business goals in a sustainable way that delivers both reliability to the customer experience across all channels and a method to operationalize innovation more effectively.

This book was written for the executive of a growing or large organization to illuminate the robustness of the techniques discussed and empower you to lead from wherever you are in the org chart, to help you defend against the coming disruption to your existence. This book is also written for the founder/entrepreneur or early stage company leader building a vision from the ground up to take on an inefficient and impersonal giant in the industry. Disrupt away, brothers and sisters!

Throughout this book, we will highlight some great examples from your peers in both regards, as they have navigated the bumpy road of proliferating a *Digital Sense* across the layers and silos of their organization to build a social business strategy that delivers a better customer experience each and every day.

Mostly, however, we wrote this book for anyone who wishes, as Steve Farber says, to "do what you love in the service of those who love what you do!" Adding what Jeff Weiner, CEO of LinkedIn, says as his personal mission statement, "To help lead with wisdom and empathy." If it is true that work is love made visible, we can only hope that at the conclusion of this book, you will clearly feel and know how much we loved working on this book together in service to you, our peers. Enjoy the journey!

Way
Zombie
People
Wiley
One
Custome
Three
Attention
Day
Organizatio
Digital
Book
Chapter
2
Digit
Motivatables
Bein
Mind
Time
Up
Level
New
Out
Everyone
Idea
Same
Keep
Amplifiers
Human
Those
Hard
Truly
Through
Building
Become
Trust
Know
Find
Even
Conscious
Organization
Years
Energy
Sense
Influencers
Shock
Early
Effective
Decision
Zombie
Both
Organization
Reality
Free
Play
Head
Successful
Held
Heroes
Leadership
Percent
Agreement
Business
Event
Avoid
Ways
Meet
Awe
Organizational
Inside
World
True
Influence
Against
Seconds
Stories
Managers
Want
Change
Think
Drive
Smaller
Collective
Senior
Build
Workforce
Need
Chapter
Create
Great
Technology
Control
Subconscious
Mind
Team
Holds
Extremely
Provide
Deep
Mass
Back
Startups

2 Influencers, Zombies, and Everything Between

The Rise of Digital Transformation

"The realignment of, or new investment in, technology, business models, and processes to drive new value for customers and employees and more effectively compete in an ever-changing digital economy."

—Brian Solis, principal analyst at The Altimeter Group

With a combined 40 years of experience building, leading, and advising organizations from the napkin and seed stage to the Fortune 100, FTSE 100, and companies on every continent but Antarctica, both of us have realized one fact about life and one fact about human beings.

FACT 1: In life the only true constant is *CHANGE.*

FACT 2: No human being resists change, but *every* human being resists being changed!

Every fundamental and successful organizational change, large or small, happens through effective communication that penetrates the subconscious part of our mind. These facts hold true for organizations as well, where fundamental change occurs and begins to rapidly appear when a tipping point of some smaller percentage (10 to 15 percent) of the workforce accepts the new paradigm or operational order into their collective subconscious.

There are different personality types that you have to learn how to deal with effectively to facilitate positive change within your organization. For those who haven't studied persuasion or any of the masters of influence throughout history at length, we will do our best to provide you some necessary high-level clarity in this chapter to the levers that govern successful communication and shifts in consciousness. We do this so that you can lead, from wherever you are, and become a catalyst for creating a truly digital organization that is ready to sustainably compete and delight its customers in the years to come.

Anyone in marketing or sales knows, all too well, the old adage *facts tell, but stories sell.* Stories cause us to connect to our emotional (subconscious) mind. The mind that ensures that our circulatory, respiratory, and digestive systems work without us having to consciously be aware of them. The subconscious mind is our operating system and the body is our hardware. The conscious mind is where we can load software and new programs, but only the ideas that are compatible with our current OS (paradigms) will work immediately.

To put any of the framework and ideas in this book to work in your organization, you must first understand how to play the game of people and influence. The following paragraphs are our effort to level-set with you by installing the proper "plugins" to your organizational perspective before you can load some of the new software this book discusses and run it successfully. You must understand that there are only three ways (ports) to penetrate a new idea or concept into the subconscious mind, where it can be nurtured and begin to grow.

The three methods to "get in the head" of someone are below.

1. Shock

2. Awe/Fascination

3. Agreement

You will want to employ all of these directly as you attempt to implement the strategies in this book. You will also be prudent to time some of your deployment of crucial conversations around the indirect occurrences that shock or fascinate the mass workforce and key players within your organization. In other words, never waste a crisis or a high that you could use to implant some of your agenda firmly in the mind of your leadership and delivery teams.

Having worked with everything from early stage startups to middle-market turnarounds and large organizations like Sprint, Symantec, Qualcomm, and Huawei, we are always making mental notes of how these three tactics are deployed to create mass control scenarios, traction, or intrigue.

At Symantec, Travis experienced the impact (*shock*) of reorganization three times in his 2-plus years. While consulting for Qualcomm for 110 days in 2013, Chris witnessed its use twice. In contrast, for startups and early stage companies, *fascination* and *agreement* can get a lot of use as tools for mass control and direction. In any event, make a mental note that these three are the paths into the subconscious and reptilian part of the human mind. In the coming paragraphs, we will talk about the four types of people you will meet along the way to drill this point home further.

Think for a minute of how hard it is in a large company to get agreement on an idea. Think even more about how hard it is for managers across an organization to create a sense of fascination or awe. Certainly, you can think of some of the masters at this, such as Steve Jobs, but the one thing that works time and time again for getting uniformly in the subconscious mind of your entire organizational chart is a reorg. They create a visceral level of uncertainty and stress that can be utilized to weed out the detractors, put potential uprisings back in their place, and realign power centers under the most entrenched or influential leaders. At the end of the day, however, it is all about getting your undivided attention, so that some other news or communication can be delivered unabated into the heart of your mind.

Think about why news organizations always lead with what bleeds. And notice how pundits, anchors, and talking heads often show up on screen in four boxes screaming at each other, only for the station to go to commercial every few minutes with some product designed to eliminate other stress in your life—whether by a pharmaceutical remedy, an enticing vacation, a gluttonous meal, or an adult beverage. Even when you put the news on mute, to lessen the shock and adrenal burnout, they have artfully placed camera angles showing the amazing legs of the female anchors—fascination—to keep your eyes engaged while they use graphics and the news alert ticker to feed you the same information in repetitive nature. Today, the BREAKING NEWS alert can include anything from a terror attack to a tweet war between Kim-ye and Taylor Swift. It's all designed to get and keep your fleeting attention just long enough to jam a message deep into your subconscious.

The way that successful startups use these three tactics to gain traction in the mind of their intended targets is even more fun. It is the old game of *Villains, Victims, and Heroes*, where they typically have some narrative around the inefficient or human injustice (*shock*) they are out to eradicate with their solution. They leverage every aspect of their youth, boldness, and apparent fearlessness to create a cascading sense of *awe and fascination* about the disruption they contend is imminent in a space that nobody thought could be toppled. They take early adopters and use growth hacking to proliferate the stories of their users who love being set free from the burden of the old way to amplify and create agreement that this is the future of (insert industry here).

When your customer experience or marketing team endeavors to surprise and delight your customer, this is a combination of positive shock and awe in full effect. The point is that you must also be willing to deploy these three tactics to get your organization to align around the idea that the present and future battlefield is around customer experience.

Our bold belief is that customer experience is truly the one metric that matters most. Organizations that align their total focus around optimizing their departments to provide the most seamless experience at each touch point in the journey will take home the lion's share of all rewards in the coming decade.

We highly recommend that you check out the efforts and CCXP™ certification at *The Customer Experience Professionals Association* (CXPA.org),[1] if you are looking for a complete road map and operational aptitude to unify your managers around the discipline of CX. They are great friends of ours, and they provide an amazing level of best practices forums, white papers, and research to keep you sharp.

Those who fail to achieve and maintain great customer experiences across the customer journey will be relegated to a distant second place or put completely out of business.

Attention and Trust

Attention and trust are the two most important (and hardest) currencies to attain today and for the foreseeable future. They will also be the easiest to lose once attained. You already know that attention has long been the asset most coveted by marketers. In the digital world, however, attention is becoming nearly impossible to gain and retain over time. Too much noise out there and not enough signal. Consumers are being bombarded with advertising, content, social updates, texts, and app notifications 24/7/365.

A recent study, by Microsoft in Canada, found that since the year 2000, *our attention span has dropped 30 percent from 12 seconds in 2000 to 8 seconds in 2016.*[2] By some accounts, we have the same attention span as a goldfish! Have you ever held a meaningful conversation with one of those? Better yet, have you ever gotten a goldfish to give you their credit card?

You didn't need Microsoft or us to tell you that attention spans have dropped. Hell, you have probably answered a text or watched part of a YouTube video while you were reading this chapter and popping an Adderall. Many of the people who picked this book up may have gotten so distracted that they never even made it to this page! So kudos to you. You're a champion and we love you for making it this far.

MILESTONE: To reward you for getting this far, tweet @teedubya & @chrisjsnook that you're a champion with the #imachampion hashtag. Add a picture of your favorite winning moment, if you like, as this will condition your subconscious for winning. Do it now and we will give you some RT love!

Attention isn't enough for winning more market share year over year. Trust is also required for that to occur. Trust to attention is the equivalent of carbon to steel. You need attention in enough compounding moment-by-moment proximity to gain a level of trust that builds with each micro-transaction or touch point. You must consider it your organization's sole purpose to build real relationships (think deep friendships and marriage-level quality) with each customer, at scale. This means you will work at it day in and day out.

This also means that breaches of trust will occur from time to time and that how you repair that trust (while you still have the customer's attention) will be as important as how well you maintain it day in and day out. To truly be world class, to sustainably hold on to happy customers, and to not be vulnerable to massive disruption, you can no longer consider this optional. As a matter of fact, it is fundamental to survival. The good news is that you can use digital sense and powerful communication tactics to lead your team into a fully transformed digital organization and leap ahead of your competitors.

Influencers, Amplifiers, Motivatables, and Zombies

We mentioned in an earlier paragraph that every organization, and even society at large, is made up of approximately four general archetypes of people. It is important to have high-level understanding of this phenomenon as you go about being a change agent to not only be more effective but also to give you context that will help alleviate your frustration and self-doubt that you are somehow running into a unique situation that means you're doomed for failure. Everyone who has succeeded or will succeed in shifting their organization to a customer-centric organization will have gone through the same issues. People are people. There are no truly unique cases. It is not a matter of whether you are able to succeed; it will come down to what you are willing to endure to make it happen in your organization.

Look at the two pyramids in Figure 2.1. On the left you will see the typical layers of an organizational chart along with their primary decision-making lens/view. On the right, you will see the generic archetypes of the people that fill those spots. The Influencers (I), Amplifiers (A), Motivatables (M), and Zombies (Z)—everyone's favorite antihero. This graphic doesn't imply that all the Zombies are in the rank and file or that you don't have Influencers buried deep in the organization. Each archetype can penetrate all echelons of an organization, but this is where you will find each in their most native setting.

Starting on the left side, let's baseline our understanding that any time a decision is being made at a different layer of the organization, that the lens by which that decision is assessed is as follows:

- Inside the C-suite, decisions are based upon the overall enterprise-wide impact.
- At the SVP or VP level, the decision criteria are usually centered around the business unit or division-level impact.
- Senior directors and directors focus on their department-level impacts and budgets.

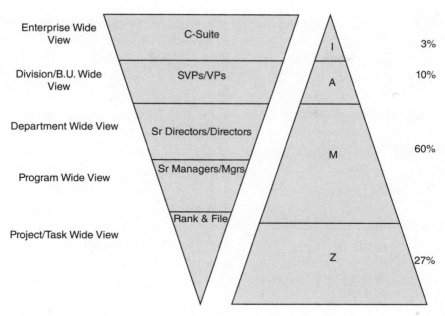

Figure 2.1

- Senior managers and managers are concerned primarily with how it will affect the program objectives they are being held to achieve.

- Lastly, the rank and file merely want to know what is going to make their task or project go more smoothly.

None of this is new to you but, it serves as important mutual context as we discuss who you will meet, and need to leverage (or avoid) along the way, as you endeavor to implement some (or all) of the recommendations in this book. Humanity always falls into statistical buckets, and this chart represents more than 40 years' combined experience in the trenches, leading organizations, consulting to organizations, and building businesses and teams from the ground up to exit. These are not exact percentages, but the percentages are *good enough for government work,* as the saying goes, and will serve you as a good barometer as you go about leading change.

Roughly 3 percent of the population are what we consider to be **Influencers**. They are also commonly identified as *motivators.* These are the masters of human persuasion. They lead effortlessly and we all want to follow. They are master motivators, orators, communicators, visionaries, and catalysts. (These aren't the same type of Influencers, however, that we'll discuss in Chapter 10). For every 100 businesspeople, three or fewer will fall into this category, and you will notice them immediately. If you read the energy of the room, it will always gravitate toward them. In the rare event that an Influencer cannot shift the energy of a room or a conversation to their agenda or liking, they may leave that room, company, or conversation, never to return.

Next up are what we call the **Amplifiers**. They represent roughly 10 percent of humanity, are extremely self-motivated, and have the innate drive and raw talent to become Influencers, but they must be placed in fertile soil to develop the nuances of that well-rounded mastery. They are intrinsically ambitious but many times can be constrained by blind spots in their own personality. They can show signs of frustration at times as they bang their heads against the same wall until someone masterful shows them another way around it. They are never short of effort but sometimes can be short of insight or tact.

Amplifiers are the foot soldiers of the Influencer. They lead by example, and they are critical players in turning a vision into tangible reality and proof points. They love the challenge of doing things that others say can't be done. They find personal fulfillment in being different than the masses, but they are not satisfied with their place in the world and hunger for higher tiers of influence, money, success, and notoriety. These are the people who will die for ribbons of acknowledgement and validation. They seek mentorship. They love to be a part of a winning team. Some are selfishly motivated, egotistical, and only stable in the organization because the leaders have found a way to tie their incentives to the goals of the organization. Others in this category are extremely altruistic and willing to build others up as part of their leadership expression. In any event, the Amplifiers are the critical fuel to the fire that is ignited by the Influencer and are, often times, the tangible day-to-day heroes inside of your organization.

As we move into the largest segment of humanity, we come across the **Motivatables**. These are the *motivatable people inside of your organization* and make up roughly 60 percent of everyone you know or will meet. Motivatables have the less than effective and often tiring habit of being people pleasers. They don't do it with malicious intent. They do it to blend in. Motivatables are masters at thriving and surviving in any environment. Like chameleons, they are wired to adapt. It comes from any number of prior experiences and early childhood software downloads that told them to be safe, nice, and polite even at their own expense. They dislike conflict and crave the comfort zone.

Motivatables can tend to be your passive-aggressive types. These are your political players, the most savvy of which have worked their way up to the higher levels of the organization. There, they can rule a silo and find personal significance through championing the inspired cause of an Influencer/Amplifier while falling back on a victim-type dominance when things imply change that forces them out of their comfort zone too quickly. Motivatables become who they hang around. Like chameleons, they adapt to their environment and rarely/almost never create it.

By the way, there is no judgement passed by us for people reading this who aim to please. Motivatables have not yet fully mastered how to stay on the productive side of that line. Their intention to create harmony is right, but their method leaves them vulnerable. Our hope in giving this example is that you will become more self-aware of where you fit on this leadership continuum and endeavor to lift yourself and others up to Amplifier and above.

Organizations that do well with culture have a solid and active maintenance by the Influencer and Amplifiers that causes the Motivatables to appear to have the same characteristics as the Amplifier. Over time, Motivatables who hang around Amplifiers long enough can morph into them, but the likelihood is smaller that they will ever become Influencers simply because they tend to be wired to be risk averse. Because of this risk aversion, the Motivatable can be an extremely vulnerable segment of your organization, if you allow too many of the fourth segment to exist in your organization.

The **Zombies** represent 27 percent of humanity, and inside your organization these are the truly unmotivatable people. They have the same smartphones and access to information, noise, and pop culture as everyone else, and therefore their power to proliferate poison is even greater than it was just 15 short years ago. Truly unmotivatable, they combine Debbie Downer with Negative Nancy. Wah wah wahhhh. If you handed a Zombie a gold brick for a Christmas bonus, the Zombie would drop it on their foot and sue you for gross negligence and max out their workers compensation claim.

 The Zombie gets off on one thing. Turning other people into Zombies.

You cannot let Zombies get their teeth into a Motivatable or anyone else. Your Influencers can smell Zombies from miles away and will never be seen around them but will strike them quickly in the head the minute one comes anywhere near someone healthy.

The Amplifiers have no problem fighting the Zombies either but will, at times, spend too much time saving Motivatables from their grasp because Motivatables are too worried about being liked by everyone to run away from the Zombie.

Zombies are experts in every sordid detail of what is wrong, scary, or unsafe about society and your company's product, culture, and leadership.

How to spot the Zombies in five bullets:

- They know every piece of gossip and share it all frequently behind closed doors.
- They build or promote websites or write negative posts on Glassdoor .com when they leave an organization.
- They know every loophole in the HR policy.
- They are absolutely destructive and toxic and suck the energy out of every meeting they are in.
- They are insatiably hungry.

In every great story, there are villains, victims, and heroes. In your organization, the Zombies are the villains. The battle is constant and culture is built with each decision or indecision on a daily basis. If you want good to overcome evil in your company, you MUST avoid the traps and neutralize the Zombies as you proceed with your efforts to transform your organization and do your part to proliferate a digital sense across it. The Zombies don't want to be exposed. The Zombies win on persistence and prey on apathy and negativity. To Zombies chaos and the status quo are oxygen. The Zombies are like crabs in a bucket. They will do almost anything to keep any other crabs from getting out of the bucket and into the light. They don't want the organization to be free from its past. They are your mortal enemy.

We aren't worried about offending any Zombies, however, because we are WAY too far into this book for any Zombies to still be reading. And the chances are that no Zombie would pick up or buy this book in the first place. Although, when the word gets out that we called 27 percent of the adult workforce Zombies in this book, we are fully expecting that a Zombie will start an anti–*Digital Sense* page railing against us to the rest of the walking dead. We fully intend to leverage that, by the way, into book sales for them to burn at their Zombie-hater parties. Hey if it makes dollars, it makes sense, right? Allegedly, we know the person who owns DigitalSenseSucks.com.

Now that you know the game and the players, let's arm you with the framework, tools, and strategies to win as we proceed to the next chapter and introduce the *Experience Marketing Framework*.

Section II
Building a
Customer-Centric
Organization

Experience
Marketing
EMF
Travis
Wright
Chapter 3
Chris J Snook
Customer
Framework
Digital Sense
Wiley
Business
World
Organization
Insight
Reliability
Approach
Market
Figure
Always
Model
Well
Strategy
Plan
Work
Focus
Help
Build
Next
Day
Elements
Design
Speed
Note
Dissonance
Structure
Questions
Specific
Innovation
Success
Culture
Guided
Sense
Learn
Thin
Points
Touch
Garrett
Loop
Building
Mobile
One
Below
Over
Restore
Iterate
Ensures
Pull
Think
Measure
Tactics
Empty
Two
Ideas
Language
Through
Optimize
Roach
Way
Related
Together
Answers
Discover
Few
Papa
Till
Relates
Cycles
Each
Plane
Delivering
Introducing
Research
Never
Built
Provide
Speech
Strength
Three
Within
Take
Experiences
Executing
State
Purpose
Being
Agreements
Guiding

3 Introducing the Experience Marketing Framework

As you already know, we work and live in an always-on, always-moving, mobile-first reality, where business happens at the speed of speech and thumbs. This present-day reality will compound in speed, accuracy, and efficiency 1,000 times over in the coming decade. Qualcomm (one of the largest chipset providers in world) actually had an internal corporate directive in 2013 called "solving the 1000x challenge" while Chris was consulting for them. The Experience Marketing Framework (EMF) will help you navigate this reality with agility to find the powerful simplicity on the back side of all this added complexity.

As we introduce the EMF, please repeat the following three agreements to yourself daily for context and consider posting this prominently in full view in your workspace.

The Three Agreements to Customer-Centric Accountability Cultures

1. I admit that I am powerless over the demands of always-on marketing.

2. The power (our customer) that is greater than our organization gives me the singular focus necessary to restore my sanity and find focus.

3. I will take a fearless inventory of our insights, vision, and execution annually and score them with brutal honesty against the customer needs, competitors' strength, and external forces that threaten our existence.

The Framework to Ask Powerful Questions

It is important to note that these next few chapters are not about giving you answers as much as they are about giving you the framework to ask the right questions. The EMF was conceived in an effort to provide you and your organization a complete foundation and structure to ask the fundamental questions needed to build your road maps in a way that aligns your major business objectives to the priority needs of your customer. All of this is set within a model that can optimize the reliability of your processes and draw out the creativity of your people.

As we dive into the next few chapters, we will provide you categories of specific questions and steps to take your team through that will both baseline and enhance your approach to build your strategy with humanized tactics that are built with digital sense.

We are both proud, card-carrying, antiestablishment members of Generation X, and therefore we have a deep appreciation and love for '80s metal, early '90s hip-hop, and grunge. Music is a universal language and a perfect example of the power and beauty of conquering dissonance when properly composed. It also proves that great results don't always require months' or years' worth of labor. When top talent is free to come together in individual expression but aligned focus, magic can happen. A musical example of this is the creation of the Guns N' Roses classic hit "Sweet Child O' Mine," which was literally created in less than five minutes (see Figure 3.1).[1]

GUNS 'N' ROSES – 'SWEET CHILD O' MINE'

Axl Rose was upstairs and had overheard his fellow members of Guns 'N' Roses jamming below. He took this opportunity to write lyrics, unbeknownst to the fact it was a jam for entertainment. It was at that moment, as a joke, that Slash improvised the world-famous riff that almost anyone can recognise.

In a mere five minutes, 'Sweet Child O' Mine' was born.

Not much has to be said about the aftermath of the track's release. It was the third single released from their 1987 debut *Appetite For Destruction*, which went on to sell over 30 million copies worldwide – providing Guns 'N' Roses with the platform that would see them becoming one of the world's best-selling bands.

Figure 3.1 Guns N' Roses

Cognitive dissonance is the clash in an organization when two or more disharmonious elements or ideas try to coexist. In an organization, this is commonplace wherever the culture is weak or the objectives are unclear. In a digital world, this can be amplified in its negative impact because of the speed by which information (true or false, verified or unverified) can and will travel to each individual. To overcome dissonance as an organization in the digital world, an even deeper commitment to frequent (crucial) communication and to establishing a common language and framework from which everyone is operating is paramount.

The EMF was created after an inspiring nudge from Ethology founder and CEO, Jeffrey Pruitt. Pruitt's passion to help brands think about experience marketing and performance media at the strategic level, instead of just digital marketing as a myriad of tactics and channels, was the catalyst for building this framework. We enlisted Chris's colleague and VP of Customer Experience, Tony Quiroz (@TQ_AZ), to flush out our ideas around the initial EMF in late 2015 (see Figure 3.2). We are grateful to both of these individuals for the inspiration and insights they provided along the way to making this model a reality.

We will spend the next several chapters diving deeper into each layer of the framework, discussing what the EMF answers and avails on both a day-to-day basis, as well as in forward-looking planning cycles. We will walk through the pragmatic use of each layer and loop one at a time, but first, let's summarize the EMF with visuals and a summary description of what it will help you achieve and why it matters in the first place.

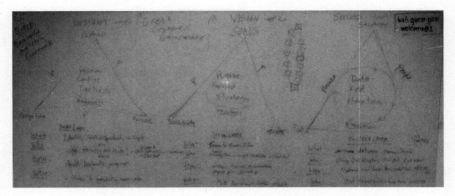

Figure 3.2   Initial EMF Sketch from Chris's Whiteboard, July 2015

The Experience Marketing Framework

- The EMF (Figure 3.3) maximizes client/customer success by delivering reliability and innovation to the customer experience.

- Experience marketing is defined as the union of purpose-driven strategy, human-centric tactics, and data-fed iterations.

- A simple "learn, plan, do" approach quickly leads to ***reliability***, which *ensures the maintenance of market share.*

  1. **Learn** the client/customer's business goals or consumer needs and persona

Purpose-focused strategy.
Human-centric tactics. Data-fed iteration.

Figure 3.3   The Experience Marketing Framework (Snook,Quiroz 2015)

2. **Plan** projects/launches/campaigns with a focus on measurable interactions.

3. **Do** the work, release to market, measure, and iterate.

- *Innovation ensures market share growth* and arises from insights. Insights can occur while executing but will be generated more reliably by adding dedicated cycles of research to your operational procedure and road map.

- A complementary "discover, design, deploy" approach leads to more seamless onboarding of innovations and commercialization of key insights gathered while executing.

  1. **Discover** the most vulnerable/opportunistic touch points in your customer journey.

  2. **Design** by assessing what's feasible (technology), viable (business), and desirable/usable (human), and build on top of a data structure that will measure what's most valued as it relates to the problem you are setting out to solve.

  3. **Deploy** and iterate based upon the data loop to optimize for reliability.

- **Vision** guides strategy. **Strategy** is the art of applying insights to specific touch points in the customer journey, guided by business goals, calibrated by scope, and prioritized to a schedule.

- **Success** = a great customer experience: well executed, uniquely crafted, and sustainable.

The EMF helps organizations and leaders deliver on the two commitments (Figure 3.4) of reliability and innovation that fellow Wiley author Jeanne Bliss (@customerbliss) called out in her book *Chief Customer Officer 2.0.*[2]

The EMF is composed of three distinct layers, interdependent walls, and two loops. As we take a look below the surface, we notice how *Purpose,*

The Experience Marketing Framework delivers on
two customer experience commitments.

RELIABILITY

INNOVATION

Figure 3.4 The Two Customer Experience Commitments

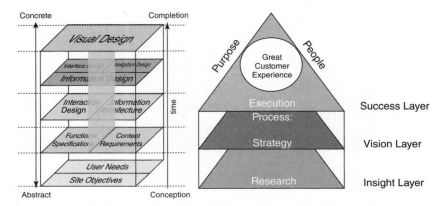

Figure 3.5 Elements of User Experience (left); Experience Marketing Framework (right)

Note to the reader: The picture on the right (EMF Snook, Quiroz 2015) is incomplete in that it does not include specific models related to human resource planning and design, market share analysis, or product development methodology. It is designed to be agnostic and plug in or play nicely with your existing frameworks for those considerations.

People, and Process hold the structure together and contribute to key phases of *Research, Strategic Planning, and Execution.*

Fans of design thinker Jesse James Garrett and his groundbreaking work in the *Elements of User Experience* will understand and see the similarities in the EMF, as we attempted to build a framework that can allow an organization to think across the silos. The goal was to develop a unified approach to diagnose the problem areas in the journey map, realize insights into actionable innovations, and optimize the reliability, all while executing in real-time. In Garrett's model for UX (see Figure 3.5), the foundational elements were the marriage of user needs to site objectives. The EMF model for CX is also rooted in a foundation consisting of the proper alignment of customer needs and business objectives.

Customer Experience Is the Battleground in a Digital World

Customer experience is not about a specific data point in the journey of interacting with your brand or product; it's the entire thing. In a digital world, where loyalty to brand is rapidly being replaced by the end users'

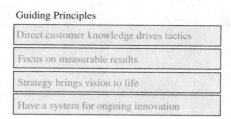

Guiding Principles

Direct customer knowledge drives tactics

Focus on measurable results

Strategy brings vision to life

Have a system for ongoing innovation

Figure 3.6   The Four Guiding Principles of the EMF

loyalty to their need in the moment, success is no longer predicated on push but is primarily related to pull. Great customer experiences will pull the market toward you, whereas empty or incomplete promises that get pushed out on top of faulty/siloed infrastructure will merely expose you. Like all structures built to last, you must have a solid foundation and a guiding set of principles. The EMF is no different and you can see the guiding set of principles in Figure 3.6.

In the next chapter, we will begin building your foundation for delivering great customer experiences guided by these principles. EMF will help you assess the forward-looking strength of your business model, value proposition, and competitive advantage as it relates to serving your customer's needs, and the conditions of the playing field on which you compete.

Takeaways from Introducing the EMF

- The EMF is designed to help you deliver great customer experiences in a digital world by providing a multilayered framework to turn insights into innovative solutions that deepen the relationship with your customer and are executed with reliability.

- The EMF is comprised of an Insights (Research), Vision (Strategy), and Success (Execution) layering. EMF enables a simple "learn, plan, do" approach in the horizontal operational plane while simultaneously allowing the vertical plane to enact regular cycles of innovation that "discover, design, and deploy" new enhancements to your day-to-day operation.

- Customer Experience is the battleground we all compete on in a digital world, and where customer service historically takes a well-honed "common sense," customer experience requires a well-honed digital sense.

Time
Digital
Sens
Wiley
Figure
Team
Insights
Industry
Data
Things
Continue
Culture
Begin
Matrix
Control
Align
Go
Important
Core
Stated
Use
Acts
Great
Documented
Decision
Understanding
EMF
Throug
Questions
More
Direct
Internal
Current
Large
Sales
Outside
Look
Two
Technology
Needs
Don
Company
Assess
Below
People
Purpose
Employees
Before
Overall
Move
Market
Process
Check
Money
Growth
Major
See
Chris
Very
Insight
Strategy
Snoo
Vision
Give
Know
Create
Etc
Strength
Customer
Version
Ensure
Services
Future
Chapter
Quadrant
Source
Making
Million
Based
Day
Need
Life
Term
Good
Access
Forces
Work
Journey
Cycle
Www
Reason
Human
Competitive
Meet
Top
Phase
High
New
Focus
Exercise
Marketing
Layer
Main
Travis
Believe
Wrig
Change
Make
Thing
Percent
Persona
Statement
Relationship
Business
Cash
Win
Transaction
Share
Relates
Way
Organizatio
Opportunity
Understand
Purchase
Defined
Increased
Experience
Reading
Come
Without
Sense
Brand
Available

4 The Insights Layer

The 2017-plus version of Fletch's statement (an iconic character played by Chevy Chase) would be *"It's all 1s and 0s nowadays."*[1] The art and science of turning insights into business growth is where the rubber meets the road for today's marketers and operators. Everything from big data to small data is available as the real-time raw material you are tasked with sense-making into strategic initiatives that drive increased growth and decreased churn.

The Insights Layer of the EMF assists you in answering several foundational questions that will ultimately help you ensure that the right customers remember your name for the things you want to be remembered for, in a disproportionate ratio to your competitors. The Insight Layer (Figure 4.1) is where you establish regular research and discovery cycles both to gut-check your current assumptions as they relate to the foreseeable future and to uncover the new assumptions you will need to flush out, as you make the effort to meet the customer where they are likely to need you/value you in the coming 12–24 months.

The heart of a great customer experience is that it feels human and reminds us that there are still other humans on the other side of our transactions, regardless of the interface by which we executed the transaction or query. When we boil down the most important takeaway value of auditing the following pillars of the Insights Layer within the EMF, it simply comes down to what insights you can operationalize that will further your organization's ability to be more human in approach at each interaction across the customer journey.

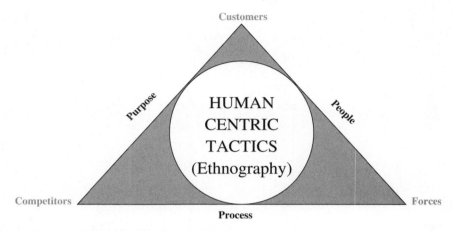

Figure 4.1   The Insight Layer: Research

The Customer Is the Main Thing

Stephen Covey tells us that "the main thing is to keep the main thing the main thing."

As you can see in this cross section of the EMF, the top of the pyramid is the *Customer*. They are the main thing. They always have been the main thing and always will be. They are our reason for existence. It is them we exist to serve, not stock price. It is the love of the customer that we want to win. It is their hard-earned money that we seek, to separate from their wallet in increasing quantities into ours, by exchanging equal or greater value through our offerings. *The. Customer. Is. The. Main. Thing.*

As we make our way down the sides of the pyramid we will notice that the other two areas of focus when we look at the Insights Layer are our *Competitors* and *Forces*. With the entire EMF, you will be assessing your insights and their impacts to your customer through three distinct lenses that represent the interdependent functions of your Purpose, People, and Process.

The output from this layer into the subsequent layers will be more humanized tactics that have come from the combination of big data trend analysis, intuition, and your ethnographic (primary) research efforts. Most of you reading this have an embedded and published corporate purpose statement. For those who do not yet have a documented purpose statement for your enterprise, the simplest way to understand the difference between purpose and mission statements is that *your purpose guides you while your mission drives you.* Your purpose statement handles the "why" about your organization's existence. Mission drills home the "how" you will achieve the vision (the "what").

Step number one in becoming a human-centric organization is to develop and galvanize your Purpose, Mission, and Vision statements, and to align everyone you bring into your organization around them in an emotionally charged way (i.e., get it into their subconscious). Your corporate purpose statement is not only important for mapping out the customer experience and the customer journey but also crucial for your social business strategy, which we will hit on later.

Since the majority of you reading this likely have a clear understanding of the purpose of your organization, this is where we do a gut check with you on an individual level that allows you—without blame or judgement—to mentally reconnect to that purpose and assess where you could improve in your alignment to that vision. In some cases, you will find that through any number of internal experiences, you cannot find your way back to a complete emotional alignment to the company's purpose. If this is the case, the brutal truth is that it is time you move on. If you cannot put in effort every day in the pursuit of this stated ideal, you are no longer a fit for that organization, and vice-versa; it is time to move on to your next adventure. Life is too short, and work that fills your soul is far too rewarding, to ignore this brutal fact.

Do not sit in an organization and get zombified! Don't rot and please don't take a check each and every pay period for something you don't align with or believe is making a difference in the world. All the money in the world cannot cure that sickness. BRAAAAAIIIINNNNSSS!!

Gandhi said to "be the change you wish to see in the world." What that means to us is that you can make the conscious decision each day to lead from where you are, with or without a specific job title or fancy corner office. You have to be willing to do work that you are not being paid for, and to have effective conversations with whomever you can that will be an asset in you moving your personal vision forward.

Napoleon Hill discussed the habit of going the extra mile in *Think and Grow Rich* (one of our all-time favorite books). This habit brings the individual to the favorable attention of those who can and will provide opportunities for self-advancement. It also tends to make one indispensable, and it enables him/her to command better compensation for their services.

You will know you are truly aligned with the company's purpose and a champion for the customer when you make decisions throughout the day based on the likelihood of a positive impact to one of two important customer groups. Those two groups consist of the internal customer (fellow employees) and the end-user customer.

Much has been written about regarding the end-user demographic, but all of us realize that the only way to truly be customer-centric in the marketplace is to first ensure that our internal culture is treated as an equally important asset. And guess what. Happy employees are among the best salespeople your organization has. Customers don't trust your brand or CEO half as much as they trust the word-of-mouth recommendation from one of your employees. Happy employees are crucial for the growth and well-being of your organization. They are your first customer!

Buying from some brands can be a religious experience, and yet for the majority of brands, each transaction is just that—a transaction. If your purpose statement is clear and up to date, you should be hiring and firing to that purpose. Who you are hiring and firing (people) is the next lens by which you will be auditing and assessing as we go through the layers of the EMF. People must embody the values of your brand (stated or otherwise) and be bought in to the purpose at an individually meaningful level. Then they must have the required skills and competencies to outperform your competitors in delivering against the promises your brand and marketing makes on a day-in and day-out basis.

People are the glue that makes the EMF work, or the acetone that takes an otherwise brilliant strategy founded in the right research and eats away at its impact with each point of execution. Although you are people powered, your processes should be designed to make sure that you don't become people dependent. Process is the third foundational piece of your puzzle before you begin to dive into the dialogues of the Insight Layer.

At the Insight Layer, you are relishing in brutal truths and insights gained about how and where your current processes are halting/accelerating innovation or optimizing/reducing reliability. The reality is that there are very few processes in any company that cannot be further improved.

In a digital world, you must increase the cycles of review around your processes as part of your quarterly or biannual reviews with the operations team. Why? Because the rate of change to your customer needs, competitive solutions, macroenvironment, and available technologies is so great that your very business model may be at risk.

An organization with *digital sense* doesn't resist this discipline but instead embraces change as the one true constant. Each process will have a different life cycle, so the value of having a clear understanding of the reason for your existence (purpose) and the relationship you wish to have with your customer (vision) will help you guide your decisions around people (who) and process (how) improvements as you march forward.

We suggest that, in your annual offsite meetings, at a minimum, you sit with your team and extended team leaders and put every person and process—even the sacred ones—on the table and run a game of KCT (Keep, Change, or Trash) on the contents of that table. This is a habit of great organizations that provides insurance against complacency at large.

Complacency and apathy are the top two killers of customer experience. The dangerous idea that you have achieved the peak of your potential already is a cancer that will slowly eat at your organization and market share until one day it is all suddenly gone, never to be regained.

Customers, Competitors, and Forces

We now live in a world where, according to CEB Global research, 57 percent of the buyer's decision in the B2B category has been made before they even contact your sales function. At any given time throughout the buyer's journey *you have 12 percent of their mindshare on average.*[2]

Think about that through your own buying habits to help ground you in those statistics more personally. How many places do you look for something online before you center in on the handful of brands you will consider doing business with to make a purchase? On the B2C side, think about how easy and fast it is for you to compare pricing online or on a mobile device for a product you have in your basket, before you decide whether or not to purchase it at that outlet or somewhere else. We both open up a price scanner app whenever we are shopping at brick-and-mortar locations. Don't you?

If you are reading this hardback book right now inside of a Barnes & Noble or local bookstore, we hope you will decide to purchase it there, but we totally understand if you decide to buy it on Amazon as a Prime member or for your Kindle, if the price is more aggressive.

The reality, each of us understands, is that when we have a need and have done our research (broad or narrow) on that purchase, we simply want the most seamless, personalized, and efficient checkout process we can get. We value not only the transaction itself or the product/service being consumed but also our belief and trust in the support system or portal by which we transacted. This is so that, in the event something is wrong or undesirable, we aren't unknowingly creating more work and hassle for ourselves.

Have you ever taken a ride with Uber? No fumbling for payment, no lag in the entry or exit of your ride; you get back your most precious asset, TIME. Digital expectations are raising all expectations.

One of the most basic tips to training a baseline level of digital sense is to have your team members ask themselves how they—as customers—would react to the decision, process, or protocol being instituted. Play devil's advocate. Never perpetuate a process that your internal team would not tolerate if they were customers.

The Customer

"Our challenge is to be in the spaces where our audiences are and understand that they will leave us if we don't work with them and understand their needs."

—*Gavin Heaton*[3]

Despite this well-known fact, there are thousands of organizations that give lip service to implementing the root changes to their operational DNA (Figure 4.2) to effect real change.

As regular air travelers, we are always blown away by how commonplace this is at major airlines. This digital example from American Airlines illustrates how difficult this is without complete organizational alignment from the top down around the customer as the number one asset. The lip service part is below in Figure 4.3 and 4.4.[4]

Figure 4.2   A Truism Depicted by an Emoji Sentence

American Airlines

The new American is arriving

We've changed our look on the outside to reflect the progress we've made on the inside, revealing our new logo and the refreshed exterior of our planes. Now, we're taking the next step in our journey to create the new American.

With the legal close of our merger with US Airways, we're one step closer to bringing you a stronger airline that offers greater schedule options, access to more destinations around the globe and a modern and fuel-efficient fleet.

See how we're coming together to create something greater

Figure 4.3   American Airlines Website Screenshot, July 2016

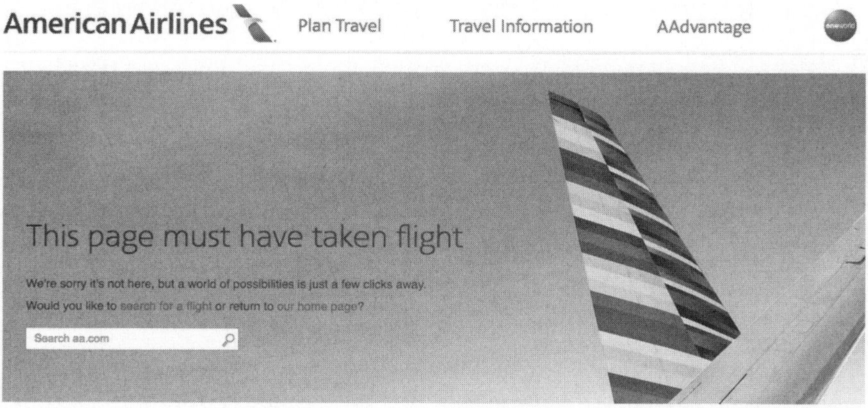

American Airlines   Plan Travel   Travel Information   AAdvantage

This page must have taken flight

We're sorry it's not here, but a world of possibilities is just a few clicks away.
Would you like to search for a flight or return to our home page?

Search aa.com

Figure 4.4   American Airlines Website Screenshot Post Click, July 2016

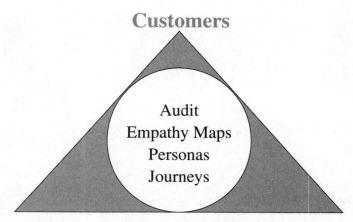

Figure 4.5   The Customer Node of the EMF Insights Layer

Figure 4.4 is the page you land on when you click through on "See how we're coming together to create something greater."[5]

The most important step to evaluating the state of your customer node as you work through the Insights Layer of the EMF (Figure 4.5) is to ensure that you have up-to-date documented personas and journey maps for each of the products/services you offer. You'll also want these for each of the known customer types that you engage with or see as a critical customer class to acquire in the present and near future.

The Importance of Persona and Customer Journey Mapping

Volumes of great material have been written about the importance of persona and journey map development as it relates to effective and efficient experience marketing. Fellow Wiley author and friend Brian Solis has some great resources in his most recent book, *X: The Experience Where Business Meets Design*. We encourage you to nerd out with Brian in the latter chapters of his book on all of the science and design thinking specifics that surround great journey map development. Also, if you aren't following him yet, do that right now: @briansolis.

The areas to audit at this layer are your detractor pipeline, your Employee Net Promoter Score (eNPS) to Net Promoter Score (NPS) ratio, your journey maps, and how well you have defined and empathized with your core persona targets. One of the problems with just looking at NPS is that as you lose detractors your score actually improves, so you also want to measure the trajectory of your eNPS and make sure that it is not heading in the opposite direction. It is a signal that something is fundamentally wrong within your organizational design and culture, and the first customer (employee) must be as big of a priority as your end-user customer.

For the sake of the pragmatic applications required to get your Insights Layer completed with a solid snapshot of your customer needs and how well you are aligning your major business objectives to them, we suggest you focus on the exercises below as your immediate starting point.

Audience Development Exercise

Purpose: Identify key personas and empathize with them

Step 1: Stop thinking first about general demographics and think first about the individual human who needs what you sell. What is their problem that you are solving?

Step 2: Assign a facilitator and define as a group the top four fictitious customers (personas) in detail that represent your ideal customer set. Give them fictitious names, ethnicities, ages, relationship and/or family statuses, and career profiles. Use the guideline list of persona elements below as a guide if you don't have a formal one.

Sample Worksheet of Persona Characteristics:

Name: Fictitious name goes here

Gender:

Ethnic background:

Marital Status:

Children:

Occupation:

Education level:

Household Income:

Age:

Websites/Apps most visited:

Hobbies:

Interests/Likes:

Values: (i.e., family, material goods, etc.)

Behaviors: (impatient, driven, multitasker)

Lifestyle: (i.e., foodie, workaholic, etc.)

Who is their boss?:

What problems are they trying to solve?:

Step 3: Gather a diverse group of team members (marketing, sales, operations, customer service, executive) that own or have impact on one of the defined customer touch points.

Step 4: Hand out a stack of sticky notepads to each person and draw the following chart (Figure 4.6) on a whiteboard or flipchart.

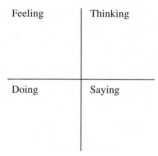

Figure 4.6 Empathy Map: Persona A

Step 5: Run through each known touch point (see Figure 4.7) of your customer's journey with your diverse group of leaders and ask the following questions about each touch point.

Empathy Mapping Group Exercise Questions:

A. How do they feel?

B. What are they thinking?

Figure 4.7 An Example of a Generic Journey Map of Touch Point

     C. What are they saying and in which medium/channel (on the phone, to a friend, via social media, in store, etc.)?

     D. What are they doing?

     Note: Each member of this discussion will write their answer to these questions on their sticky notes, and when everyone is done they will stick them on the board in the appropriate quadrant.

Step 6: Depending on which touch points you care most about (i.e., awareness, evaluation, consideration, purchase, etc.), this exercise can take as little as 30 minutes or as long as several hours for each persona. Regardless of the time you give this, don't let lack of time become a reason to procrastinate.

Empathizing with your customer sets is the single most important strategy and tactic you can engage in to begin humanizing your business and taking customer experience to a new level. It is also an amazingly efficient and telling way to uncover unknown alignment or lack thereof among your team members and address any inconsistencies or differences of opinion to whom your most valuable personas are and the associated needs they have, which you can help solve.

Look Honestly at Your Competitive Landscape

Now that you have updated your empathic understanding of your core customer segments, and their current and likely near-future needs that you help solve, we need to look honestly

> "The journey of a thousand miles begins with a single step"
>
> —*Lao Tzu*

across the competitive landscape and score how you stack up overall and align the current baseline to your stated vision of where you are headed.

Many of you assess market share using a popular framework such as Boston Consulting Group's BCG Matrix or the Gartner Magic Quadrant. We will speak to both tools and how you can use them in this node to create a clear picture of where your opportunity and challenges lie as it relates to increasing your competitive advantage and likelihood of increased success.

As you continue to work through the Insight Layer in this section with your team of internal stakeholders, agency partners, and key partners, you

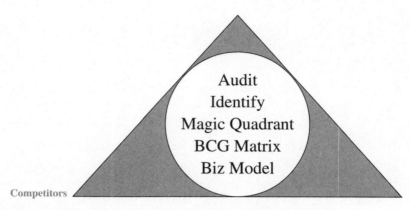

Figure 4.8   The Competitors Node of the EMF Insights Layer

will leverage research and all available data on your business in comparison to your direct competition (Figure 4.8). You will take the audits on detractor pipeline from the work done in your customer node and begin to further map which competitor you lost them to. This allows you to proactively work to discover where the vulnerability lies. You will also identify new competitors or potential competitors in the near future based on leveraging tools such as the Gartner Magic Quadrant[6] (see Figure 4.9). In some cases, Gartner will have a current-year, published magic quadrant for your industry, and in other cases they will not. In either case, we suggest that you build your own using their framework and compare the two, and discuss the implications and opportunities for you to move from wherever you are to the top right of the quadrant, most relevant to your stated goals and company vision.

According to Gartner the following quadrants are defined as follows:

How does a Gartner Magic Quadrant Work?

A Magic Quadrant provides a graphical competitive positioning of four types of technology providers, in markets where growth is high and provider differentiation is distinct:

Leaders execute well against their current vision and are well positioned for tomorrow.

Visionaries understand where the market is going or have a vision for changing market rules but do not yet execute well.

Figure 4.9 Gartner's Magic Quadrant

Niche Players focus successfully on a small segment or are unfocused and do not out-innovate or outperform others.

Challengers execute well today or may dominate a large segment but do not demonstrate an understanding of market direction.

The benefit of using the EMF in concert with Gartner's Magic Quadrant is that it will clarify an additional context by which you should rank your competitive advantage looking ahead. That added insight will be based upon your group's qualitative and quantitative assessment of how well you currently execute on the reliability of your customer experience as it relates to your competition and how complete your vision is. This will also show you how to continue innovating your customer experience as a competitive advantage in the coming years.

We will discuss how to operationalize your commitment to reliability and innovation through a social business digital strategy later in this book; until then, the visual in Figure 4.10 will help you contextualize for your C-Suite where both of these commitments play into your present and future market position within the Gartner Magic Quadrant.

Depending on how many lines of business you currently oversee, it may also be in your practice to utilize the BCG Matrix (aka Growth-Share Matrix, as seen in Figure 4.11) as part of your annual assessments and strategic planning.

The EMF will complement this effort as well. It should help you view the investment decisions and future resourcing not only around the immediate impact to the P&L or balance sheet but also as it relates to the near-term future-need-states of your customer. It may also reveal what intellectual property or assets can be repositioned or divested to allow for a doubling down on the most promising question marks, while innovating the customer experience of your cash cows to sustain your priority sources of wealth creation and growth fuel.

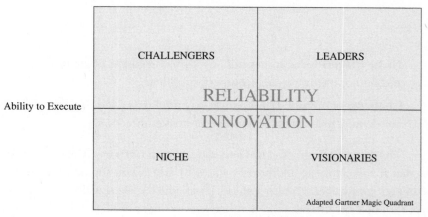

Figure 4.10 Layering the Two Commitments of CX over the Gartner Magic Quadrant

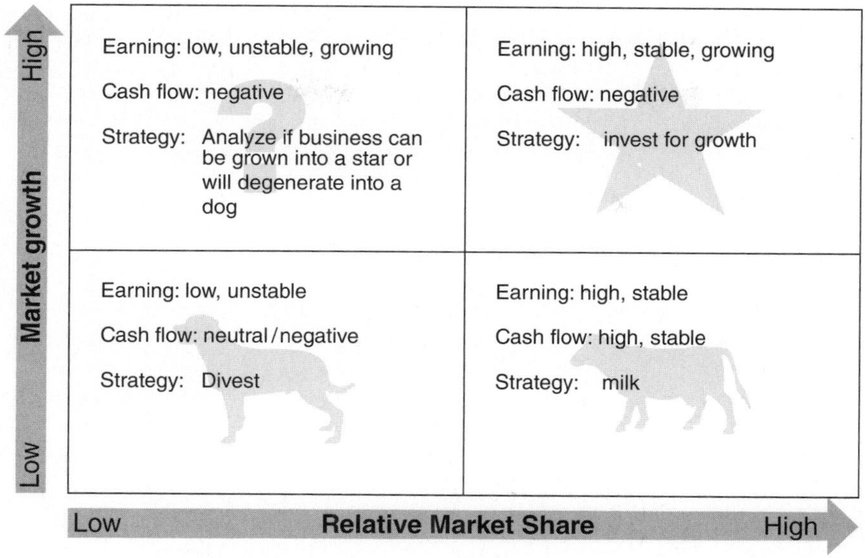

Figure 4.11 BCG Matrix

We both believe that any framework, including our own, is strongest when it is brilliantly simple and powerfully clear in its communication. However, there is an equally present potential liability or limitation due to that simplicity. The BCG Matrix has great strength in its simple elegance, but it also does not account for a detailed assessment of all the contributing factors of your overall competitive strength, especially in a high-growth market.

Market share is an important factor and leverage point to assess, but in the digital world, where business life cycles have exponentially shortened (see Figure 4.12), complacency and reliance on market share as a strength is the number one blind spot and vulnerability to your sustainability.

The Customer Is the Asset

To reduce this vulnerability in the BCG Matrix, we suggest that the EMF will help you provide through all three layers a more complete picture, as it relates to your market share, brand equity, distribution relationships,

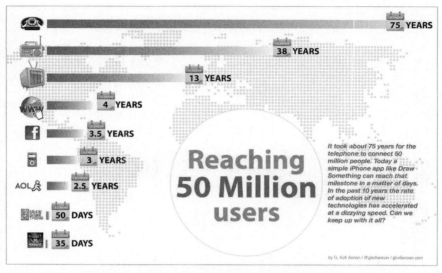

Figure 4.12 "Reaching 50 Million Users by G. Kofi Annan"[7]

Note to reader: This Angry Bird Space meme has been called "too good to check" because it makes a clear point about user adoption scenarios today versus yesteryear. It is important to call out that for those sticklers who want to know the full context. *The Wall Street Journal* (*WSJ*) did an exposé piece worth reading about this.[8]

logistics/supply chain inefficiencies, product/service line offerings, and customer loyalty/advocacy.

The BCG Matrix, on its own, is most valuable as a reasonable measure of competitive strength in low-growth markets—cash cows and dogs—but it is going to be a much less accurate predictor of your overall health and stability in high-growth, highly fragmented markets. The other limitation of the BCG Matrix (other than the fact that different publishers of it move the boxes around from version to version under the guise of artistic expression, we guess) is the large middle section where many of your offerings/brands or business units may be plotted. There is no inherent tool in the BCG Matrix alone that allows you to know which decision to make as it relates to items in the black hole (Figure 4.13).

Therefore, we believe that as you dive into the competitor node of the EMF, it is important to assess your relative strengths against competition in

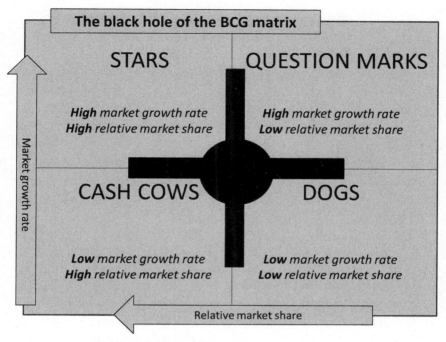

Figure 4.13 BCG Matrix Black Hole[9]

both the BCG and Gartner frameworks. Each has its value in helping you benchmark where you stand today and where the potential opportunity to leap ahead will be in the future.

DIGITAL BIT: Download your free Excel template for creating a BCG Matrix with or without known market share data here: DigitalSen.se.com/FreeBCG.

Now that you have a good handle on how and where you sit in relationship to your customers in comparison to your direct competitors, it is time to take an intuitive and logical—data-backed—look at the unknown future of outside forces (Figure 4.14) that are possible or likely to have an

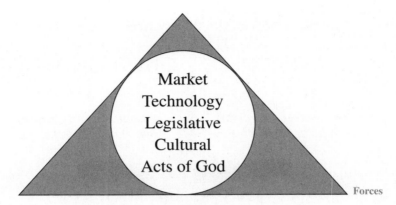

Figure 4.14 The Forces Node of the EMF Insights Layer

impact on your customer, your competition, your industry, or society at large. We have bucketed forces into one of five categories and developed some simple questions for the forces exercise to help you get a well-rounded view what is at play around you, so that you can develop a core group of insights worth acting upon.

"Use the Force, Luke!"

As it relates to market forces, you will pull together historical analysis of market trends (bubbles, bursts, election cycle impacts, Fed Funds rates, quantitative easing cycles, employment and productivity data, etc.) and have it at the ready as you ask the group the following directional questions.

1. Do I/we believe that the general stock market value has a direct or inverse relationship to our growth potential?
2. Do we believe that within the next five years we will be in a recession, coming out of one, or in a full-blown bull market?
3. As it relates to our customers and the needs we solve for them, what impact does an uncertain market, growth market, or down market have on their buying potential, loyalty, or psyche?

4. As it relates to our competitors, who is vulnerable or well positioned from a capital to growth trajectory ratio if the market and access to capital changes significantly in the coming years?

5. Is that an opportunity for us to consolidate our industry or be acquired under favorable terms?

The next category of things outside of your control that must be considered are technology forces. In his book, *BOLD,* Peter Diamandis talks about the six phases that industries go through due to technological forces. It is worth familiarizing yourself with these phases as context because you will want to assess which phase you believe your industry is currently in. You'll also want to assess where current near-term capabilities will be in the coming 2–5 years, especially as you map a plan to stay relevant and in front of your customer's needs with your solution and infrastructure to support them.

The 6 Ds (Phases) as Classified by Peter Diamandis

1. **Digitization:** The reason why you and your organization need a digital sense is because today, anything can be digitized—represented by ones and zeros—and everything will be digitized in due time. As Marc Andreessen stated in his August 2011 op-ed in *The Wall Street Journal,* "Software is eating the world."[10]

    If you are still wondering why this is happening and how it can happen, consider that we are now more than 60 years into the computer revolution and more than 20 years into the rise of the modern Internet. We are no longer in the low trajectory of the exponential compounding of Moore's law or Zuck's law; we are at the knee-bend heading into full vertical. Technology that can transform industries overnight through software is now readily and widely available, affordable, and getting cheaper by the second. When things are digitized, they can spread at the speed of light, constrained only by the current speed of our Internet connections.

2. **Deception:** This is the phase that follows digitization, and in many ways, this is where the masses of society consciously live. This is the phase where most of the exponential growth and compounding goes unnoticed

and is mistaken for linear improvements, because our biological evolution happens over millions of years, but we manufacture new complexity in picoseconds.

The classic exercise to show humanity's bias to think linearly vs. exponentially is *The Penny or $1 Million Dollars Exercise:* (Figure 4.15)

Step 1: Ask your group to choose between accepting $1 million in cash today or a single (one-cent) penny that doubles every day for the next month.

Step 2: Tell them they have 15 seconds to choose.

At first blush, most people will do some quick finger math ($0.01 Day 1, $0.02 Day 2, $0.04 Day 3 $0.08 Day 4, $0.16, and so on until you call time.) People will get impatient or fearful of losing out on some percentage of the $1 million in cash by guessing, and based upon their miniscule returns in the first week, they will project a plodder's progress of linear growth on the month and opt to take $1 million today. However, as you can see (in Figure 4.15) they would have left a lot on the table by making that choice.

Those who chose the penny-doubled option are sweating it a bit at day 20, but as their minds begin to grasp the visible and conspicuous disruption of the compounding, they get very excited. At the same time, when you begin to realize that this holds true for all truths and realities we hold dear today, it can become threatening, scary, and overwhelming.

What does all this mean to your business reality moving forward? Consider that the smartphone you hold in your hand today has more

Day	Value	Day	Value	Day	Value
1	$0.01	11	$10.24	21	$10,485.76
2	$0.02	12	$20.48	22	$20,971.52
3	$0.04	13	$40.96	23	$41,943.04
4	$0.08	14	$81.92	24	$83,886.08
5	$0.16	15	$163.84	25	$167,772.16
6	$0.32	16	$327.68	26	$335,544.32
7	$0.64	17	$655.36	27	$671,088.64
8	$1.28	18	$1,310.72	28	$1,342,177.28
9	$2.56	19	$2,621.44	29	$2,684,354.56
10	$5.12	20	$5,242.88	30	$5,368,709.12

Figure 4.15 A penny doubled for 30 days chart

access to information right now than President George W. Bush had at his total disposal when he entered office in January 2000. The equivalent device at the $1,000 price point in 2023 will have the speed and processing power of a human brain, because of this exponential doubling, and the deception phase is where we wrestle with the notion that something like that is likely or possible when the reality is it is already happening.

3. **Disruption:** In many ways one of the most overused buzzwords today is disruption, but in the most simple terms, technology forces that cause disruption are the technological breakthroughs or developments that create an entirely new market and destroy an existing one.

Think about what Airbnb has done for hospitality or Uber has done for consumer expectations and access not to just affordable ride sharing but also to payments at point of sale. The zero-friction payment interface in both of these examples not only has caused massive disruption in their direct industries (hospitality and transportation) but also is disrupting the banking industry and retail payments and merchant industry because of the new consumer expectation and interface they have deployed. Let's not even get into how blockchain technology is disrupting banking, because that's a whole other book!

You have heard it before, but we live in an exponential era and a digital world. *Either disrupt yourself or be disrupted by someone else.* Focusing on the customer and the forces shifting their overall expectations outside of your industry are the only ways, in our opinion, to stay ahead of this fact sustainably. It is the one true area to still win competitive advantage.

4. **Demonetization:** As the disruption takes root in a marketplace, it completely erodes or removes money from the model it disrupted. Skype, and now FB Messenger and the like, demonetized long-distance telephony. Travis paid his way through the University of Kansas by peddling Sprint's $0.10 a minute long distance *forever* plan! Guess what? It wasn't forever.

Ubiquitous Wi-Fi access will continue to demonetize wireless carrier plans for fees around SMS, voice, and so on. Napster demonetized the music business. Snapchat and similar applications that allow for personalized consumption and simultaneous production/interaction with media and content may soon demonetize broadcast television in the same way that Netflix demonetized primetime television and the retail movie rental business. Remember Blockbuster Video? Travis may still have some fines to pay them. Let Wayne Huizenga, former CEO of Blockbuster, know that he is truly sorry.

5. **Dematerialization:** Where demonetization relates to the disappearance of money that was once paid for certain goods and services, dematerialization relates to the disappearance of the actual goods and services themselves.

For example (Figure 4.16), autonomous driving vehicles at scale will dematerialize the need for traffic cops, auto dealerships, auto lending and ownership in general, and much more. Think about all of the luxuries that existed and were consumed by the upper middle class and wealthy demographic in the 1980s and have now been dematerialized and come standard within the lowest/most basic generation smartphone in an everyman-affordable, pay-as-you-go monthly lease contract.

6. **Democratization:** The upside of every disruption, however, is that it brings an end to the exponential chain reaction of vanishing returns and opens up an entirely new and abundant marketplace of opportunity that is more widely available for new entrants to solve problems with new innovations.

In the world ahead, everything from money, health records, and title/ownership records to corporate capitalization tables can exist in a distributed ledger, such as blockchain, with no need for intermediaries or trust agents; the opportunity is endless. In a world where cars drive for us, we will think of new opportunities to fill our time. In a world where we use mobile devices—or merge with our devices—as if it was our personal remote control, to call on-demand anything and everything, where are you positioned as a company and organization? This world is not off into the 50–100 year future. This is the next 5–15 years. The most exciting and disruptive moments in human history are happening now through 2030.

Lastly, there are also technology forces that have nothing to do with the future and everything to do with the past, that must be navigated as you attempt to become a customer-centric digital organization. Those

Figure 4.16

Source: *India Times.*[11]

forces are the legacy technology systems and disparate incentives between your IT and marketing/sales functions. We highly recommend you also pick up and read *The Inevitable: Understanding the 12 Technological Forces That Will Shape Our Future* by Kevin Kelly as a great supplemental guide to the questions below.

Questions to Assess Technological Forces

The high-level questions to ask your team to assess the technological forces that are likely to impact your business are below and give you a starting point to prioritize your plan of attack:

1. What can we do to better meet the increased frictionless expectations that our customers have about transacting with any company because of outside disruptions from Uber, Amazon, and so on to the user interface and experience of purchasing a product or service?

2. What are we doing to think of ourselves as a technology and media company, regardless of our core offering, so that we can deepen the engagement and relationship we have within our customer's mindshare?

3. What are the truths that we hold about ourselves that are not vulnerable to disruption?

4. What new cultural shift, technology, or consumer access point would make those truths and sacred cows go away?

5. Why wouldn't we endeavor right now to create them before they get created by someone else?

6. What legacy technology systems do we rely on that can or are inhibiting our ability to seamlessly align around customer experience?

7. Do we have a documented and widely known and drilled set of protocols in the event of an act of terror, direct cyber attack, or indirect cyber attack against one of our major partners that will secure the assets and data of our employees, customers, and partners?

The remaining forces include acts of God, cultural, and legislative forces that are outside of your control (sometimes even if you own and fund the political lobby). As you address these in your EMF planning, the following questions are good high-level catalysts to stir up your brainstorm.

Acts of God Questions

1. Do we have an up-to-date disaster and recovery plan documented in place for our employees and our customers?

2. Do we have a marketing and promotional plan and communication strategy to respond in real time to natural disasters that communicates an on-message proactive response to our employees and customers?

3. Do we have a robust set of supporting partners or internal programs to help our people through emotionally trying times or life events and have we empowered HR to create and invest in this strategy for when bad things happen to our good people and customers?

Cultural Forces Questions

1. Does our internal culture, office esthetic, policy, and procedure design meet the needs and desires of tomorrow's workforce and talent?

2. Is our compensation model clear, equitable, and fun? Do our incentive structures line up to us achieving our major business objectives while simultaneously causing customer-centric decision-making across departments?

3. Are we at risk of having talent poached by direct competitors? If so, what postmortems have we run to assess where we can shore up vulnerability? What one change could we make in this coming quarter to mitigate future losses immediately?

4. How aligned are the growth trajectories of our eNPS scores to our customer NPS scores? Are we focused on giving our first customer (the employee) the attention and clarity of purpose they need and deserve?

5. If our culture is one of our greatest assets, how are we leveraging this story to be told through our marketing and communications plans as a key differentiator? Are we doubling down on this or deprioritizing?

Legislative Forces Questions

1. What have election cycles (lame duck periods and media inventory costs) done to our projections of conversion rate, cost per lead, length of sales cycle, and so on in the past? What sensitivity analysis and assumptions are we making about this next few years as we look forward?

2. Are we investing appropriately in political capital locally, regionally, and nationally depending on our business footprint? Are we inefficient or inactive in this regard? Are we missing an opportunity?

3. If our industry gets deregulated (or regulated) in the coming few years, does our strategy have a parallel plan in place to capitalize on this type of shift and either preserve our core business and customer relationships or take market share away from our competition?

4. Will legislation that is reactive to acts of terror, acts of God, or shift in political control cause us an increased cost burden to maintain compliance? And what will our plan be to maintain our customer relationships on smaller budgets as we meet any of these new requirements?

Congratulations! You have now arrived at the end of the Insights Layer and now have a couple of dozen questions from each node that you can formalize a meaningful discussion within your team immediately to begin building your insights into a social business strategy with humanized tactics. As you contemplate this chapter, you may also come to the conclusion that your very business model is at risk of rapidly becoming obsolete.

Business model is best defined simply as "how you make money sustainably to survive and grow." As you think through the customer needs, the competitive landscape, and the various forces described previously, you may come to the conclusion that you need a new vision and business model all together. As G.I. Joe said, "Knowing is half the battle!"

Takeaways from the Insight Layer

- The major insights you will gain come from taking a deep look at the needs of your customer, your current and attainable near-term position in the competitive landscape, and the forces outside of your control.

- In a digital world there are six phases of the business life cycle: Digitization, Deception, Demonetization, Disruption, Dematerialization, and Democratization, which then leads to a remonetization.

- You must assess the insights, opportunities, threats, strengths, and vulnerabilities through both the internal customer (employee) lens and the external customer (market).

After the exercises in this chapter you may come to the conclusion that your very business model is on the near-term trajectory to obsolescence. In any event it is a wise practice to use EMF to disrupt yourself and find new ways to win the customer relationship before someone else does.

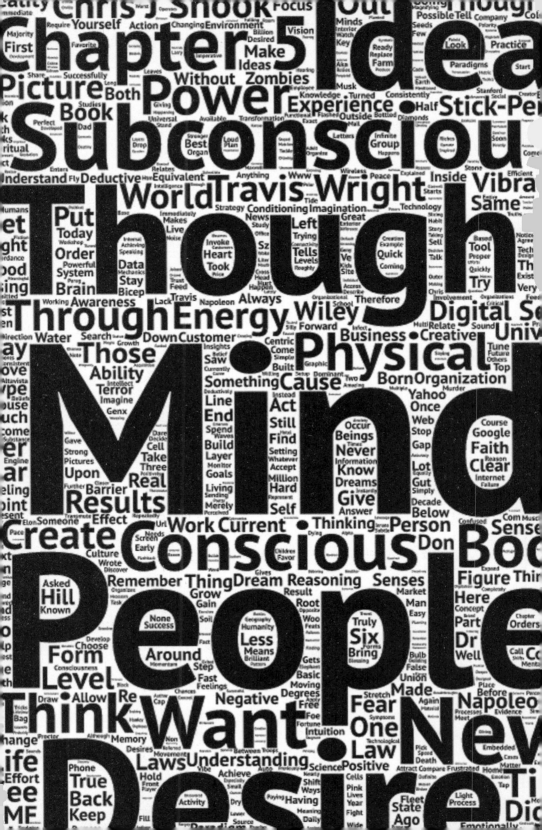

5 Mind over Organizational Matter

♫♫*Drop the negative vibe*
and draw a hard line
No fear, no doubt
I'm in control of my mind
Stand behind me
'Cause I was born to lead
My truth is your dare
Cause today I'm a player♫♫

—Playa's Anthem (Orpheus Hanley Soundstation Records 2009)

"By wrapping the world in seamless and digital connectivity we move closer to a world of interdependent economic peace and prosperity. Connectivity is destiny. Functional geography over Political geography."

—PARAG KHANNA IN HIS BOOK *CONNECTOGRAPHY*

We know that by now a digital sense sounds like something out of Elon Musk's next brilliant bag of science-fiction-turned-reality tricks. For those of us under the age of 65, in our lifetime there probably will be a true digital sense—sixth sense—layer of consciousness available to allow human beings to keep pace with our technological and AI inventions. Many futurists, from Ray Kurzweil to Gerd Leonhard, have predicted the singularity will occur as early as 2023.

At the 2016 RE/CODE conference,[1] Musk even hinted that he believed a digital layer embedded into our consciousness would be a good idea for humanity, as a means to augment our painfully slow evolutionary biology, and that it was possible to achieve in a short window of time. However, since he is busy changing the world in three other significant ways right now, this book will have to do.

For the immediate pragmatic purposes of helping you transform your organization into a digital organization, centered around customer experience and great culture, you need a practical approach and understanding of how and where transformation and paradigm shifts occur in your mind. It is also imperative that you can help others around you (*the collective organizational mind*), tap into the power of their minds, to create groundswell momentum and digital sense to successfully realign purpose, vision, goals, systems, and tactics around the customer as the one metric that matters. It is with this in mind that we will spend this chapter diving deeper into a simple yet powerful visual of how you can put your mind to work to create a new subconscious operating system. One that is focused on achieving this desired end. This will keep the zombies from derailing your efforts and infecting your motivatables, as you make the effort to build your brand into one that differentiates on customer experience across all points in the buyer journey.

To successfully implement the EMF, to gain buy-in across the executive rank, and to motivate/lead the body of your organization in this new direction; you must have a clear picture in your mind from which to work.

Mind and Brain Mechanics 101

Mind is the activity and movement of the spirit. Our brain is the system/organ that organizes and distributes the activity called "mind." We are all spiritual beings, blessed and empowered with an intellect, living in a physical body and having this human experience. Spirit is not to be confused with religion. Religion is merely a vehicle that studies spirit, and there are many flavors of religion. Pick your favorite one, or none at all, and this truth about how our creative power works will hold true. Mind is the master power that can transmute the spiritual desires given to us from the divine/ethereal form into their physical equivalent.

Let's travel back to a time when you didn't have an e-mail address. Remember or imagine with us when you didn't own a cell phone. Now, about half of you reading this book can't remember that time, because you were born after 1990, but a good majority of you can remember when that was your reality. However, within the last 5 years, the one thing that almost all of us (Boomer, GenX, GenY, Gen Z, and our kids of Gen Alpha) have in common is that we are all completely reliant and even somewhat addicted to our digital devices—our sixth sense—aka "smartphone."

The power of this can't be understated. Even those of us from GenX and the Boomers who remember living an adult life without a smartphone or even an e-mail address will have a hard time recollecting how we made it through our day without those technological breakthroughs. Going to the bathroom has never been the same, right? Less than 27 years prior to the printing of this book, there was no such thing as the world wide web/Internet. Bottled water was a new concept that some critics touted as silly, saying, "Why would I pay for bottled water when I have a faucet in my house?" If you have stayed in a hotel room lately, you will agree that those convenient bottles of water on your nightstand for only $4.50 per liter are a blessing if you wake up with dry mouth.

How did these "necessities" of today become our reality when they didn't even exist 30, 20, or even 10 years ago? The amazing thing is that when the Internet went up as we exited the 1980s and entered the 1990s, the Google founders were barely in high school. Yet, in the year 2017, the idea that Sergey Brin and Larry Page dreamt up a decade and a half ago, for a "search engine" to organize all of the world's information for people on this relatively new thing called the World Wide Web, joined five other tech companies in the six largest (by market capitalization companies in the Fortune 500, as seen in Figure 5.1) with only Exxon representing a nontech company.

Symbol	Company	Cap Rank on 8/9/16	Market CAP on 8/9/16	1d Chg on 8/9/16	1m Chg on 8/9/16	12m Chg on 8/9/16
AAPL	Apple	1	586.3	0.4%	12.5%	−5.8%
GOOGL	Alphabet	2	555.0	0.3%	12.5%	21.5%
MSFT	Microsoft	3	453.5	0.2%	11.3%	24.5%
XOM	Exxon Mobil	4	367.8	0.1%	−5.2%	15.4%
AMZN	Amazon.com	5	364.2	0.2%	3.0%	47.0%
FB	Facebook	6	359.1	−0.2%	6.7%	32.6%

Figure 5.1 Market Capitalization of the Top 6 Fortune 500 Companies in 2016

In 2007, 10 years ago, Google (now Alphabet) boasted over 11,000 employees with revenues of just under $1 million per employee and was ranked seventeenth on the Fortune 500 with market value at $143.6 billion! Not a bad 9-plus year growth in value of over $411 billion as of 2016.[2]

Substance Is all Around Us. We Just Need the Thought.

"Every block of stone has a statue inside it and it is the task of the sculptor to discover it."

—MICHELANGELO

The way to fly the plane was here long before the Wright brothers tuned in their awareness to the discovery of it. (*Note:* Orville and Wilbur are no relation to Travis, although he will tell you that they are. Don't believe him though; he's bulls#%ting you.)

Similarly, the way to build the incandescent light bulb and all the materials were already here, but it was Edison's persistence, organized effort, and mind power that made it physical reality. (*Note: Screw Edison and J.P. Morgan lol. As badass as they were as shrewd monopolists, Nikola Tesla was a much cooler and important inventor in our opinion*).

MILESTONE: Let us know you made it this far and share your preference with us by tweeting either #TeslaOverEdison or #EdisonOverTesla to @teedubya @chrisjsnook.

What is the point? Every desire in your heart, every dream, every *idea* starts in the mind. The understanding and development of your mind and its interdependence with the Universal Mind will allow you to quickly realize that the creative genius in those mentioned above resides equally in you for your desires.

It has been said that a picture is worth a thousand words. We think in pictures, and if we said, "Think of a car," you would agree that you instantly saw a picture of either a car you want or your current car. You would be able to describe in detail the color of the exterior and interior, the level of cleanliness, etc. You would not think of the letters *c-a-r*. If we said, "Think of your house," you would not see the letters *h-o-u-s-e*, you would see a picture of your house as it flashed across the screen of your mind, and it would replace the car.

The opposite works, as well. Let's try this quick exercise. Right now, do *not* think of a pink elephant.

It's nearly impossible to *not* think of a pink elephant in that instance. So, think of what you want, in a positive way, not about what you don't want. It may sound woo-woo, but stick with us because your ability to communicate and achieve desired objectives will be forever impacted for the better if you can apply this chapter in your life moving forward.

When we ask you to think of a picture of your "mind," what do you see? If you are like the majority of people, you may have seen a picture of the brain. Having trained and done this exercise with thousands of people and hundreds of organizations over the last decade, we have seen that roughly 65 percent of people's immediate knee-jerk answer/picture to this question is their brain. However, we mentioned previously that your brain is not your mind any more than your fingernail or pancreas is your mind. Brain is the system/organ that organizes the movement of mind. Mind is flowing in every cell of your body—even your heart has cells that are part of the collective mind.

If you have ever been startled by something, you have felt the "fight or flight" response of your sympathetic nervous system kick in instantaneously. Why? Because the activity of mind activated your adrenal gland and shot adrenaline through every fiber of your being to prepare your body for a quick and efficient exit from perceived danger! When you are trying to lead change or create a new paradigm without a picture of your mind—read, goals or business objectives—you are left with unordered chaos of your knowledge and thoughts and the inability to consistently reproduce the desired result.

Thoughts are invisible waves of energy. You can't see them—much as you can't see Wi-Fi, AM/FM radio, or antenna TV—but you know they are there. The more you feed the thought, the stronger it gets. For example, if you dwell on how bad you feel, or something you fear, that thought gets stronger, and the chances of it happening increase. You can see their results when you tune into the right frequency positively or negatively.

If thoughts become things, but you—like the majority of people— are absent a proper picture of your mind, you lack the ability to give order to your thought patterns and knowledge. Given this it should be no secret why many people are frustrated by the acquisition of more knowledge, methods, and frameworks without seeing an increase shift in end results.

Fortunately, Dr. Thurman Fleet gave humanity a picture to work with in 1934 when he started the Concept Therapy® movement in San Antonio, Texas. The concept was further developed into a honed curriculum and has been delivered to millions of people and thousands of organizations globally by one of our partners at the Proctor Gallagher Institute over the last 40 years. In the coming paragraphs we will share a magical "Stick-Person" graphic with you and explain how to use it daily, and in complement to the EMF, so that you can cause meaningful and lasting change in your organization in a digital world.

Dr. Fleet, a chiropractor, was intrigued and frustrated by the practice of treating symptoms and not the root cause of people's ailments. He was committed to a holistic healing regimen with his patients while paying close attention and providing treatment to their acute symptoms and complaints. He found that without a picture of their minds, his patients could not invoke the laws of the universe effectively to begin healing the root cause in their thinking, which was continuously bringing back the symptoms of their disorders. Fleet gave them a picture called the "stick-person" that transformed their results dramatically in record-breaking time. This same concept of the "stick-person" has become a foundational element of all our consulting/ workshop programs.

When Bob Proctor first shared it with us over a decade ago, it took our client results and personal effectiveness to unprecedented levels of growth and satisfaction in less than six months. We are excited to share its basic explanation and diagram with you below and encourage you to study it thoroughly from now until you leave this planet, as we remain committed to do.

The Stick-Person Explained

Human beings are the only known living things that can choose their thoughts—that we know of—and by doing so, humans have the creative power of the universe in their hands to discover, make, and mold the life of their dreams.

"I bring you today, both a blessing and a curse."

—MOSES, DEUTERONOMY 11:26.

Moses's words there are the best way to describe this wonderful power of *free will* that the Creator/Universe has bestowed upon you. When you and your team can grasp that your reality is *always* the result of your dominant thoughts (which create), your feelings (what we give focus to), and your behavior and actions (the result of your vibration), you can truly begin to live a life of peace and enjoyment. W. Clement Stone said, "If you can see it, and believe it, you can achieve it." He was, and still is, right.

We all think in pictures. For instance, when we asked you before to think of a car, you will notice that a car flashed across the screen of your mind. Now, if you saw your current car or your dream car, with all the details of the exterior color and interior design, that is because you were emotionally involved with that idea. We think in pictures of the things with which we are emotionally involved. We could have either a positive or negative emotional involvement with any idea, but that doesn't matter. The idea will begin to unfold from thought form into its physical equivalent the minute that we attach emotion (positive or negative), feeling, and meaning to the idea!

This is critical to understand because many of the people living today focus on *what they do not want* instead of giving thought and energy to *what they do want*.

The law of polarity tells us that everything in the universe has an opposite that exists simultaneously. Therefore, the high, or goal, you seek in your business is present at the same time as the low, or failure, you may be currently experiencing and giving more energy to. Whatever thoughts we give emotion and feeling to will expand and begin immediately to move into their physical form, or reality, and they do this by the law of perpetual transmutation of energy.

DIGITAL BIT: You can learn more about the
7 Universal Laws in a free audio podcast by visiting
DigitalSen.se/the7laws.[3]

When most people are asked to think of a house or car, or any other material thing including their body, they instantly get a clear picture on the screen of their mind; however, when you ask them what their MIND looks like, they draw a blank. Our minds are the most powerful creative resource in the universe, and we have never been given a clear picture to work with. Many people feel confused and frustrated because they have knowledge of how to do what they want but are unable to organize it into a meaningful course of action and a definite purpose that moves the thought into its physical form with speed and accuracy.

We use the power of our intellect to experience our physical reality. The largest gap in human experience is the gap between what we know and what we do. With the picture below (Figure 5.2), you will begin the journey of rapidly closing that gap in your performance from here on out.

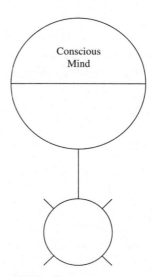

Figure 5.2 The Conscious Mind

Understanding the Mind Using the Stick-Person Graphic

Let the top half of the circle represent your "thinking mind" or conscious mind. This is where you have the ability to accept or reject any idea you choose. When thoughts come to you from the world around you, this is your filter to choose only those with which you will get emotionally involved. This is where you can create the thoughts and dreams that you want for your life and for your organization as well. After all, if you have built or are building a company, you thought it into existence. You believed in your idea and executed consistently to make it happen.

When you create a thought or dream that you want, you can repeat it over and over, until you get the feeling of joy or abundance that you desire, and then the thought will move across the line into the subconscious or "feeling mind" where the order will be carried out to manifest it in physical form.

You can never outperform your self-image. Neither can your organization. All these laws will do for you is attract to you more of who you are, and never what you want and are unwilling to become first.

It is estimated that today, you are bombarded through multiple forms of media and experience with upward of 60,000 images per day. This is up from 10,000 images per day less than a decade ago. Of these images, we can effectively capture or process only 1,000 on a conscious level. The Information Age democratized access to smartphone technology, and this societal benefit has magnified the complexity of our lives while simultaneously—law of polarity—making our lives more efficient and easy through the "app for everything" culture. Without the understanding of the difference between your deductive and inductive reasoning, it is very possible to relate to your reality primarily through the use of your five senses and your smartphone digital appendage. When you do this, you can consciously accept thoughts or ideas that you do not want to "think" on the subconscious level, where they must and will be followed as "orders" by your effort.

Ask yourself how often you notice when you have gotten emotionally involved with a disturbing idea simply because you listened to it or saw it on the news. How often do you find yourself feeling down or upset or fearful the rest of the day? When you watch the news before bed or first thing in the morning, or get overly involved with the gossip at work, you are deductively—using your visual and hearing senses—accepting those thought patterns into your subconscious. This will set up your present-state vibration and dictate what you choose to act on and inevitably how you feel. This sole reason is why neither one of us watches the evening news or horror movies. We want to keep that stuff far away from our subconscious mind.

We both consciously decide to not view those forms of media because in both of our cases we have noticed that it negatively impacts us and siphons power away from our productive focus.

If you want to think, feel, and act more positively, you must guard your subconscious (Figure 5.3) with your conscious mind by being watchful of what ideas you get emotionally involved with and what images you are repeatedly viewing. The greatest gift the Creator/Universe bestowed upon humans was "free will" to choose what we want. You need to exercise that tool in your favor, with the understanding that if you don't monitor your thoughts, you are a Motivatable for people, organizations, and advertisers, which will be more than willing to inundate you with their dogma and attempt to bend your will to their own.

This is the "emotional mind" or "feeling mind." The ancient Greeks called it "the heart of hearts." The subconscious mind only has one answer to all commands it receives from the conscious mind, and that answer is "YES!" The subconscious mind has no ability to accept or reject the thoughts that we

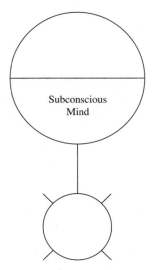

Figure 5.3 The Subconscious Mind

get emotionally involved with; it can and will carry them out by sending orders to the body below as fast as possible.

The universe loves speed! This is why it is important to monitor the thoughts and ideas you are getting emotionally involved with. If you worry or have doubt about some negative idea happening, the subconscious will begin to move you in the direction of having that negative thing happen. Likewise, if you create a positive idea of how you want things to go, or how you want to handle the unfortunate things that happen, then the subconscious mind can and will move you into that positive vibration and begin to manifest that result!

Remember that if the conscious mind is "the general," the subconscious mind is the "troops" and will always carry out the orders that come down from the general. It makes no difference if these orders will help you or hurt you. The beautiful thing is that you can monitor your conscious mind and, more important, use autosuggestion to *create the thoughts that you want* and make those thoughts the orders that your general gives to your troops!

Maxwell Maltz, MD, FICS, who penned the classic book *Psycho-Cybernetics* in 1960, had this to say: "A human being always acts, feels, and performs in accordance with what he imagines to be true about himself and his environment. This is a basic and fundamental law of the mind. It is the way humans were built."[4,5]

Why not imagine yourself successful in establishing alignment and digital sense across your organization? Maltz wrote extensively about how scientists discovered that your subconscious mind operates as what is referred to as a negative-feedback servomechanism. Servo-what? Okay, imagine you are in your house and it is summertime. It is 90 degrees outside, and you decide to set the thermostat to 70 degrees. Someone in the house leaves and doesn't shut the front door. Some of you may flashback to your childhood when your father or mother yelled to you, "Why am I paying to air-condition the whole neighborhood!? Were you born in a f$%^ing barn!!?" Regardless of the flashback moment, your thermostat senses the differential between the outside temperature and the internal setting. Thus, immediately the fan kicks on, and it begins to work overtime to maintain 70 degrees inside the house. This is a negative-feedback cybernetic mechanism. The goal is set and known, and therefore only negative feedback is necessary for the goal to be achieved.

Each of us has a subconscious mind that operates in the same way as everyone else's. The engineers who built things like thermostats, autopilots, and heat-seeking missiles knew how to build them because of their under-standing of how the subconscious mind works. When you get emotionally involved with a dream or goal and it enters the subconscious, the mind "locks in" on the desired outcome. Then, all future negative feedback is processed as guidance and reverse-engineered, to make a conscious correction, take actions to get back on course, and to achieve the chosen and subconsciously embedded destination successfully. This is comforting because the minute that you have your goal on the subconscious level, you possess its spiritual equivalent and cannot miss your target.

The law of gender is what predicates and determines the gestation period of that specific goal's transmutation from its spiritual form to its physical equivalent. This law does not allow you to know when you will "reap," but it does guarantee that "as you sow, so shall you reap."

In his masterpiece, *The Power of Your Subconscious Mind,* Joseph Murphy tells us to "quiet the mind and still the body. Tell the body to relax; it has to obey you. It has no volition, initiative, or self-conscious intelligence. Your body is an emotional hard-drive disk that *records* your *beliefs* and *impressions.*"

The body (Figure 5.4) is the physical form and the machine that is cre-ated and recreated daily by your dominant thoughts and actions. The body is energy in a massive and constant state of vibration. The body is always

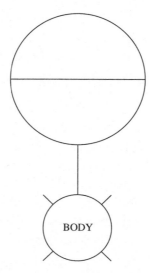

Figure 5.4 The Body

changing or staying the same based upon your thoughts and feelings. It releases 50,000 cells per second back out to the universe, which means that some parts of your physical body are regenerated every day. Roughly every 7 years, you have a completely new body at the cellular level. The results you are looking at, in your physical environment—current business—were produced by the same thoughts and feelings that set up the vibration of your body. In your business enterprise, the body is the physical embodiment of your dominant cultural vibration.

For you to change your current results, you must first change the thoughts and ideas that you get emotionally involved with. When you change the thoughts you give the most focus and energy to, you set up a new feeling/vibration in the subconscious mind, which changes what is acted upon and attracted to the body. This is how you bring any and all ideas from the spiritual plane down to their material equivalent in the physical plane that we all call reality.

This baseline understanding of your mind is also how you proliferate a digital sense across your team and organizational mind. Beware the Zombies in this regard, and ground yourself in the truth that Zombies in your organization—and life—are masterfully on autopilot, leveraging every aspect of this tool to cause you and your people to get and stay emotionally involved with negative and destructive thoughts.

The Zombies are operating from a purely animalistic/survivalist set of subconscious paradigms with no ability or willingness to consider a new way of thinking. They will immediately reject or neglect any new ideas. Quarantine them away from your most important initiatives. Remember that their true power of being on autopilot is equally available for you to use as yours for good. The war is won or lost at the level of the subconscious mind. Master this mind power and harness it for good, and model it for your Motivatiables each and every day as you train them on how to master it as well.

Normal functioning human beings are born with five senses (Figure 5.5): *sight, taste, touch, hearing,* and *smell.* Those of you who are still reading this book, will have six. ☺ #sixthsense

By the age of five, most children have a complete understanding of their ability to use their five senses to understand the world and environment around them. These are our deductive reasoning faculties. The five senses are

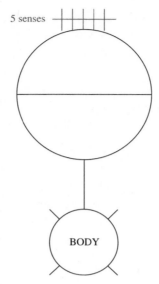

5 senses

BODY

Figure 5.5 The Five Senses

limited to telling us and showing us what already "is." The five senses have NO power to create, and therefore we cannot consider ourselves to be "thinking" when we are looking at our world and results with our five senses. *The five senses are merely feedback loops providing real-time analytics of our experience.*

The Six Intellectual Faculties

1. Reasoning (both deductive and inductive)
2. Intuition
3. Perception
4. Will
5. Imagination
6. Memory

These are our creative faculties and our "thinking muscles." For you to utilize your mind in its intended way to provide you the life or business of our dreams, you must develop these mental muscles. It is also imperative to understand that these six intellectual faculties are always "on" and "perfect" in design. However, they may be weak or strong depending on how much and how often you exercise them. It may be helpful to your understanding to compare these mental muscles to the physical muscles in your body.

For instance, you have a bicep muscle in your arm. Some people have 24-inch "pythons" like the ones Hulk Hogan would always boast about, and other people have tiny little arms. In both of those cases, the bicep is there and will provide the body with flexion at the elbow joint. The bicep's lifting capacity, and its aesthetic appeal, is directly proportional to how often and consistently you exercise it, specifically in its natural plane of motion. If you exercise your bicep consistently, it will grow and expand. However, if you ignore the consistent exercise of it, then it will atrophy.

Your six intellectual faculties operate by the same laws. Your ability to have the life of your dreams starts with your "thinking power." Your "thinking power" is proportional to the development, integration, and strength of these six faculties. Start exercising them consistently in your life and your ability to persuade people to your way of thinking will improve incrementally, and then exponentially!

Reasoning

Reasoning is your innate ability to think. We discussed that deductive reasoning is not thinking with your own mind, but is instead a default way of thinking that ensures you are going to continually be a product of your environment. Motivatables spend a lot of time with deductive reasoning. Deductive reasoning relies on your habitual conditioning at the subconscious level for guidance. This is harmful, because when you are deductively reasoning, you will quickly reject anything that doesn't match your current understanding or paradigms.

Culture is best defined as nothing more than group habit. Therefore, if your culture is deeply embedded with people in the status-quo comfort-zone of deductive reasoning, it will require some real effort in strengthening of the inductive reasoning muscle within the core group of Amplifiers to make a real shift occur as it relates to implementing the EMF and a social business strategy. Deductive-reasoning-heavy organizations are guaranteed to continue acting on ideas that keep the current paradigm in place, which means your leadership will be highly likely to reject an idea that would move your business forward in a sustainable way. This is the same reason Western Union didn't adopt telephone technology. Alexander Graham Bell offered to sell the patents to them for $100,000 in 1879. Western Union turned them down as they were in the paradigm of the telegraph. Western Union should have also become like PayPal, but they didn't switch their paradigm.[6] And Yahoo! LOL at Yahoo! They could have purchased Google for $1 million in 1998. Instead Verizon made a bid to purchase what was left of them for $4 billion in 2016.

The following excerpt from *The Google Story* by David A. Vise highlights Google's earlier buy-out offer to AltaVista and seems to suggest that Yahoo! too would have been asked to pay in the region of $1 million:

> Seated in Palo Alto's Mandarin Gourmet restaurant in March 1998, Page and Brin prepared to pitch Paul Flaherty, a Stanford Ph.D. and an architect of AltaVista, on the merits of their superior search engine technology. AltaVista, they hoped, would pay as much as $1 million to get access to the soon-to-be-patented PageRank system . . .
>
> With the help of Stanford professors and the Office of Technology Licensing, Brin and Page tried unsuccessfully to sell their PageRank system to Excite and other search engines. Yahoo!, seemingly a logical buyer because it relied on directories edited by people and didn't have a fast way to scour the entire Internet, also turned down the chance to buy or license the Google technology. In part, Yahoo! rejected it because the firm wanted computer users to spend more time on Yahoo![7]

You are purely deductive when your environment creates you, and you are being inductive when you create your environment's vibration.

Inductive reasoning—true thinking—occurs when we use our intuition, perception, will, imagination, and memory to analyze new insights or problems and move immediately to create and support the picture of what we want to see manifest with new thought patterns.

Intuition

Often referred to as our "sixth sense," coincidentally—not digital sense—intuition is our ability to recognize someone else's vibration without even knowing them or speaking to them. When we meet someone who immediately makes us feel good or positive, that person is in a positive vibration. When we meet someone who makes us feel negative or scared, they are in a lower or more negative vibration.

Napoleon Hill's *Think and Grow Rich* explained that when you demand a definite plan from your subconscious, it will and must answer you; but it will do so through inspired thought, or the sixth sense, along with hard work and action.[8] When the still small voice answers, you must ACT immediately, and failure to do so, without delay, will be fatal to success.

You have more than likely had a gut feeling about something only to deductively—logically—talk yourself out of moving on it and had it come back to haunt you. Travis had this with NASDAQ: APPL stock in 2001. He intuitively knew that with Jobs leading and with the release of the iPod and the new iMac, Apple was back. The only problem with that was Travis didn't invest NEARLY ENOUGH, and he sold it way too early.

The bottom line is—*Trust Your Gut*—and develop your intuition to tune in at the highest level of those around you. This will allow you to see through all the noise coming out of the data feeds and mouths or people, and get right to the essence of what they are saying and who they are. Malcolm Gladwell is the best-selling author of *The Tipping Point, Outliers,* and *Blink: The Power of Thinking without Thinking.* In the latter, he discusses a term he calls "thin-slicing," which is the phenomenon of taking the smallest amount of information possible and using it to make a judgment or decision. He illustrates, through numerous real-world examples and scientific research, that when you properly learn to "thin slice" in the area of your business, personal, or financial life, your quick judgments and analyses are often more insightful and better than those made with more information. He refers to the "adaptive unconscious" as a giant computer that quickly and quietly processes a lot of the data we need to keep functioning as human beings in forward direction.[9]

Thin-slicing relies heavily on the intuition and can either work for you or against you depending on which paradigms are ruling your subconscious. If properly developed, however, Gladwell quotes volumes of scientific data that support the accuracy of decision-making when relying on the intuitive "gut" reaction.

Perception

This is the mental muscle you use to make "meaning" of events or experiences in your life. This is where your existing conditioning (truths that we hold dear) will creep up and give us an interpretation. Everything in the world just "is" until we put something next to it and compare it.

For example: What is $20,000 per month? Some may say that $20,000 per month is a lot of money, and some may think that $20,000 would be a terrible pay cut or what the company spends per day on sponsored employee lunches. The point is that $20,000 per month just "is." It only has meaning when we use our perception and invoke the law of relativity to compare the thing that "is" with something else. For example: murder "is." Murder is "BAD" only after we compare it to our moral compass or to "Thou shalt not murder" in the Ten Commandments.

Will

This is your ability to hold any image, idea, or thought that you want in your conscious mind and focus until it has the chance to embed itself into your subconscious mind. You do this so that the idea can become your default paradigm and begin to move into its physical form.

The sun has an outer visible layer called the photosphere, and its temperature is 6,000 degrees Celsius. (Which is almost as hot as Chris J. Snook's hair-metal mixtape, which he made back in 1989.) The sun is 93 million miles from the Earth, and that is why you and I can go outside and over the course of a few hours of being in the sun's energy get a golden tan (or, in Chris's case, a BAD sunburn). However, most of you will remember grade-school science when you took a magnifying glass and placed it between a piece of gum on the ground and the sun and watched that same energy that gives your skin a darker color burn the gum into a ball of fire in less than 60 seconds. (Travis thinks this is an especially fun experiment to do to light firecracker fuses). The magnifying glass is the instrument that harnessed all that energy—6,000 degrees Celsius—into a single focus. *Will is the magnifying glass for our mind.*

Imagination

This is your creative power. Humans have the ability to create such amazing innovations as airplanes, fax machines, the Internet, the automobile, and the light bulb against all doubt and odds. Why? Because of the power of imagination when combined with the other five intellectual faculties. Your imagination is either concocting how you can do something or telling you all the ways that you can't. Start using it to fuel what you want, and put the brakes on using it for coming up with reasons why you can't.

If you imagine all of the constraints around organizing a multi-disciplinary working group inside of your company to tackle the EMF conversations, research, and planning, you will find those constraints to be very real and strong. You can also imagine an amazingly passionate, customer-centric, dedicated group of change agents within your organization, which efficiently join small multidisciplinary working groups to tackle the digital transformation of your company. Combining all of this new understanding with the EMF as your foundational framework to deliver great customer experience, you will attract and find the resources you need.

Focus on what you want your organization to look like, with a clear vision, and chances are, it will manifest, once you adopt the right actions to move it forward. You can have the business relationship with your customers and employees that you dream of, and, frankly, deserve. Napoleon Hill tells us that you have two complimentary forms of imagination with which you can work.

1. **Creative Imagination** is what works with the infinite intelligence to bring forth a new plan previously unaware to you at the conscious level to turn your insights into real world innovations.

2. **Synthetic Imagination**, on the other hand, is where you take your current pool of knowledge, data, and resources to create.

Hill also called your imagination the "workshop of the mind." Inside this workshop, you need to be using and developing your skill for both your creative and synthetic imaginations if you are to produce the results you desire.

Memory

This is your ability to recall previous events and experiences. Many people tend to remember only their failures, but your memory can also produce images of success. We want you to use your memory to bolster your confidence and self-esteem as you try something new because at one point everything was new to you. No baby is born with the ability to talk, walk, or ride a bike, and yet most of you today, as adults, do all three with no regard to how difficult those things once were. You need to exercise your memory to work in your favor and remind yourself that you can do anything you set our mind to!

What to Do When the Zombies Attack

Now that you are armed with a clear picture of the faculties you and your team will leverage, along with infinite intelligence and the EMF to create a massively differentiated and lawfully sound social business strategy, powered by purpose, people, and processes, you must be prepared for the guaranteed standoff with the Zombies. The Zombies are the widely known, and yet undiscovered, dream-killers that plague the universe we operate in. They are not divinely inspired, but they are extremely powerful. Their most common weapon of choice are seeds of destruction also known as "Other People's Opinions": OPO. These Zombies are subtle cancers that live in and leverage the Motivatables, whose easily persuadable nature and dominant habit of deductive reasoning create your most common vulnerability. OPOs are seeds planted by Zombies and watered by Motivatables in discrete moments, and they grow into the tall weeds (which the Zombies feed upon) that infect your dream space, while your newly planted creative crop is still early in its gestation.

OPOs are the catalysts for worry and doubt in the conscious mind, and if emotional involvement with these proceeds, fear manifests in the sub-conscious mind, thereby setting up a vibration that results in anxiety at the body/physical plane. This puts you in a fight or flight state waiting for the Zombies to appear and takes your focus off of creation.

The reason the Zombies are dangerous is that these subtle seeds of destruction they plant don't require that they be directly seen or in striking range of your wrath. They can actually cause more direct havoc on your momentum because they, oftentimes, go undetected until they have grown substantially strong in key minds around your support network.

Break through Your Comfort Zone

There is a sneaky, conniving, and fraudulent internal foe to the very spirit that each of you must constantly negotiate. It is the only fertile soil inside of us that doesn't serve your interests in personal growth. That foe is your individual *comfort zone*. The laws of the universe work cohesively and in accordance with one another to create an orderly universe by which effects may be repeatable. One of the outcomes of this body of laws governing all things in the physical plane is that of "create or disintegrate." This could also be explained by saying "that which is not growing is dying." The fraud of the "comfort zone" is that it hides behind the law of gender and fools us to believing that things stay the same, because you do not see an immediate "death" in the physical plane when you stop your spirit from driving forward or growing in a certain direction. The death of all dreams, aspirations, and things happens slowly over time and could be likened to you running through a field of thorny rose bushes and then taking a few years to bleed to death.

Nothing Stays the Same!

Everything is in a state of constant change! To think otherwise is to advertise your ignorance of—or about—the indisputable laws of nature. The worst thing about comfort zones is that they don't hurt. They feel comfortable, and in the worst and most paralyzing states, they may even feel good! You are most vulnerable as an individual and an organization when you put too much value on being comfortable.

We want you to pause and think about a couple of things for a minute as they relate to the laws of the universe.

1. Have you ever seen water boil at 211 degrees Fahrenheit? NOPE! It always boils at exactly 212 degrees (at sea level).

2. Have you ever wondered how scientists can predict the exact time of the sunset on any given day, or the timing of the high tides and low tides?

3. How in the world did they figure out how to make a wireless device called a smartphone that can simultaneously transmit the sound waves of your voice through a satellite into the receiving end of a friend's phone in an airport terminal in France and allow you to three-way call your sister on her wireless phone in New Jersey, *while* you scan pictures of the trip on Facebook before snapping a selfie of yourself accomplishing this and posting it to Instagram or Snapchat before hanging up?

The exact science that allows brilliant people to engineer such techno-logical feats must be studied and applied to bring forth anything in the "great order" that is our universe. That same order governing water's boiling point, the high and low tide, and the feats of wireless transmission governs your income, your health, your organizational dynamics, everything! However, your current comfort zone (Figure 5.6) contains all the information that you are ever going to have and all the awareness of opportunity that you will currently and continually have. If you do not stretch your comfort zone and gain new awareness through the setting of goals outside of your current understanding, what you have in all areas of your life today is all that you will ever have and all you'll ever be!

Russell Conwell wrote *Acres of Diamonds* and spent his entire speaking career talking with people about the tremendous opportunities that lay right in their own backyards but that they lacked the awareness to see. If you're not familiar with the story, the speech begins with an anecdote about a man who owned a large farm and was "wealthy and content" until he learned of the riches of diamonds. He became so desirous for diamonds that he sold all he had and left his family to search the world for the gems. In the end, he found none. Broke and exhausted, he committed suicide. The man who bought the farm from him soon discovered that soil and earth underneath the farm was filled with diamonds and became filthy rich. Ouch![10]

The lesson for you is that every organization (backyard) has issues, and although it may seem as though you have to go outside of it to find the value, more often than not, you can find it below your feet, if you are willing to apply your intellectual faculties to the situation and stretch out of your comfort zone. Use the EMF and the power of the stick-person to become a

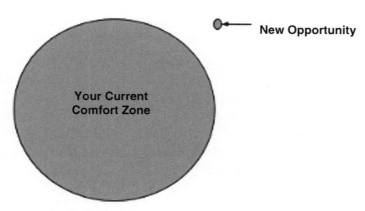

Figure 5.6 Your Comfort Zone

more powerful leader who leads digital transformation across your organization by attraction vs. promotion.

Charles Haanel wrote definitively about "life as an enfoldment" in his book, *The Master Key System.*[11] The infinite power of energy is always moving into form, through form, and out of form. It is never stagnant! It is equally present in all places at all times. It is just as much in front of you as it is behind you. Just as much to your left as it is to your right. It is just as much in us, as it is present in you. But it's never stagnant and never still.

Fear is what is holding you back, and the false Terror Barrier is a beast that the Zombies love to use, that we will show you how to slay on the upward climb to your dreams of building a more customer-centric digitally sensible organization!

The picture of the stick-person in Figure 5.7 graphically depicts your comfort zone. Let "x" represent an idea or thought that comes into your Conscious Mind. Assuming that you also have x-type conditioning or paradigms, then you will be quick to accept the x-type idea, and this will reinforce the x-type conditioning in your subconscious. The subconscious mind will setup an x-type vibration in the body which will take action in that accord and manifest into physical reality as an x-type result (R). At no point in this

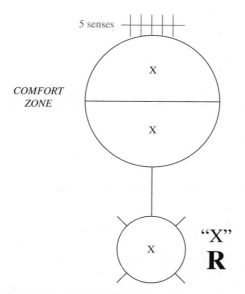

Figure 5.7 The Mechanics of the Terror Barrier

process will you feel "uncomfortable" because the "x" idea that enters your conscious mind matches your underlying subconscious conditioning and you will relate to it as "good" using your deductive reasoning.

What frustrates many people is that they will ask for advice from somebody on how to get new results, but they are unaware that they are only going to accept an idea at the conscious level that matches their current conditioning. They will, therefore, never reason inductively (truly "think") about the idea's actual impact on results. They will falsely expect that they will get new results, but, as the previous drawing clearly indicates, this is simply not possible.

You may be reading this book and others like it, in the sincerest effort to learn how to apply the EMF and some of our recommendations, but if you have paradigms and beliefs in your subconscious mind about how politically stifling or resistant your team or organization is to change, you are setting the table for an interaction with the Terror Barrier. The drawing in Figure 5.8 depicts what happens once the person reaches past aspiration and begins to act and "stretch" their comfort zone by "reasoning with a new idea or goal."

Whenever you set a truly worthy goal you will know, because when you set a good goal, achieving it will require you to increase your awareness and stretch your comfort zone to allow the new "how" to permeate your stream of consciousness. In other words, when you are honest about what you "really want" you will see you have no idea how to get it inside your current awareness level.

 DIGITAL BIT: For an audio podcast on the 7 Levels of Awareness visit Digitalsen.se/7Levels.

When this happens we will let "y" represent a new idea or goal. When you have autosuggested your new desire consistently enough to your mind, you will be successful at creating a "positive" emotional involvement with the y-type idea and it will cross the border of your mind and enter into your subconscious mind. At this point your new paradigm ("y") will be going into

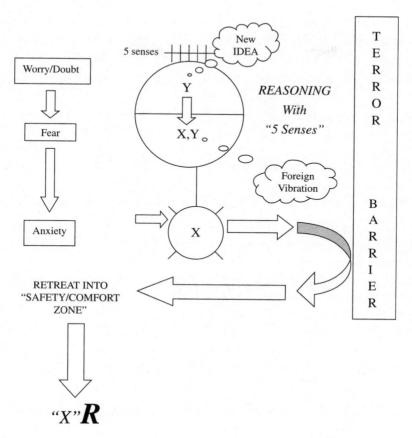

Figure 5.8

a head-to-head battle with your old "x" paradigm for precedence in the subconscious mind. Your old paradigm will begin a sabotage pattern to prevent "y" from dethroning it by sending signal patterns to your conscious mind to rely on your five senses to look for physical evidence in the outer world. It will enlist all the Zombies it can around you to infect the Motivatables on your team, your advisory group, and even potentially your supporters at home to cause the chain of events depicted in this graphic. Since the "y" idea is in process of moving into "form" from its spiritual state to its physical equivalent, you will not see physical evidence through your five senses. The old paradigm knows this, and it will effectively create the notion of worry/doubt in the conscious mind.

If you decide to get emotionally involved with worry/doubt, your old paradigm will win the battle, and you will invoke the pattern of fear in the subconscious mind. The vibration will set up the manifestation of anxiety in the body, causing you to hit the terror barrier and retreat back into the "safety" of the comfort zone. This will cause you to continue to get x-type results and fail to break through and materialize your stated goal and objective. *We mentioned it earlier but remind you again how critical it is to remember that you can never outperform your own self-image.* Your goals are not wrong. You wouldn't be given a desire in your heart if you weren't capable of having it manifest. You must develop a congruent self-image that is in line with that which you want and not let fear of the unknown derail you.

In his study on the self-image and his work on *Psycho-Cybernetics*, Dr. Maxwell Maltz noted that human beings are only born with two innate fears as a means of survival: Fear of falling and fear of loud noises![12] Every other fear is "man-made" or, better yet, "paradigm-made." Another point to remember is that you are never actually speaking to a person when you are trying to enroll them in your way of thinking. You are always speaking to their paradigms and narratives. Everyone can be right in their own mind from their perspective. To overcome this, you must raise your own vibration first, and attract those of similar mind to the mission.

Our personal acronym for fear is *Feeling Excited And Ready*! What the stick-person is illustrating is that in almost all cases (except falling or loud noise) the "Terror Barrier" is a mirage that limits us only because we let it.

The only way through the Terror Barrier is faith! Faith is not something you get from religion. Faith comes from understanding. Faith comes first from an expectation, which becomes a belief after repeated and consistent expectation. Belief becomes faith after repeatedly finding evidence and understanding to believe in that something time and again.

Now and from here forward, you have a conceptual understanding that when you feel worry and doubt at the conscious level, you need not sweat. It will take practice and repetition, however, to trust that and change the way that you relate to feelings of worry and doubt from here on. When you bust through the false Terror Barrier, it is truly a time to CELEBRATE, because your new idea or goal has successfully moved from a wish and dream to the realm of the subconscious mind (Figure 5.9).

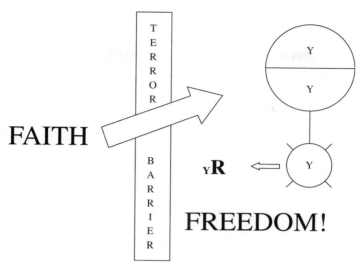

Figure 5.9

Remember that the subconscious can only say "yes" to whatever you give the most emotional energy to.

Faith and doubt cannot exist at the same time any more than night and day can. You will feel worry and doubt because your y-type idea will be battling with your x-type conditioning and trying to replace it. The uncomfortable part is not in wanting the y-type idea. It is when you have to step forward in faith, believing in the physically unseen with the understanding that everything is moving from "thought"—spiritual equivalent—into "thing"—physical form—through the power of your mind.

When you focus on faith in "y," the worry and doubt will not vibrate as fear, and you will step through the Terror Barrier into freedom from your old "x" conditioning! Once you have successfully replaced the old "x" with the new "y," it will become your present conditioning, your spirit will seek expression and fuller expansion again, and your "y" will become the new "x." That is the cycle of our spirit unfolding, and it is the miracle of life and of achievement science!

Remember that Emerson said, "Whatever you give energy to, grows!" Now you understand why you will feel thoughts of worry and doubt as you begin to put the EMF into practice using the exercises in this book to bring clarity and collaboration from your cross-functional teams into reality. You also now know how to step forward with increased faith, because you understand that your dreams are finally trying to move "through" your subconscious mind into the vibration of the body, to attract the necessary items to manifest your dream in its physical and observable equivalent!

Practice doesn't make perfect, but practice does make permanent. Now you have the perfect model of your mind to work with to practice making your efficient and consistent use of the EMF a permanent fixture in your planning process.

Emerson also once called the law of cause and effect, "the law of laws." Most people understand the law of cause and effect incorrectly. They have comprehended the basic tenets of "the more you put into something, the more you get out"; however, they thought that the actions they took were the *cause* and the results they got were their *effect*.

You now visually understand through the stick-person that they are mistaken, and the cause is at the level of thought. The effect is at the level of vibration—paradigms and conditioning of the subconscious mind—and the vibration is what dictates the action taken, which produces the results we can see and observe in our visual reality through our five senses! This is why merely changing the action—such as by reading this book and doing the EMF exercises—without changing the root cause (thinking) typically leaves a person frustrated, with more of the same results (a siloed organization, lacking digital sense, that is not customer-centric) and thinking that this book or—even worse—the universe is letting them down. Now you can see that this is just not true.

The power is within you. The EMF is fluid and dynamic and agnostically integrates with any other processes you currently deploy. Use the stick-person to firmly implant the vision for where your company is going in your mind first and it will be an unwavering beacon for the rest of your team to align with as you work through the bulk of the EMF nodes and put this vision into a plan with milestones.

The law of cause and effect (Figure 5.10) is illustrated below inside of the stick-person to further drill this home.

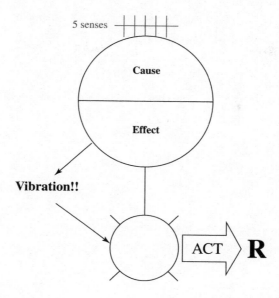

Figure 5.10

Now that you are working with a clear picture of your mind and the universal laws you are working with, you are ready to wield your creative power. You are ready to dive back into the EMF and set up and/or optimize your purpose-focused strategy in the Vision Layer.

6 The Vision Layer

"If you are working on something exciting that you really care about, you don't have to be pushed. The vision pulls you."

—Steve Jobs

Your business is a relationship, more than it is any other thing. Don't rush on to the next paragraph. Think about that for a minute.

Wikipedia defines *business* as "*a commercial operation or firm engaged in commerce that seeks to achieve volume and profits by transacting its goods and services.*"[1] However, we are here to tell you that, although that definition holds true, your business is a relationship, first and foremost.

Your business is one of the most complex and important relationships in society; it moves the world forward in aggregate. Business is the engine of humanity's progress and it could, therefore, be said that business is humanity's most important relationship in the evolution of our species. However, focusing solely on profit motives—without regard for other people, species, and the planet—is not a good way to run your business. Either way, you definitely have a relationship with your business, good or bad. So, if you will think about your business from here on out as a relationship, we believe that you will be well on your way to leveraging the EMF to its maximum benefit as you transform to a customer-centric digital organization.

All of the great relationships in business, music and entertainment, sports, and everyday love stories have one thing in common. They all have a vision for where they are going together. Think of the great business partnerships, great rock bands, or great baseball teams like the 2015 Kansas City Royals, and think about why they work. It begins with painting a clear inspiring picture of where you are going and how you are taking each person with you. Charlene Li of the Altimeter Group says, "The biggest determinants, by far, of whether you will be successful at social business are leadership and culture." (Sidenote: Travis added the 2015 Royals because (1) they were awesome and (2) the Royals beat Chris's favorite baseball team, the New York Mets, in the 2015 World Series. Chris left this in the final edits because karma is real and vengeance will be his in the next book . . . he hopes. ☺)

For relationships to work and last, an ongoing alignment and a shared vision are necessary.

Your employees, your stakeholders, and your customers all crave—and deserve—to know, and have the chance to align with, your vision. For that matter, your spouse does too! However, your vision without a prioritized plan is nothing more than a pipe dream. You must schedule and calibrate the scope. It has always been true that the vital few in society who can see the future and simultaneously work their face off to create it have carried the many who can merely just hope and dream.

MILESTONE: The following mental break is sponsored by our fictitious foundation: ATTENTION DEFICIT DISORDERLIES OF AMERICA. And now that you've made it to this part of the book, we just want to thank and congratulate you. According to publishing analyst Dan Poynter, 87 percent of people will never read this far into a book they purchase.[2] In fact, to let us know you have made it this far, stop reading right now for a few seconds and tweet @chrisjsnook and @teedubya with the funniest Bro picture that you can find, bro.

Don't say anything else. It will be our inside secret that you are nearly halfway through the book! Here's one of our favorites. We'll cover *b*usiness *r*elationship *o*ptimization in a later chapter, #BRO!

The Vision Layer + Social Business

In the Vision Layer (Figure 6.1) of the EMF, you will clearly state and anchor your vision into a social business strategy that aligns to purpose, deploys human-centric tactics, and course corrects with data-fed iterations.

Later in the book, we will provide plenty of "how to" ideas and resources as they relate to specific tactics, technologies, and life hacks you can deploy to leverage your newly enhanced digital sense into more meaningful results. Since strategy always should come before tactics, let's focus on how you can leverage the EMF to build your strategic plan and the questions you need to ask and answer within your team to ensure that your strategy is holistic and human at its core.

The Vision Layer Exercises

Dive right in with your team to the Vision Layer with the momentum gained from your efforts at the Insight Layer by starting with an audit of your current business goals (aka, major business objectives) as they relate to the clarity you gained around your customer's needs. The first step here is to ensure that your major goals (Figure 6.2) align to the needs of your customer and will allow you to achieve your higher purpose.

Building a solid *social business strategy* is the art of applying insights to specific touch points in the customer journey, guided by business goals and calibrated by scope to the resources available. This all begins with a clear

Figure 6.1 The EMF Vision Layer: Strategy

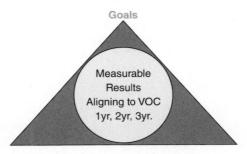

Figure 6.2 The Goals Node of the EMF Vision Layer

focus on the *top three business goals* that deepen your relationship with your customer and employees, in a way that drives increased volume and profit to your financial statements.

Time to complete exercise: 50 minutes to 2 hours (depending on the organization)

Setting the stage: On the whiteboard should be the top three major business objectives for the coming year. The facilitator will quickly state aloud the major business objectives on the board and check for alignment amongst all the working group team that those objectives are clear and aligned on.

Confucius said, "Man who aim at nothing—sure to hit it." He also says, "Man who stands on toilet is high on pot." But that's irrelevant.

Step 1: In this Vision Layer exercise of the EMF, each member should write out their top three to five department-level goals for the coming year on sticky notes.

Step 2: Each member will place those sticky notes underneath the most relevant major business objective that they support or impact.

Step 3: The facilitator and remaining working group will discuss and verify that you have clear metrics (KPIs) by which you are measuring your progress to each of those goals. If you do not, either pause to define the valued metric related to each or throw that goal out and replace it with something you are willing and able to measure.

Note: Data should drive decisions today, but the data is made valuable only when we hold each other accountable, as a cross-functional team, to define which measurements provide the most relevant value. When you measure the right stuff and observe the data through your five senses, you will benefit most from the continued mental muscle building of each individual's intellectual faculties. This allows your group intuition to grow stronger and more aligned. Intuition is the faculty you will use to uncover insights from the data and then imagine and create the innovations that you can operationalize in the future as you seek to optimize reliability in the customer experience.

Step 4: Discuss your Lean Six Sigma and Voice of Customer (VOC) data,[3] NPS scores, survey feedback, and detractor pipeline data, and look at how the happy and lost customers have prioritized their needs, and make sure that you helping them achieve those needs. Only this will allow you to achieve your stated business objectives in a sustainable way. Don't forget to give equal weight to considering the needs of your internal/employee customer as well as your external/end user customer in this regard.

Step 5: Wrap up this session by revisiting the original major business objectives that are up on the whiteboard along with the three department level goals each leader is driving toward. Gut-check that they are stated properly and adjust them as needed to formalize the goals node as a group.

Step 6: Document this and publish it everywhere it is appropriate and share with your department teams. Some example questions to help catalyze your goal alignment to customer needs audit are as follows:

1. Do our department level metrics and KPIs all map to and connect to our management by objectives (MBO)?

2. Does the impact on our customer rank number one in our department-level decision criteria?

3. If the answer to question 2 is "no" or "not sure," instead of asking why, which will just cause a justification of the current department level processes and KPIs, ask question 4.

4. What if we put the customer (internal and external) first in priority across the company? What current decision criteria and KPIs are we governed by that would violate this new edict?

5. How can we leverage our social business channels, tools, and incentives internally (Officevibe, Yammer, Slack, Facebook groups, and so on), to build a relationship between our people to these business goals, as a mutually beneficial and dynamically human thing?

Now you have up-to-date and documented 12-month goals. The good news is, if you are in a politically toxic environment, but you can't quit or won't leave, you can actually have these conversations with yourself and build out your own path to map your day-to-day team efforts to aligning around the customer and your current stated objectives. If you are reading this book, you are not a Zombie, which means you can make a difference if you are willing to try. Recruit one or two other people and start small. Remember always that *much gathers more!*

As Margaret Mead famously said, *"Never doubt that a small group of thoughtful, committed people can change the world; indeed, it's the only thing that ever has."*

The EMF is here to help you organize your own thoughts as well as your teams so that you can lead from wherever you are. A small group of committed people with digital sense and the customer at the heart of their efforts can make a huge impact even inside of siloed organizations.

Please don't mentally check out here if you feel yourself saying that, *"This is great, guys, but it will never work in my f#@ked up company."* Remember that your relationship to your own enjoyment of your work is as important as anything larger. Master this effort for your own purposes. Never underestimate the power of you as a force for greater customer experience.

There is nothing wrong with self-interest as long as it is enlightened. If you are aware of and serve your personal goals and needs in alignment to the enterprise goals, you are acting in enlightened (mutually beneficial) self-interest, which is a worthy ideal for any company to enable. Depending on your rank in the company, its size, and its years in business, an official purpose statement may or may not be in your control. If your company has a clearly articulated purpose statement, you want to get yourself in relationship with that purpose at a renewed, visceral level. If you can't get yourself excited to embody that purpose day in and day out and you don't own the company, start looking for more meaningful work. If you do own the company and don't feel an unquenchable passion for the current or stated purpose, stop everything right now and get honest about what purpose inspires you to get out of bed every morning and grind. You must have a strong WHY to personally be your best, to inspire your team, and get their best output on a daily basis.

At Ethology, we realized in year 5 that we didn't have a clearly concise purpose statement that all team members would jump out of bed for and commit to hire and fire against. At the beginning of the fifth year, we embarked on a 6-month process that yielded a simple but powerful purpose statement, "To earn the compliment of being each client's most trusted business advisor."

Now we have a purpose that every leader internally can hire and fire to. This purpose is both achievable and fragile in every single business and client interaction and represents an accountable relationship.

- It is human to earn a compliment. It is human to strive for continual improvement.

- It is also human to f#%k up and have to eat s#%t, apologize, and find a way to make it better with the follow-up interactions.

- It is human to crave trust and respect from our closest relationships

- It is human to not give our trust and respect out to others flippantly.

All of these truths make this purpose something extremely visceral for the organization and therefore make it a great purpose statement. What is yours? Can everyone on your team and in your organization state it out loud if called upon? If not, you don't have a clear purpose, and at a minimum, you need to remind people what it is and help them find their own conviction on why it matters. Strong culture is glued together by a clear and meaningful "why."

A purpose-focused social business strategy must have a strong *why*, a clear *what*, and a manageable *how*. Redefine it if it needs redefining, or put it up on the whiteboard now and get everyone in your circle to share how and why it matters to them. Build a frothy energy of aligned purpose and bask in the productivity it will produce as you move through the rest of this layer with your team.

Customer Journeys

As you move around the nodes of the Vision Layer to the bottom left corner node, we will get into an audit of how you deliver at each of the key touch points in your customer's journey (Figure 6.3).

You will run an audit against each product/service line, update and/or establish documented personas, journey maps, and the associated channel strategies you deploy for each. You will also decide how aligned your KPIs for each touch point map to your overarching channel strategy goals and your major business objectives. You will replace or redefine the data you capture and care about to ensure this is the case.

The most common mistake made in defining your social business strategy is not technology or choice of platform or channel. It's not necessarily the user experience either. All of those things play into your results, but before a line of code is written, a blog post or editorial calendar is conceived, or a dollar in advertising has been deployed, *you cannot forget to answer the simple questions that your target has at each point in their journey.*

In this section of the Vision Layer, you will unpack your major customer touch points along their journey from Awareness to Advocate and everything in between. You will begin to score yourself by how well you clearly solve and engage with them in a relevant way at each touch point or moment of truth. You will also build on the information gained at the Insight Layer around your competitors by benchmarking how well you stack up to competing solutions in the marketplace on relevance and engagement at these key touch points.

The bullets that follow cover the baseline understanding you should go over with all members of your cross-functional working group to level set the team around this section.

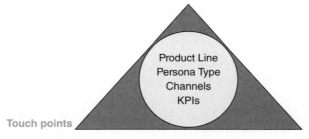

Figure 6.3 The Touch Points Node of the EMF Vision Layer

- A journey map is a formal and customized business document that makes your customer experience *visible and tangible* by injecting thoughts, actions, and feelings into the process.

- It also helps you pinpoint key "moments of truth" in which decisions are made and positive vs. negative impressions are set—so that you can give those special attention.

- These "moments of truth" happen at a handful of digital and or physical touch points with your brand along the buyer's journey.

- For each key persona and product/business line offering you will potentially have an associated journey map.

- You will likely have a minimum of four documented personas and associated journey maps that represent the core value driving offerings of your business.

- A buyer persona is a semifictional representation of your ideal customer based on market research and real data about your existing customers. When creating your buyer persona(s), consider including customer demographics, behavior patterns, motivations, and goals.

If you are newer to the world of customer journey map design and persona development we recommend our fellow Wiley author and friend Brian Solis's latest book *X: The Experience When Business Meets Design* as a phenomenal resource for architecting experience with deep process dives and visual examples of how to design and develop customer journeys for your organization.[4]

 DIGITAL BIT: If you would like a very practical facilitator's resource for your working group that is 100 percent free, visit DigitalSen.se/nssg* and download The Not-So-Secret-Guide to ALL Our Secrets *from Ethology. It includes step-by-step instructions for how to set up and facilitate everything from a business blueprinting session to a content workshop, journey map, tactical plan templates, heuristic audits, ROT content audit, design studio, how to benchmark competitors, and more.*

*Adapted from *The Not-So-Secret Guide to All Our Secrets.*

The resources above are invaluable to you and the free download is easy to print off and duplicate in PDF so that you have a step-by-step process for how to facilitate each internal working session. To start you off with an example of an exercise you should do with your team immediately, we have broken out elements of an audience development session below:

The Journey Map Touch Point Exercise

Tip: You should use both analytics and direct observation (ethnographic) research when informing your journey map and audience development efforts.

Setup: A large whiteboard (preferably 4 feet high and 8 feet long) or posterboard surface. Tape (using masking tape) a line that separates the top and bottom in equal parts across the full length.

Materials Needed:

♦ You will need a stack of 5″ × 8″ and 3″ × 5″ index cards

♦ You will need several packs of multicolored (yellow, purple, green, pink, blue, etc.) sticky notes

♦ You will need Sharpie markers and/or pens for each participant.

♦ You will need one team member as facilitator and should aim for a cross-functional working group that includes a representative from marketing, sales, operations, delivery, customer service, and finance with direct customer knowledge from their domain.

Time to complete: 2–3 hours

Step 1: Identify the key steps that a customer takes as they progress through the buyer's journey.

♦ DON'T limit this to just the interactions/touch points with your brand, but take a broad view to see their entire experience.

♦ The facilitator will write each phase on one of the 5″ × 8″ index cards

Step 2: On the top half of your whiteboard/poster board the facilitator will place these steps in order of how they occur, from left to right.

Step 3: Identify what your customer is doing at each step in their buying journey

♦ Have each team member write every action they can think of for each step on a yellow sticky note

- Place the yellow sticky notes directly below the corresponding step above the tape line

Step 4: Identify what your customer is thinking and feeling during each step.

- Write every thought/feeling on a purple sticky note directly below the corresponding step, below the tape line.

Step 5: Examine the touch points in the journey (these are where your brand has the chance to interface with the customer such as search engines, websites, apps, social media, people, employees, retail stores/service centers, call centers, etc.).

- Have each person write these touch points on the green sticky notes.
- Place the green sticky notes below each corresponding step to identify which touch points are in play at each step of the buyer's journey.

Step 6: Identify your customer's pain points during each step.

- Write every pain point on a pink sticky note.
- Place the pink sticky note directly below the corresponding step, below the line

Step 7: Now you are ready to discuss the opportunities to improve the customer's experience and prioritize which areas will generate the largest impact/delta in ROI and get investment and focus in the coming year as it relates to budget and scope.

- Each member writes the opportunities as they see them on a blue sticky note and places them at the bottom of your board

Recap:

- Yellow sticky=Customer action
- Purple sticky=Customer thoughts/feelings
- Green sticky=Touch points in the journey
- Pink sticky=Customer pain points
- Blue sticky=Opportunities

Step 8: Identify the moments of truth

- Have each team member consider what your customer is doing, thinking, feeling, and experiencing every time they think or interact with your company and write each of these moments of truth on a 3″ × 5″ card.

- Place the index card next to its corresponding phase/step in the journey

Step 9: Pop your favorite adult beverage because you have just mapped your customer journey. Now you can use this map to audit your existing customer experience and key touch points and make a plan to improve areas of concern.

Scope

Scope is the range or view, aim and purpose, length, and limit by which you will address any given opportunity or challenge you uncover as you complete your Vision Layer. It is the clear definition of any operation that you will undertake as it relates to improving key customer touch points that align to customer pain points/needs and generate the most impact toward your stated business objectives. No Vision Layer (Figure 6.4) can be complete without calibrating resources, time lines, and opportunities to a defined scope.

Your strategy becomes ready to execute in the Success Layer once it has been put to a proper scope that defines how you will satisfy your strategic objectives/goals. Scope is your written governing document or road map that translates the customer needs and your product/service objectives into specific requirements to improve the infrastructure and messaging at key touch points, and defines who within your organization or vendor network will be tasked with implementing them and at what budgetary cost.

Taking time to define the scope is both a valuable process and a valuable end product. It is valuable as a process because it allows you to uncover land mines, budgetary conflicts, or internal political issues that could derail the project before it gets started and work to find a compromise in advance. It is a

Figure 6.4 The Scope Node of the EMF Vision Layer

valuable end product because it provides a document for governance and measurement that can be shared and executed across the silos to maximize buy-in and efficiency.

Step 1: Begin by defining the requirements.

◆ This seems obvious but it important to know what you are building and for what objectives. The second and equally important reason to define the requirements is to identify what it is that you are not going to build.

◆ If you have completed the Goals and Audience Development/Journey Map exercises from earlier, then the second half of these defined requirements is easy to complete. We suggest writing these defined requirement statements as follows: "We are building a *(insert project here)* to address the *(insert specific customer pain point here)* at *(insert touch point impacted here)* in the buyer's journey, for the sake of *(insert the associated major business objective/goal here)*. List of requirements and phases would be expanded in each case below this summary statement.

EXAMPLE: "We are building a mobile-first customer app portal to address the customer's need for real-time access to account information and transaction ability while on the go at the USE touch point, for the sake of increasing cross sales and customer loyalty by 10 percent this year."

Phase 1: Requirements and time line (derived from direct customer knowledge and feedback)

Timeline of the sprint: January 15 to March 31, 2017

Requirements:

◆ Simple, reliable, app interface that works reliably even in low-bandwidth environments

◆ Ability to see balance and recent transaction history in real time

◆ Ability to send or receive money or transfer to and from linked accounts.

Phase 2: Requirements and time line

Budget to complete Phase 1 and 2: $50,000

Internal team members required:

◆ Director of Mobile Payments, director of IT, compliance officer, general counsel

External resources needed:

◆ Front end developer, backend developer, UX/UI specialist

Step 2: Prioritize the requirements.

◆ In the example above, we began to show a simple theoretical example of what a prioritized requirements document might look like.

◆ It is very important (although sometimes difficult) to put in the time to be very specific with the requirements of each investment you will make to optimize a key touch point in your customer's journey. It is not enough to stick with vague words like "*a hip, cool interface that looks good to our customers on a mobile device.*"

◆ You have done rigorous work in this layer and the Insight layer before to gain a clear picture of the thoughts, feelings, and actions your customers will be guided by at each point in the journey. As you think through these requirements, you will want to be as specific as possible and provide access to that summary persona data and journey map to whoever is building or executing the project for you.

◆ You will also need to negotiate with other department leads and budget holders depending and ensure that the scope stays well defined and as tight as possible despite the human nature of each new participant to want "it" to do one more thing for their specific domain of concern.

◆ It is very common to see one requirement impact or tie back to multiple strategic goals or objectives, and this is important to map out as well so that you can use this data to make the tough decisions on what gets cut when budgets and statements of work (SOWs) are in conflict and something must get cut or put on the shelf for another phase.

◆ Feasibility is a key determinant in how things get prioritized as well. For instance, you may have an executive order to hit one of the major business objectives within 2 months, but as you begin to scope out and define the requirements to get your current idea to market, it will require 4 months or not be possible for 12 months within that budget range. This lack of feasibility is a real constraint but is valuable to uncover because it can cause you to rethink your product strategy or find a whole new way to hit the major business objective. A design thinker mentality will look at the problem first (i.e., "hit this major business objective in 2 months") and find the most feasible and efficient method to achieve that outcome.

◆ A hidden value of prioritizing and detailing the defined requirements of your scope with teams is that in some cases you will find that features and efforts you begin to see as requirements will not align completely to your defined goals section. This is a sign of either a doomed strategy that has not properly addressed constraints and feasibility and jumped to defining requirements too quickly, or that has not yet clearly ranked the priority of each major business objective to provide proper top-down guidance.

The key things to come away with from the Vision Layer of the EMF is a documented process and aligned rationale as to what the prioritized strategic goals for the organization are moving forward in the next 12 months in concrete terms, and not necessarily the proposed means of getting there. You will likely need to define scope more than once as you begin to phase into execution, and find ways to approach this process with urgency and accuracy and agility as environments, people, and markets shift in real time.

A great understanding of design thinking will help you and your teams navigate this balance, and you can find 45 amazing resources on implementing design thinking into your organization.[5]

Takeaways from the Vision Layer

What: You have defined your three major business goals and aligned them to your customer needs. You have audited and mapped your buyer's journey and assessed key areas to improve at certain touch points. You have calibrated scope and prioritized projects to budgets and feasible timelines, and identified available internal and external resources.

Who: Project stakeholders in a cross-functional working group, executive sponsor, client/customers, agency partners.

How: Conducting workshops, ethnographic research, data analysis, building project plans and requirement docs, revisiting recommendations, and making decisions to prioritize.

Why: The purpose of this layer is to get to a point where you have made decisions about how you will attack the coming year and put it all to a plan and schedule.

7 The Success Layer

"Success is not final. Failure is not fatal: it is the courage to continue that counts."

—Winston Churchill

The EMF has been influenced by a DNA strand that comes from a deep admiration by both of us for the Japanese philosophy of Kaizen, which was made most famous in the late 1980s by the Toyota Production System. Kaizen was the precursor to the widespread adoption of the lean-manufacturing movement and continues to inspire innovation today, as the last decade has seen an immense amount of use and press around the lean startup, lean design, and lean everything movements.

The Kaizen process has been known as the Deming Cycle, the plan-do-check-act (PDCA) cycle, and the Shewhart Cycle, but regardless of vernacular, centers around the interplay of these four tenets: Plan, Do, Check, Act. Kaizen is a philosophy for constant and never-ending improvement.

In the Success Layer (Figure 7.1), we have chosen to simplify that a step further into a slightly modified and customer-centric model of Learn. Plan. Do. We have ordered it this way because, as you read earlier in this book, the first guiding principle of the EMF is that *direct customer knowledge drives tactics.* While you are executing you will need to prioritize *learning* from your customer and your macroforces environment in real time, because the business environment today is shifting and evolving so quickly. When insights arise, they arrive from this learning- and customer-focused feedback loop. From there, we have shown you how to *plan* in the Vision Layer, and now we will discuss the key components of successful execution to round out the surface layer of the EMF, which allows you to deliver optimal reliability and ongoing innovation around your customer experience.

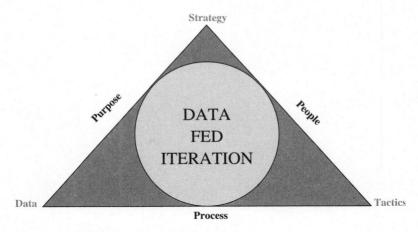

Figure 7.1 The Success Layer: Execution

The remainder of this book will be about executing and ways to continue improving the digital sense of your entire team on a daily basis, so they can run the cycle of learn, plan, do as a lean, mean, customer-centric machine.

Success is an ongoing journey, and never a destination. It is a marathon run in daily sprints! In the world of business today, you are truly only as good as your most recent iteration. The customer is all powerful and loyal to needs above all else. You don't want to be the next Yahoo! or Blackberry. (LOL at Yahoo!, again) Legacy matters only if that legacy is continually built upon putting the customer center to your decision-making, and using your people and processes to create holistic data that can be refined to feed all future iterations. As the architect of your customer experience, you will use the success layer to implement your purpose-focused social business strategy with human-centric tactics, and small data (measuring what is valued) versus big data (valuing what can be measured), to yield relevant audience intelligence. Relevant intelligence can help you iterate your performance media and your marketing plan to achieve your stated business objectives.

The Success Layer begins with executing your social business strategy. There are a handful of key execution elements to your social business strategy, which include your business strategy, marketing strategy (from the

Figure 7.2 The Strategy Node of the EMF Success Layer

Vision Layer), content strategy, and audience intelligence (data) strategy (Figure 7.2).

Volumes of work and several great operational frameworks exist around the larger and highly researched concept of social business and developing a social business strategy. We will mention a few of them below for initial context; however, we will keep this chapter as common sense as possible, with some practical exercises to help you understand and execute a content rich and engaging social business strategy.

One resource we are excited to support and be contributors to is *The Digital Continuum.*[1] Originated by Universal Mind and launched in late 2016, the Digital Continuum has combined many of the industry's digital best practices into a map of what it would look like within a single organization. Human-Centered Design, the Scaled Agile Framework, the Competing Values Framework, and Continuous Delivery are just a few of the best practices that make up this mapping of a digital organization in its ideal state. We are excited to provide future derivatives of our digital sense thought leadership and the Experience Marketing Framework to this resource, in complement to this amazing effort of best practices. This mapping allows organizations to move beyond the theoretical and into a real example that they can use as a blueprint. We encourage you to bookmark the site today and sign up for their newsletter/drip list.

Your social business strategy goes end-to-end from mission and values to DevOps, deployment, and it encompasses how you communicate, how you deploy, and how you drive toward your major business objectives. Social business strategy is a prominent focus in the area of business transformation these days because in the past several years digital and social technologies have reduced the cost of communication by orders of magnitude. All organizations are nothing more than hives of people communicating and collaborating to execute business processes "work."

Prior to digital and social technologies, collaboration and innovation were slow and expensive. Today, however, if (and it's a big IF) an organization can learn how and when to use them, collaboration can be inexpensive and innovation cycles can happen rapidly. Since every company and every industry is dealing with a customer who has unprecedented access to information and choice, becoming a digitally transformed social business is an imperative operational strategy, upon which you can layer the EMF to produce world-class customer experiences.

What Is a Social Business?

A social business is one built upon a foundation of learning, growing and a strategy that starts by asking, "What people and environment must we have to achieve our objectives?" and "What processes must we excel at to deliver value to our customers and meet our business and financial objectives?" It also asks (as you did at length in the Insight Layer), "What do our customers value?" and "What do our shareholders expect?"

If you are looking for another great resource to help you map your social business strategy (Figure 7.3), you can check out the team at LeaderNetworks.com for some great ideas on how to build your social business value chain from development to social selling to delivery.[2]

Lastly, a great must-read article by Christopher Rollyson goes in-depth on the most common "Social Business Strategy Use Cases."[3] And it will help you quickly assess where in the Social Business Life Cycle of transformation your company is currently residing and what steps are most relevant to take for continued evolution. The most immediately relevant value from this piece will be for chief data officers (CDOs), chief marketing officers (CMOs), chief compliance officers (CCOs), and CEOs, to reflect on which choices they are facing today to either improve ROI or simply remain relevant in volatile markets moving forward.

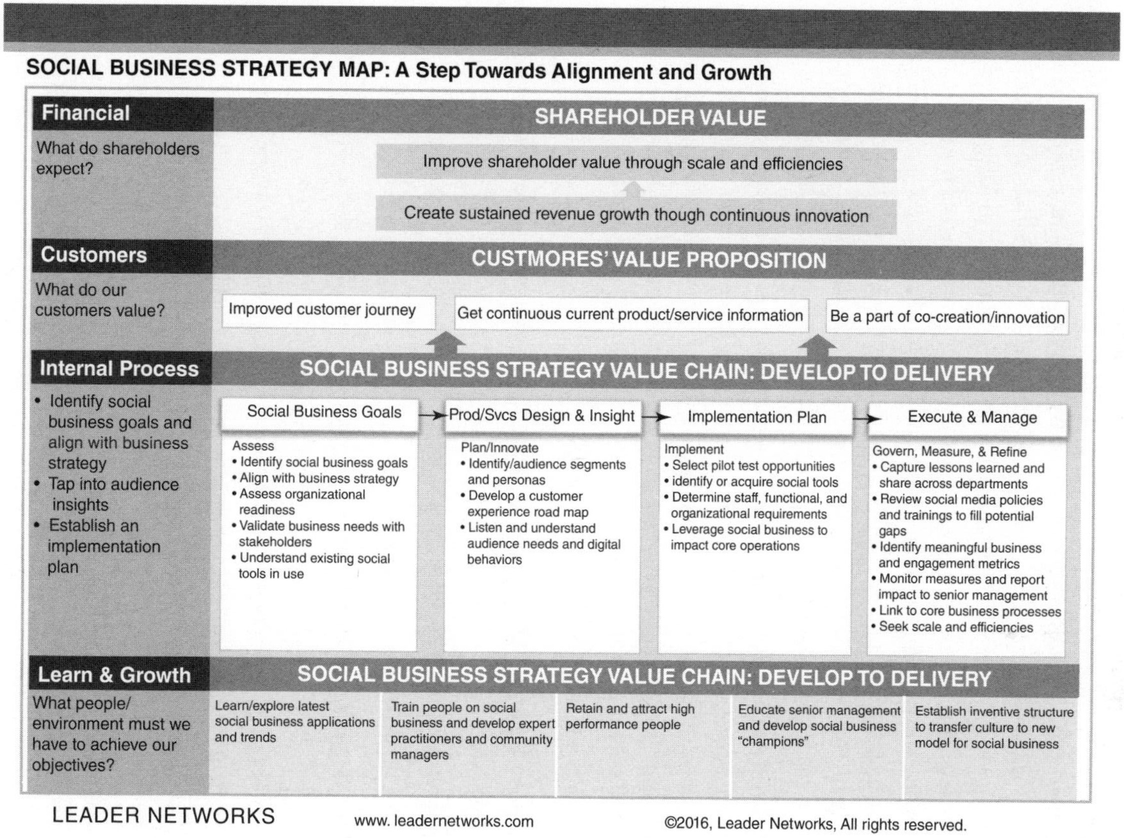

SOCIAL BUSINESS STRATEGY MAP: A Step Towards Alignment and Growth

Financial
What do shareholders expect?

SHAREHOLDER VALUE
Improve shareholder value through scale and efficiencies

Create sustained revenue growth though continuous innovation

Customers
What do our customers value?

CUSTMORES' VALUE PROPOSITION
Improved customer journey | Get continuous current product/service information | Be a part of co-creation/innovation

Internal Process
What do our customers value?
- Identify social business goals and align with business strategy
- Tap into audience insights
- Establish an implementation plan

SOCIAL BUSINESS STRATEGY VALUE CHAIN: DEVELOP TO DELIVERY

Social Business Goals

Assess
- Identify social business goals
- Align with business strategy
- Assess organizational readiness
- Validate business needs with stakeholders
- Understand existing social tools in use

Prod/Svcs Design & Insight

Plan/Innovate
- Identify/audience segments and personas
- Develop a customer experience road map
- Listen and understand audience needs and digital behaviors

Implementation Plan

Implement
- Select pilot test opportunities
- Identify or acquire social tools
- Determine staff, functional, and organizational requirements
- Leverage social business to impact core operations

Execute & Manage

Govern, Measure, & Refine
- Capture lessons learned and share across departments
- Review social media policies and trainings to fill potential gaps
- Identify meaningful business and engagement metrics
- Monitor measures and report impact to senior management
- Link to core business processes
- Seek scale and efficiencies

Learn & Growth
What people/ environment must we have to achieve our objectives?

SOCIAL BUSINESS STRATEGY VALUE CHAIN: DEVELOP TO DELIVERY

Learn/explore latest social business applications and trends | Train people on social business and develop expert practitioners and community managers | Retain and attract high performance people | Educate senior management and develop social business "champions" | Establish inventive structure to transfer culture to new model for social business

LEADER NETWORKS   www.leadernetworks.com

Figure 7.3

111

Begin with the End in Mind

Designing the most practical elements of your social business strategy, as it relates to your customer experience and marketing efforts, begins with the end in mind. You will need to look at your business objectives and figure out what you stand for and where your company is headed. You really need to envision all of the ways that social media can help your business. Social media is not just for marketers. Your customer service should be socially activated. Your sales team should be activated with social to help them build relationships with your prospects. Your HR team should be activated with social, to help bring in the top talent that isn't actively looking for a job. Your operations team and any other team that is customer facing should be looking for ways to integrate social within their department, channel, or product.

Our friends at Altimeter Group produce some amazing thought leadership and research around the current and future state of social business, and you should subscribe to their newsletter and webinars if you are newer to (or in the middle of) the process of social business transformation and looking for best practices and benchmarking tools.[4] Their infographic (Figure 7.4) on social business is about as good as it gets.[5]

- **Clear Business Objectives:** without them, you don't know what you're shooting for.
- **Clear Vision:** without it, you don't know where you're going
- **Buy-in from the C-Suite:** without it, you can't get started.
- **Strategic Road Map:** without it, your organization's social business initiatives won't align with your organization's business goals.
- **Establish Guidelines and Processes:** without them, your social media team may tell someone to "cc get a clue."
- **Build and Train Your Team:** without doing that, you'll get the wrong people on the bus.
- **Invest in the Right Technologies:** without doing this, you'll end up buying the newest fandangled technology, which doesn't serve any real business goal.

Once you figure out your objectives, use your data and analytics for insights. Use those insights to help you map your content strategy and your audience intelligence strategy. Almost every fiber of your day-to-day activity

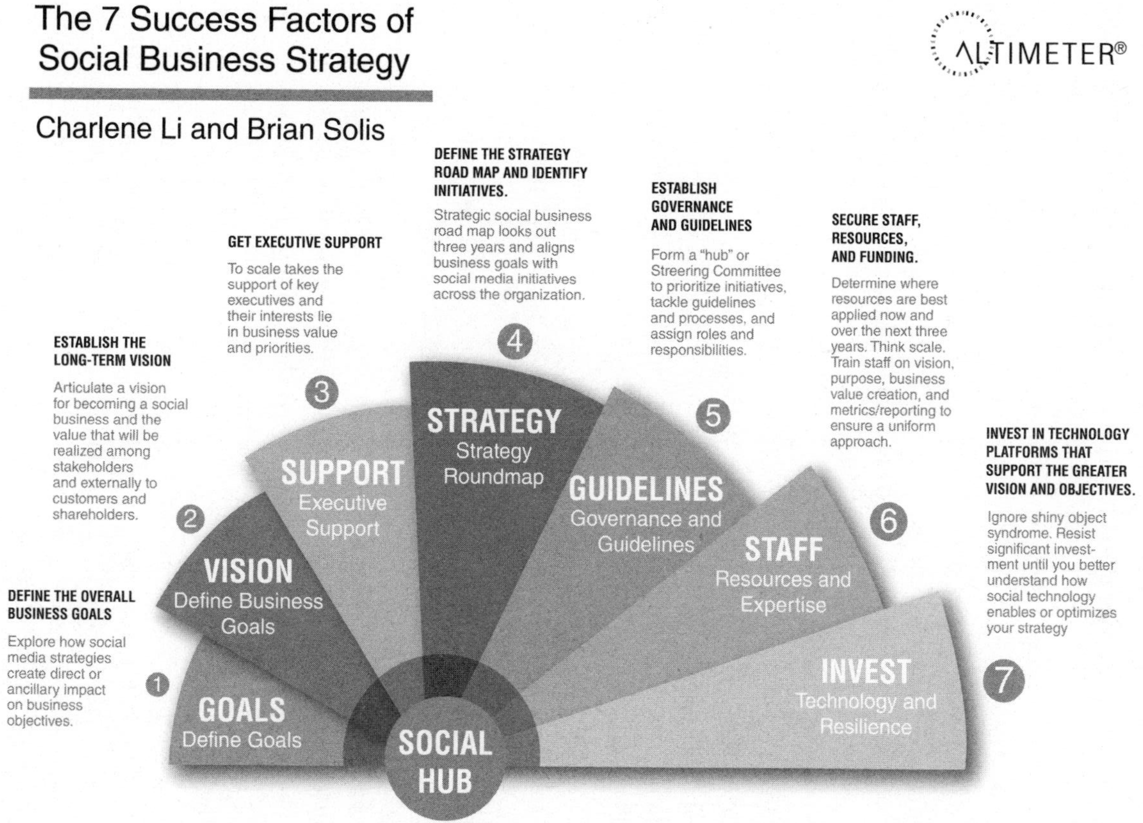

The 7 Success Factors of Social Business Strategy

Charlene Li and Brian Solis

ALTIMETER®

DEFINE THE OVERALL BUSINESS GOALS

Explore how social media strategies create direct or ancillary impact on business objectives.

ESTABLISH THE LONG-TERM VISION

Articulate a vision for becoming a social business and the value that will be realized among stakeholders and externally to customers and shareholders.

GET EXECUTIVE SUPPORT

To scale takes the support of key executives and their interests lie in business value and priorities.

DEFINE THE STRATEGY ROAD MAP AND IDENTIFY INITIATIVES.

Strategic social business road map looks out three years and aligns business goals with social media initiatives across the organization.

ESTABLISH GOVERNANCE AND GUIDELINES

Form a "hub" or Steering Committee to prioritize initiatives, tackle guidelines and processes, and assign roles and responsibilities.

SECURE STAFF, RESOURCES, AND FUNDING.

Determine where resources are best applied now and over the next three years. Think scale. Train staff on vision, purpose, business value creation, and metrics/reporting to ensure a uniform approach.

INVEST IN TECHNOLOGY PLATFORMS THAT SUPPORT THE GREATER VISION AND OBJECTIVES.

Ignore shiny object syndrome. Resist significant investment until you better understand how social technology enables or optimizes your strategy.

① GOALS — Define Goals
② VISION — Define Business Goals
③ SUPPORT — Executive Support
④ STRATEGY — Strategy Roundmap
⑤ GUIDELINES — Governance and Guidelines
⑥ STAFF — Resources and Expertise
⑦ INVEST — Technology and Resilience

SOCIAL HUB

Figure 7.4

will be influenced or impaired by the presence or lack of these two things, your content strategy and your targeted audiences.

It is important to distinguish content strategy from content marketing. The easiest way to think about this is content strategy is like the blueprint to a new custom-built house, and content marketing is like the tools you will use to build it. Each of these serves important but completely different purposes.

Similarly, audience intelligence strategy is focused primarily on the activity of defining the processes by which you will collect, measure, and make sense of the "small data" that you value. Audience intelligence does not imply the buzzword of big data strategy where you collect and measure every data point imaginable just because you can.

In his book *Small Data,* Martin Lindstrom talks about the tiny clues that uncover huge trends and emphasizes numerous use cases, from Lego to McDonalds and Euro-Disney, that illustrate the power of blending hard analytics data with direct ethnographic research. This allows you to laser in on the metrics that most impact your results within each customer persona.

In 2016 the average shopper required 28 brand interactions before making a purchase decision, according to aggregated client data gathered from interviews with the founders of GeniusMonkey.com, a programmatic platform technology provider.[6] Also, the average shopper spends only 5 percent of their time online searching and 95 percent of their time engaging with content. You can understand then, why success at the level of execution requires that a sound content and audience intelligence strategy (blueprint) of how you will build and deploy your messaging. You also must measure its impact across the customer journey, and across every department in your company, with documented and clear processes for governance in place.

Measuring what matters is the key at this layer. The integration of the orbiting Operational-*Learn, Plan, Do* Loop (Figure 7.5) as a rapid way to optimize reliability, and the Innovation-*Discover, Design, Deploy* Loop to operationalize new insights ensures that you will hone in on the most relevant data to make the most impactful iterations as you execute on the current and future strategies. Below, we will take a deeper look at how you can customize and utilize these interlocking loops, as you execute on a day-in and day-out basis.

Loops, Love, and ROI

As an organizational leader and marketer, your job is often reduced to the qualitative metric of making customers L-O-V-E your brand, while being judged by the quantitative metrics of sales, profits, and ROI. The challenge of innovating and simultaneously providing a positive state of reliability in the customer experience has many of our clients tripping over each other or in a codependent relationship between the marketing, IT, and operations silos, which ultimately causes breakdowns in achieving the desired results while internal frustrations mount. This effect will be compounded further in the coming years as platform fragmentation and disintermediation continue to increase at unprecedented rates of speed. The layers and loops model (Figures 7.5 and 7.6) with the EMF are an attempt to solve this problem.

These two loops interlocked in orbit (on horizontal and vertical planes), ensure that there is no need for a matched cadence between your cycles of innovation and day-to-day execution. In this architecture, a renewable and prioritized dynamic to operationalize future innovations within your existing customer experience is possible while you continue to deliver your existing processes to your customer.

The Operational Loop will be applied to each discipline area for which you are executing and seeking to create a greater contribution impact to the overall customer experience. You will have dozens of these across the enterprise, each with their own data measures and KPIs, which ultimately roll up

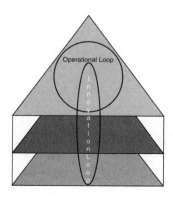

LAYERS AND LOOPS

The Operational Loop is in the horizontal plane focused on executing the current strategy to achieve reliability through constant improvement and refinement to maintain customer experience.

The Innovation Loop is in the vertical plane running across each layer as needed to turn insights, into prioritized strategies and plans with a schedule to be operationalized at the success layer.

The orbital interlocking of the Operational and Innovation Loops allows for a difference in cadence and speed within each business unit as it relates to innovation and service reilability without the risk of collision or fracture.

Figure 7.5 Orbiting Loops Influenced by Buckminster Fuller's Theory on Orbiting in Love

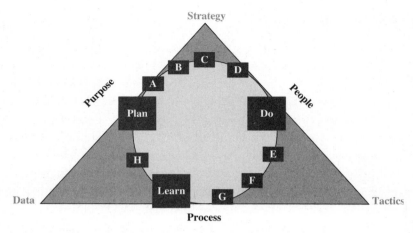

Figure 7.6 The Operational Loop: Execution Reliability

into the overall domain-level strategies and department-level KPIs. Within this horizontal plane, there may be several micronodes that management implements as milestone checkpoints between the primary nodes of Learn, Plan, Do to further illustrate the process by which your team will ultimately deliver increased reliability over time within each discipline.

As we mentioned earlier, you will, without doubt, discover opportunities for innovation from insights gained while executing. Depending on the maturity of your business and industry, you will be able to invest in these insights in varying degree and with varying priority. However, the key thing is that you have a model by which you understand and can communicate to all the stakeholders. You will set out to create predictable cycles of innovation, and operationalize those innovations into the same execution layer, that you have set up to manage the customer experience consistently.

In Figure 7.7, you notice the Innovation Loop overlay with its major nodes of Discover, Design, and Deploy and its micronode milestones that can be customized in number to fit within whichever innovation methodology and process you subscribe. For example, if you were using a lean startup methodology for innovation, you would likely consider the micronode number one as "ideation," number two as "early validation," number three as "front end prototyping," and so on.

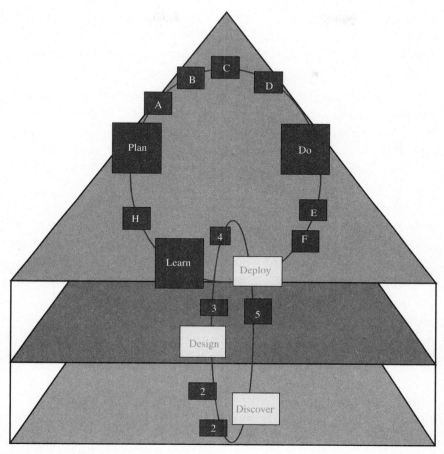

Figure 7.7 The Innovation Loop

It is both an offensive and defensive strategy to build the internal model and infrastructure to listen to the voice of the internal customer (your employee base), as it relates to insights and ideas for new market opportunities. Using the EMF to plug in your lean methodology and agile design processes will give you a powerful yet flexible model by which you can create more frequent cycles of innovation.

A great example from recent years of a company that has done this brilliantly is Mercer. When Julio Portalatin took over as CEO in 2012, the company was turning 37 years old. Mercer is a nearly $4.5 billion/year, wholly owned subsidiary of Marsh & McLennan Companies (NYSE: MMC) and operates in 140 countries as a leading global consultancy that helps firms maximize the health, wealth, and careers of their most precious asset, their people.

With more than 20,000 employees, this company was not in any way what you would consider to be a nimble startup, yet under Julio's leadership, it has been able to innovate brilliantly and continue to disrupt itself. They have achieved this by putting processes and business units in place, like the Mercer Innovation Hub and its internal Global Innovation Challenge launched in 2014 under the leadership of Partner, Jo-Anne Bloch.

The Mercer Innovation Hub received more than 200 ideas from people across the enterprise in its inaugural challenge. A small number of these ideas were selected through a rigorous vetting process using lean methodology. A diverse innovation team was formed to take these ideas forward to commercialization.

Along the way some ideas progressed, others were dropped, and new ideas emerged. Some have become services that have migrated from ideation and validation through to incubation and soft launch. They are in the market and available to clients, today as Mercer Match™ and Mercer Candidate Care™.

Mercer continues to maintain a pipeline of new innovation, through this challenge annually. Mercer has even invested in a dedicated CMO for the Innovation Hub as of 2016. She works directly with the innovation teams and reports into the C-Suite of Mercer. The role is to help complete the full commercialization potential of its new offerings and to ensure these can flow seamlessly into the overall Mercer customer experience. Mercer executives and managers continue to draw inspiration and insights by looking at external forces such as VC capital flows and customer needs.

Mercer Candidate Care was developed based on industry research that identified for every open job requisition, roughly 219 people applied. Since inherently only a handful of people will be contacted to interview, and only one person will end up with the actual employment, they noticed significant statistical data that brand dilution and loss of equity was occurring in many companies due to a lack of communication and "care" to the candidates that did not make the cut.

Think about the problem they discovered this way. Brand XYZ has raving fan customers and has built a tremendous amount of brand equity over the years through investment into all the right channels of customer communication and experience. Bob Smith is a loyal brand advocate and notices that XYZ is expanding or opening up a job in his market for which he is qualified in his mind. He begins to feel the excitement as he mentally envisions what it would be like to finally work for XYZ after being such a raving fan for all of these years. He completes the online application process and hits submit. Days, weeks, and months go by and he hears nothing. There are no personal portals or people following up with him to allow him to know where he stands in the process. All he has to go on is the autoresponder (DO NOT REPLY) e-mail he received acknowledging his resume and cover letter submittal at step one.

This common occurrence was happening hundreds of times per job listing and causing companies from telecom to consumer electronics to inadvertently turn raving fan customers into lost souls who felt shunned by their beloved brand, and nobody had built a solution to solve it. Now when a company leverages Mercer Candidate Care in its hiring process the other 219 people that applied for each job not only received personalized communication throughout the processes but also were made aware of resources such as Mercer Match™ so that Mercer can help its client companies find other placements for those candidates outside of the organization as a valued added service.

Mercer's innovative efforts have taken months off of the average hiring cycle for candidates out of work and the benefits have been accretive to their clients' brand equity versus dilutive. Mercer Match (download the app free at MercerMatch.com) was launched as an Android and iOS application that utilizes gamification to identify key persona traits, skills, and strengths and uses algorithms to match specific talent efficiently to jobs and cultures where they will best thrive. Through the blend of the internal culture of keeping the customer central in the decision-making process and the investment made to commercialize the best ideas through the Innovation Hub, Mercer has been able to open up new markets for their methodology while keeping ahead of the disruptive forces and capital formations that are impacting the future of HR, recruiting, and personnel management.

The EMF with its layers and loops works as a flexible and malleable resource. It will allow you to make decisions based upon your overall assessments, knowledge, and plans derived from the Insights and Vision Layers. Depending on how mature your business is within your industry and life cycle, you will put a different weight on how much emphasis and depth you leverage the operational loop and innovation loops. EMF is also flexible to constraints like budgets, bandwidth, and human capital to invest in light or deep research and development and commercialization efforts. EMF also ensures that you have a common picture and model for your teams to work with, when explaining where in the process new innovations are, what receives prioritization as it relates to resources, and which domains of the business will be impacted once execution is deployed.

Optimizing the Operational Loop

In business, as in life, there is no way to stop or slow things down so that you can get to work on something new. In fact, our goal is that you will begin to see your business in these layers and loops more clearly, so that you can calm down and speed up.

The easiest node for anyone to enter this framework is actually within the Success Layer and specifically, under the node of *Learn.* This is primarily because, regardless of your current internal organizational alignment around customer experience, you are currently executing a marketing and sales strategy today. This gives you an automatic list of areas where insights can and will be generated and where learning can occur.

By beginning with your current operation, you can run a series of simple, but important, audits that will uncover areas and gaps that can begin to be iterated. The audits serve as a catalyst of mini data points and proof points of concern, as you make the case for a deeper annual planning cycle to dive deeper into the Insight and Vision Layers.

Humanizing your tactics starts with a series of audits across your current digital universe. We will cover some of the high level areas to consider tackling below, that historically have shown to be great fodder for further discovery and organization commitment. We have also provided some resources or quick exercises you can use to run these audits.

Audit 1: ROT Content Audit

One of the most common issues we find with brands today, as it relates to their digital presence, is that they have invested heavily in content creation and digital asset creation over the past few years under the idea that "more is better." Thus, in many companies, this has resulted in an unnecessary amount of digital and financial waste.

Even some of the largest and most popular brands—from Starbucks to Disney—have found that their digital presence is filled with tons of ROT. **ROT is an acronym for *Redundant, Out of date, and Trivial* content.** ROT is content that lives in the universe of your digital experience, but serves little to no relevant value to the customer you are seeking to engage.

Think about your social media feeds filled with pictures of people's food and selfies and completely useless drivel or clickbait. How many times have you considered deleting your Facebook account only to continue to persist with it? We (all humans) crave better content, not more content.

The Content Marketing Institute (CMI) surveys show that only 37 percent of companies in 2015 had a documented content strategy while only 10 percent of companies could tell whether the content was effective at driving increased performance.[7] All of this activity leads to piles and piles of nonperforming content and over the past few years companies have responded by creating more, using the proverbial *"throw spaghetti at the wall and see what sticks"* approach. This resulted in an estimated $1 billion in wasted investment related to content creation in 2015 according to CMI.

The following exercise was developed by Anna Hrach at Ethology and is a powerful but simple exercise you can perform immediately to rid your digital presence and website of ROT.[8]

R=Redundant (overly wordy and duplicate content)

O=Outdated (expired offers, broken links, out-of-date content and materials)

T=Trival (not relevant to your brand or customers, doesn't speak in the brand voice or tone, doesn't reflect your brand values or adhere to brand guidelines)

Redundant content examples are most common across channels where they are not made to feel native to the interface. For example: A blog post around a certain topic should not be copied and pasted into your Facebook feed, and a piece of creative around a promotion on Instagram should not be reused without thoughtful creative on LinkedIn, Snapchat, Facebook, or Twitter. Coordinated campaigns across channels requires coordinated creative that ties everything together but does not lack a relevant and native feel to the user experience expectation of each channel. A great visual using beer to explain (Figure 7.8) context before content helps illustrate this to help improve your digital sense around what would make content feel native and not redundant across popular channels.[9]

For a great manual on how to create engaging and native content that is not redundant across channels, we highly recommend Gary Vaynerchuk's *Jab, Jab, Jab, Right Hook.*[10]

Outdated content is extremely common in large brands and small brands alike. It is primarily a result of a lack of proper governance. Out-of-date content is harder to spot than redundant or trivial content. It can be an old phone number or extension that no longer works. It is a reference and bio/headshot of a staff member who is no longer part of the organization. It is the events that are over and never got removed from your event calendar. It is the products mentioned on other pages or blog posts that have been discontinued. This is the content you will find deep within pages or subsections of your site.

One approach is to archive content such as news and events after an agreed amount of time in automated way at the time of publication. This removes the content from site search and navigation but allows it to stay available for those that need access to it for other internal reasons.

What about content with a less obvious end date? The best approach is to establish a policy to enforce content review on a frequent basis be it quarterly or semiannually depending on the volume you are producing. This will make sure content producers check their content to ensure it is not out of date. Another way to automate this internal auditing is to use the last modified date in your CMS to trigger an e-mail telling the person who created the page to check it. You should cc the department distribution list and admin as well so that it is dependent on the system, not an individual, if that original author has left the company and nobody else is supporting the content. In either case your content needs flagging.

Since content that produces little traffic is also less valuable, you could automate a notification based upon traffic flows to notify the producers when it has failed to reach a minimum traffic baseline or dwell time. Be careful with

Social Media Explained With Beer

f — I Like Beer

🐦 — I'm drinking #Beer

in — Drinking Beer is one of my skills

P — Here is a board of pictures of Beer

○ — Here is a vintage photo of me drinking Beer

g+ — This is a Hangout for those who drink Beer

✓ — This is where I drink Beer....a lot

ⓐ — I'm listening to a song about Beer

You Tube — Watch this video of me drinking Beer

t — Here's a GIF of someone drinking Beer

v — This is a 6 second looped video of me drinking Beer

Infographic made by JBERTHO.COM

Figure 7.8   Social Media Explained with Beer by jbertho.com

this, however, since the traffic and dwell time are soft metrics and not great indicators for all types of content as it relates to their value.

Trivial content is the hardest to deal with typically because there can be disparate opinions within the team as to what is trivial. This is where having a clear and up-to-date document on brand guidelines that includes voice and tone parameters is valuable. The other three most common criteria by which you should assess trivial content are below:

- Analytics (traffic, dwell time, etc.)
- Users' top tasks (that you want them to complete)
- Business objectives (How it maps to achieving your top three)

You can start by looking at how much traffic the content is getting. Remember however, that this is not the greatest indicator because we have seen a frozen enchilada product company think that homemade Mexican food recipes were a great piece of content on their site because it drove tons of traffic. However, none of that traffic wanted to buy frozen Mexican meals, so conversions were next to nothing. This is why the assessment of how that content is doing related to the top tasks you want them to take because of that content and which business objectives it is mapping to are equally important markers. It is trivial if it doesn't have all three and if it has high traffic but not the other two is potentially decreasing the findability of more relevant content.

Some content that is trivial must be there for compliance reasons, so not all of it needs to be removed. You just want to always ensure that ROT content is not decreasing the ranking or findability of your most relevant and engaging stuff. Flagging these for review and instituting governance around how content is published and reviewed gives you a good systemized approach to managing the content monster and ROT.

DIGITAL BIT: For an easy to use ROT content template (.xls) from our friend Anna Hrach you can visit www.DigitalSen.se/ROT.

Base Content vs. Peripheral Content

Sujan Patel, a growth and content hacker, offers us this advice: think about your content in the terms of base content and peripheral content.

- **Base Content:** is what your niche is all about. It's what you do and care about.
- **Peripheral Content:** is what your audience cares about.

From his e-book, *Content Marketing Playbook*, which is a goldmine full of content marketing nuggets, Sujan gives this example, of you owning a cooking school that has a niche blog that focuses on baking. Your base content will be recipes for cupcakes and other content related directly to baking. Your peripheral content is all about what your audience may like, such as reviews of baking equipment and ingredients, cookbooks, baking events, and kitchen apparel, along with diet and health tips. With peripheral content, you are putting yourself in the mind of your customer and giving them stuff that suits their interests.[11]

Audit 2: Brand Guidelines Audit

A deep dive into how to develop your brand guidelines is outside of the scope of this book, but KISSMetrics offers a great article on why you should do a brand audit and a simple way to start.[12]

Audit 3: Heuristic Audit

A heuristic audit will help you uncover what is working and not working on your site as it relates to overall usability for your intended audience. It will identify the short and longer term fixes and areas of concern as you prioritize the touch points you will invest in to drive the most impact.

DIGITAL BIT: You can download a Heuristic Audit Checklist at DigitalSen.se/heuristicaudit.

Good Governance Guidelines

What rules and governance do you need for your content strategy? The ideal content continuum will look something like Figure 7.9 below:

The most basic and powerful rules for good governance around your content strategy and publishing efforts are to establish the following and document them for clear awareness, training, and reinforcement within your teams.

- When are the scheduled cycles for planning and updates?
- When, how, and to what metrics do we assess how content is performing?
- When do we audit our workflows and processes?
- When and how often do we update our process?
- When (and by what criteria) does content get prioritized for creation, promotion, and featured publication?

As we conclude this chapter, we want to encourage all of you to think of yourselves as designers—practical, creative problem solvers. The reality of what great designers do is they solve problems using a variety of tactics and tools through a process of discovery, planning, creativity, and execution.

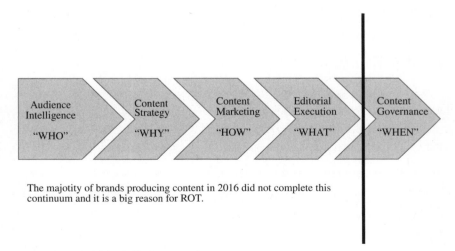

The majotity of brands producing content in 2016 did not complete this continuum and it is a big reason for ROT.

Figure 7.9 Content Strategy Continuum

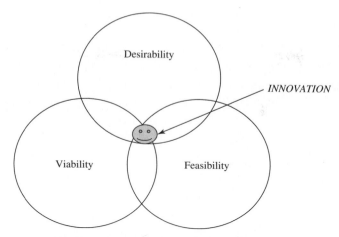

Figure 7.10 Design Thinking's Sweet Spot Graphic

Design thinking is human-centered and integrates the needs of the customer, the possibilities of technology, and the requirements for business success. Figure 7.10 shows the sweet spot where innovation in any process occurs and design thinkers never lose sight of this and use the EMF to help define the problem and opportunities more effectively so that they can focus their energy and resources on finding the solution in the center.

As you move on to the remaining sections of this book and begin to build your ultimate technology stack and arsenal of tactics, we will sunset this chapter and section with a simple summary of how you can "DO" design thinking, even if you have never considered yourself to be a design thinker.

The EMF will support each and every one of these functions as a framework, so you will be well on your way to hacking your way to more efficient optimizations around your day-to-day efforts and overall customer experience.

Design thinking operates in three spaces: Inspiration, Ideation, and Implementation. The EMF mirrors this with its Insights Layer, Vision Layer, and Success Layer. The design thinker approach to the Insight Layer (Inspiration) would be to gather insights, empathize with the customer, define the core problem, and reframe it. At the Vision Layer (Ideation) the design thinker would then brainstorm to generate ideas around how to achieve the stated goal, uncover unexpected areas for exploration, prototype a solution, and gather feedback to validate and iterate design requirements. Lastly, the design thinker would begin to implement at the Success Layer by making the solution real, make it rain, test more ways to make it rain, and iterate.

There is a saying that you can approach the center of town from any angle and it remains the center of town. You have now been armed with the framework and mental models for how to design your organization and enroll all stakeholders around the notion that a great customer experience is the one metric that matters for continued growth and sustainability.

You know how to keep the Zombies at bay, and now it is time to show you how to build the customized data and analytics platforms and tactical plans to go obliterate your competition!

Takeaways from the Success Layer

What: At this layer you have implemented a process to optimize reliability around your customer experience, and implemented repeatable measurements of value and a culture of iteration based upon the Kaizen philosophy of never-ending incremental daily improvement.

Who: Discipline leads, executive sponsor, agency partners, front line teams, analytics department, and customer success team members.

How: Audience intelligence/analytics systems, voice of customer (VOC) programs, performance media tactics, NPS/eNPS, detractor pipeline, and financial support

Why: The purpose of this layer is to meet your stated business objectives on time and at/or under budget while creating a fluid feedback and feedforward loop for future planning and funds for continued innovation.

Section III
Social Business Strategies and Tactics

8 Social Business Strategy for Marketing

As we dive into the tactics section of the EMF and help you level-up your overall digital sense of the methodologies at your disposal—many of which you are already deploying daily—we will again focus on the most practical and pragmatic approach to integrating these disciplines (Figure 8.1).

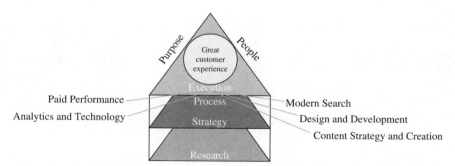

Figure 8.1 EMF with Five Core Tactical Methodologies and the Tactics Excerpt from Success Layer

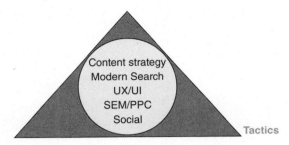

Figure 8.1 The Tactics Node of the EMF Success Layer

Much has been written on the topic of social media strategy. Many great minds have conquered that subject. This book is more about customer experience and social business permeating through your entire organization. The fact is, we are marketing to humans in a digital world where everyone is tethered to a mobile device and everyone has the attention span of a goldfish. Good luck!

Case Study: The $1 Billion Dollar Growth Hack

In many C-suites even today, social media is an afterthought. A tactic tacked on at the end of the campaign, an "oh! by the way . . ." That doesn't work. This is less the case in 2017, but it still amazes us how social media (what Gary Vaynerchuk appropriately refers to as "the current state of the Internet") still confuses so many C-suite leaders.

While at Symantec, Travis was the global social media strategist for the Norton brand, working directly under Mia Dand, head of Global Social Media and Analytics, and now, the CEO of Lighthouse3; and Rhonda Shantz, the head of Consumer Marketing for Norton. However, Travis was able to work with more than

11 different silos within Norton and Symantec, to help be a change agent. That's the equivalent of a running back running for a touchdown in American Football without any offensive line.

One of the major problems that Norton Antivirus had was a huge churn. Each year, a Norton Antivirus 60-day trial software was placed on hundreds of millions of original equipment manufacturer (OEM) equipment, such as Toshiba, Compaq, Dell, and other desktop and laptop computers. After the 60-day trial, more than 280 million demos were uninstalled or expired. 280,000,000 UNINSTALLED OR EXPIRED SOFTWARE TRIALS! That is a huge number. As Trump might say, YUUUUGE.

Travis thought, "Wow, if we could move the needle even 1 percent, that would be an additional 2.8 million paying customers, at an average of $64 per sale. That would be new net business revenue of $179 million. That's a lot of cheese."

First they needed to understand why the software trial wasn't performing as well, so Travis acted like a customer, installed it on his laptop, and waited the 60 days to see what was going on. While experiencing this trial, Travis noticed that it was nearly invisible the first 30 days of the trial. Then on day 31, it started giving you FUD (fear, uncertainty, and doubt). Trial users would see messages like:

- "You have 30 days to renew Norton Antivirus to protect your stuff."

- "Your computer is in jeopardy of becoming a zombie computer; your trial ends in 15 days!"

- "Your whole family is going to die a violent death if you don't renew now!"

Okay, that last one was hyperbole. The point is, Norton was trying to scare people into buying their product. Travis had an idea of wrapping social shareable facts, tips, and the ability to share messages into the software trial. The hypothesis being, maybe people

(continued)

(*continued*)
would find more value and have an overall better customer experience. By weaving social media into their product through the lens of customer experience, they tested adding more helpful messages and changing the tone of the messaging from fear to added value. *For example:*

Day 1: Welcome to Norton Antivirus. We help you protect your stuff that matters. We are giving you a 60-day free trial, instead of our normal 30-day trial.

Day 2: Norton has found over X number of viruses since 1982, when Peter Norton founded Peter Norton Computing with $30,000 and an IBM computer.

Day 3: Connect with Norton on Facebook & Twitter for tips on how to protect your stuff!

Day 7: Norton discovered 87 new threats this week. Your complimentary protection lasts 53 more days.

By changing the tone, during the initial beta test they had increased conversions by a whopping 4.87 percent! After the initial tests in messaging and imagery, they continued optimizing the messaging and subsequently, the conversion percentage increased to 6.59 percent. Let's do the math: 6.59 percent of 280,000,000 is 18,452,000 new conversions worth $1.36 billion. The testing was a resounding success.

Abruptly in late 2012, the Symantec board decided to fire Enrique Salem, CEO since 2009. They then hired Steve Bennett, who eventually called for a complete reorganization of the company. Under Salem, Norton and Symantec were essentially run as two different business units that operated independently. During the reorg, entire organizations were moved or dissolved.

Robert Enderle, of CIO.com, reviewed the reorganization and noted that Bennett was following the *General Electric* model of being product-focused instead of customer-focused. He concluded,

"Eliminating middle management removes a large number of highly paid employees. This will tactically improve Symantec's bottom line but reduce skills needed to ensure high-quality products in the long term."[1]

In March 2014, Symantec fired Steve Bennett from his CEO position and named Michael Brown as interim president and chief executive. Including the interim CEO, Symantec has had 3 CEOs in less than two years.[2]

The funny thing is due to the reorganization, Symantec never fully rolled out the software with revamped social messaging. The talent needed to make it happen was let go. The data on conversion increases was documented, but lost in the noise of cutting to profitability. Digital sense, anyone, anyone? Nope.

The lesson: many balls can get dropped and opportunities can be missed when reorganizations happen and massive layoffs occur without an attempt at a transferal of knowledge. It was only a billion dollars or so, though. No big deal, right?

Appropriate Campaign Goals

In marketing, public relations, and communications, there are many different campaign goals that your organization could be trying to accomplish. Are you trying to build more awareness? Are you trying to launch a new product? Are you trying to grow your audience? For the sake of simplicity, the EMF should be used to help tie your social media marketing goals and other marketing goals directly into your achievement of your major business objectives. At the most basic level your goals as a marketer should be to:

1. Increase conversions
2. Generate revenue
3. Increase market share
4. Customer acquisition/retention

SOCIAL MEDIA MARKETING CHECKLIST

Step 1: Do a complete social media audit.

◆ Which networks are you currently active on?

◆ Are your networks optimized (photo and cover images, bio, URL, etc.)?

◆ Which networks are currently bringing you the most value related to the four KPIs above?

◆ How do your profiles compare to your competitors' profiles?

Step 2: Identify your ideal personas (you have heard this before and here it is again).

If you don't know who your ideal customer is, how are you going to market to them? We gave you tips and a template on this earlier, but Hubspot also has a quick and dirty persona generating tool at MakeMyPersona.com. It will walk you through a bunch of questions and then generate a Word document for you.

Step 3: Identify key success metrics for tracking and reporting.

You need to be able to define your success ahead of time. By mapping out and identifying your metrics ahead of time, you can begin working on optimizing those areas of your marketing campaigns. It will help you think about and ask the right questions. Data don't lie, baby. A few metrics worth measuring are:

◆ Conversion rate

◆ Time spent on website

◆ Reach

◆ Brand mentions

◆ Sentiment

◆ Total shares

◆ Customer acquisition costs (CPC)

◆ Likes/fans

◆ Clicks

- Backlinks to your website
- E-mails added to your lists

There are many other metrics out there that may be relevant to your business. Choose wisely and remember to *measure what is valued more than you value what is measurable.*

Step 4: Create a Dominating Content Marketing Strategy.

Content in the proper context is king. And it really is a driving force to affect business performance when you have adopted the philosophy of creating and curating informative, helpful content for your ideal customer. In fact, content is VITAL to your business. Content shows up in several ways not limited to the categories below:

- Video
- Images/infographics
- Text/articles/blog posts
- Audio/podcasts
- Links
- Live events
- Hiring processes and protocols
- Paid media and advertisements
- The social media posts of your employees and executives both personal and professional

DIGITAL BIT: We strongly recommend that you create a content marketing calendar to help with your content strategy and planning. A great tool to check out is DivvyHQ.com. It will help you organize and schedule your content in many ways.

There are many types of content out there, as you can see in the following graphic from Michael King, @iPullRank

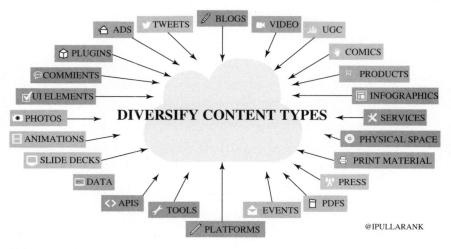

Figure 8.2

(Figure 8.2). So, you'll want to mix and match it up. Keep it fresh. Keep it relevant.

Step 5: Invest in Social Media Marketing Tools & Technologies.

Modern marketers use tools to help them in their daily efforts. As you will see in our accompanying "Marketing Technology Glossary" (available at www.digitalsen.se/mktgtools), there are hundreds of categories of tools, which reference thousands of actual tools.

Some of the general types of social media tools that you may have:

◆ Monitor social media conversation.

◆ Schedule your content

◆ Discover & curate content.

◆ Maximize your audience.

◆ Interact with influencers and customers.

◆ Measure results

DIGITAL BIT: We aren't going to go into all of the tools in this book, because they are always changing. However, if you go to DigitalSen.se/mktgtools, there is a curated collection of some of Travis, Chris, and Kevin Mullett's favorite tools. We promise to update this frequently and welcome your comments and crowd-curation as you become aware and test kickass stuff in your daily efforts.

Anyone who has been to a social media marketing conference should know Kevin Mullett, @kmullett. He and Travis are constantly trying to one-up one another on their tools. They finally decided to quit competing and work together. You get the benefit of that collaboration with a frequently updated Digital Bit resource.

Step 6: Track, Analyze, and Optimize your Efforts.

This is key when it comes to succeeding on social media. Even the most seasoned social marketer will fail; that's to be expected. Testing, experimenting, and optimizing campaigns are part of the fun. It might seem basic, but tracking your results, analyzing the data, and optimizing is essential to excel in this space. Let the data flow through you.

Social media strategy has been written about ad nauseam in the past decade. Many organizations still haven't figured out how to value it across the enterprise and see it as more than just a silo of tactics in the marketing department. Hopefully, this simple audit checklist will help you finally make the plunge to becoming a more socially integrate business.

Content Marketing and Paid Media Amplification

We could talk forever on content marketing, but there are plenty of great books and blogs out there. ContentMarketingInstitute.com is one of the best resources on that topic. QuickSprout has a great definitive guide on content marketing, as well.[3]

We aren't going to teach you anything that they won't; however, we can teach you some sweet content marketing hacks. We will talk about some later in this chapter in the social selling section, and it rings true with any great piece of content.

Can you relate to the following? You create a magical piece of content for your ideal targeted persona, you post it on your blog, and all you get is crickets chirping. Ever have that happen? It's infuriating. Well, if you take that same piece of content, and put a bit of paid media behind it—specifically Facebook, Twitter, LinkedIn, Pinterest, Instagram, or even Reddit ads—you have a chance to get that content in front of exactly the right people. If you have built out your personas, you can target those exact people with advertising. That's one more reason why building out personas is an important task.

One trick for social marketing is creating an idea that can break through culture, giving you an unfair advantage on earned media reach. Basically, making an idea that can be digested and pushed around the Internet with headlines. The key to virality in 2017 is still headlines, not brand pages. Headlines are the artifact that people can exchange and share. Put the right paid dollars against something and build an idea that journalists can't resist.

Many brands have found out that the easiest way to break through and amplify what they do in social media is by designing the idea to travel through all channels of media. Designing the idea through a process of writing the headline first. They've figured out that people rarely share posts from a brand page—what they share most is headlines and links to trusted media sources. The anti-affectionate term for much of this content is clickbait, but when it is done strategically and with relevance, it is extremely powerful. Travis sometimes calls this *PR hacking*.

Kentucky Fried Chicken (KFC) is one brand that we've been keeping an eye on that has really proved themselves to be skillful at this media jujitsu, with back-to-back headlines about weirdo products that smell like chicken. Nail polish that tastes like chicken (proving that they're still finger-licking good) and sunscreen that smells like a bucket of extra crispy. The latter was able to garner over 90 blog posts from medium to large publishers in just 6 hours following the release. These products don't even have to be real or commercially available! Only two bottles of the nail polish were made, but that's enough to get a picture, and it makes for a headline that journalists can't resist.[4]

HEADLINE: KFC's Fried Chicken-Scented Sunscreen Will Keep Your Skin From Getting Crispy

For when you want to make yourself smell finger-lickin' good

During the writing of this book, Travis visited Kansas City–based ad agency, Barkley, where media hacking has become part of their offering. "Our job is to bring our brand's ideas to life in the real world," says Joe Cox, head of Consumer Engagement at Barkley. "To do that, we have to have a deep understanding of what makes media tick. It's not just social, it's the relationship of social, earned, and paid together that will bring a modern idea to life."

Barkley worked with Dairy Queen this past Valentine's Day and helped them with an idea to promote their February Valentine's Blizzard. It's tough to break through the noise of V-day with a product, so they built a story around it that made it interesting to media. It wouldn't just be a V-day Blizzard, but a *Singles Blizzard*. This was based on data, which they had commissioned, saying that 2016 was the first time in U.S. history when there were more single people than married people.

HEADLINE: Dairy Queen Has Something Special For Singles This Valentine's Day

This headline has a lot more social equity in your feed than a picture of a DQ Blizzard by itself. *DQ trended nationally on Facebook & Twitter within 12 hours of the release.*[5]

"Things have so massively changed since Oreo did *Dunk in the Dark* at the 2013 Super Bowl. Honestly, it's time for brands to drop

(continued)

(*continued*)

Real-Time Marketing. It's over. You can't break through anymore and the juice isn't worth the squeeze. Don't be ambulance chasers of real time events." says Joe Cox, Head of Social Media at Barkley.

Joe continued, "Very few brands are able to be publishers. That's a ton of resources and money that I'd rather them spend on updating their digital infrastructure or organizing their purchase data. Brands can't speak just to speak, but only need to speak when they have something to say and then light that shit on fire with really specific targeted social amplification."

Barkley has a command center that they call Houston, which is a wall of televisions and monitors that help them keep up with what's going on in real time with their brands. It's quite impressive. They have screens that show the sentiments for the various brands, where you can click the sentiment, see where it is, and then respond. For community management, it's badass. They even have a screen dedicated to the amount each emoji has been used that day. Not surprisingly, the purple eggplant is used quite frequently. And the ☺ is typically used most often.

Barkley's community managers aren't just looking for that one moment; they are tracking trending hashtags and their meaning, what articles are trending, what's in their community's feeds, and how they can be relevant.

Real-Time Marketing isn't dead, per se, but it's definitely more saturated now. That's why putting social amplification money against content that isn't even your own, but articles about how amazing you are from third parties, works so well.

A great tool to check out that takes social listening, sentiment analysis, and scoring with automation of the one-to-one communication of triage or offers is Earshot.com. It can even recognize brand logos on clothing and so on in pictures where the brand may or may not be mentioned. It scores against relevance, risk, and sentiment and allows for a single dashboard to automate your promotional and reactive responses in a highly personalized, one-to-one way at scale.

Another example of content amplification, Mike "Jortsy" Gelphman, CEO of the Disruption Institute, a mobile app and coding school in Kansas City, puts on a yearly conference called Compute Midwest. This is a premier event, but not many outside of the region know about it. Kansas City? That's right. Hailing from the first city chosen for Google Fiber, Compute Midwest is one of the world's leading future-focused tech conferences. More than 1,000 attendees exploring the technologies transforming tomorrow and learning how the world-class speakers overcame enormous challenges to create breakthrough innovations. Topics include self-driving cars, robots, space travel, and artificial intelligence.

Since this is a great conference, Travis included it in an article on *Inc.* magazine featuring seven other top tech conferences happening around the world.[6] Gelphman was then able to use that piece of content to build trust and convince other people to come to his event. He was even able to leverage it to gain additional sponsorship dollars. This conference has attracted some of the world's most innovative and influential people in tech over the past 5 years, including Robert Scoble, Alexis Ohanian, Stephen Wolfram, Cynthia Breazeal, and John Underkoffler.

> *"I've been fortunate enough to speak all over the world, but what I found at ComputeMidwest was something really special—entrepreneurship has a great stage in KC thanks to this conference."*
>
> —ALEXIS OHANIAN, COFOUNDER OF REDDIT

The key point here is this. It is better to have someone else talk about how great you are than to blather to everyone about how great you think you are. If you get a good piece of press, don't just tweet it a couple of times and share it on LinkedIn. Put some ad spend behind it and really target the eyeballs of the people you want to see that content.

This is just one example of what you can do with paid media and content. Try to think outside the box a bit, and get eyes on some of your more valuable content. Also, take that content and repost it on your site with a link back the original work. Why? Because you can tag visitors with a retargeting pixel and you can market to them all over the web. Keep in mind that reposting content that was originally posted elsewhere won't help you with search rankings at all. But it will help you with amplifying the right content to the right people, as you build custom advertising audiences, and then retargeting them later with Adroll, Facebook ads, or the Google Display Network.

Case Study: Fort Collins Startup Week Goes Global on $2,500

Chris was able to leverage a strategy like this in 2014, when he and his wife decided to create, brand, organize, and promote the first ever Fort Collins Startup Week with only 102 days to execute.[7] At the time not too many entrepreneurs or venture capitalists outside of Colorado could point to Fort Collins on a map. The Snooks had lived in the city for only 8 months and were on sabbatical, having moved there from Southern California on a whim with no prior contacts in the state. However, by creating a multipronged guerrilla-content heavy marketing and sales strategy, they were able to attract 3,221 attendees from 16 states and the Commonwealth of Puerto Rico in less than 102 days!

In 2015 they bested that effort with over 3,500 attendees from 25 states and 11 countries on five of the seven continents. To our knowledge, no other regional startup week anywhere in the world has attracted such a broadly dispersed audience of domestic and international attendees. This was all done on a grassroots budget that left less than $2,500 for total marketing spend each year.

It started with producing a SlideShare guide aggregating all of the local resources and startup community players called "The Definitive Guide to Fort Collins Startup Scene" (*which got 24,709 organic unique views* on Chris's page[8] and *16,500 views* on Brianne's[9]).

The Snooks placed four paid PR national wires to announce the event and also highlight key milestones of momentum through the eReleases.com service to create media pickups nationally that could be reshared. Against these third-party pickups they ran light retargeting and personally sent social media messages to each new follower as they came alive on the Fort Collins Startup Week Twitter feed. They also leveraged offline efforts by recruiting more than 117 speakers and mentors to be part of the 5-day, 102-event festival. You have heard of FOMO right? Fear. Of. Missing. Out. It was leveraged to the hilt and made Fort Collins the place to be Memorial Day weekend the last two years. The effort impressed Eric Schurenberg, editor in chief of *Inc.* magazine, so much that he wrote about it in his Editor's Letter in July 2015's issue "How They Do It In Flyover Country!"[10] Talk about some valuable earned media!

Modern Enterprise Search Marketing

We define modern search as follows from your customer's perspective and from your company's perspective.

1. Your customer sees it as self-directed real-time problem solving on demand.

2. You see it as the proper blend of SEO, SEM, local search, UI/UX, Content Marketing, and Analytics to optimize the discovery and post click engagement with potential customers in their time of need, to garner more traffic and increase the volume of your potential opportunities to generate revenue.

Search Engine Optimization (SEO)

Travis started in search engine optimization before it was a thing and well before Google hit the scene. The under-30 reader just thought "there was search before Google?" He intuitively knew, for example, that if you were a plumber living in Kansas City, you should consider owning KCPlumber.com. While selling yellow page advertising in the mid to late '90s, he started consulted with businesses and working side by side with them to establish their web presence.

In the beginning, SEO was a black hat cowboy's uncharted Wild West. There were so many ways to manipulate the search results, because the search engines were nowhere near the sophisticated tools we're used to today. For example, Travis quickly figured out that if you wanted a webpage to rank for a term like "Britney Spears" all you needed to do was put the words "Britney Spears" in a <div> that was the same color as the background. Then you could move that <div> off the edge of the margin, so that only the search engines would find it. Simple hacks like this ruled the SEO industry for the first years, until the search engines smartened up and began rolling out penalties to websites breaking their published guidelines. Those days are long gone. And Travis hung up his black hat long ago. He now wears a more grayish hat, typically with a KC Royals logo on it.

Search engine optimization has evolved into an entirely different beast today. With all of the algorithm changes and rules by Google, it's no longer about gaming the engines. It's truly about meeting the customer at the center of their intention as they query. With Google's Penguin, Panda, Hummingbird, and other major search engine algorithm updates, your site's search engine rankings can plummet overnight if you aren't up to speed on the latest mandates from our Google Master Overlord.

The key to success with the search engines these days is all about the long game and customer intent. It's based on establishing a solid foundation of on page optimization and growing your site's authority in the eyes of the search engines as well as providing a solid experience of relevant content for your customers. A simple way to design a successful website is to constantly review it for user experience. Not only will your customers be happy but also Google bases many of its ranking factors on user experience, so it's a win-win. Now ask yourself, "What do people looking for something online want?"

Key Determinants Impacting Your Organic Search Ranking

Page Speed: How quickly your site loads is huge for keeping your customer on your site. Nothing will make someone click away like a slow page load. Besides it being a ranking factor, speed has become such an obsession with Google that they've recently launched the Accelerated Mobile Pages (AMP) project. This project has a goal to shift as many webpages as possible to a simplified streamlined HTML page designed to load almost instantly. The issue is that this platform is only realistic for news sites and those businesses focused on publishing a lot of content. It's just not realistic for small businesses or ecommerce sites in its current state. However, Google is dedicated to its success so it won't take long for AMP to become more user friendly for all types of websites.

Mobile Friendly: Any website that wants to be successful MUST be easily accessed from any mobile device. The format endorsed by Google, as well as all the other search engines, is responsive design. Responsive design allows the content from your website to automatically format itself for any sized device, from a desktop computer to your smartphone. Having a website that is mobile friendly gives you an advantage in the search results.

Secure Site (HTTPS): Another ranking factor that Google has been pushing onto sites is the shift from HTTP to HTTPS by installing a secure certificate on the server side of your website. This certificate is supposed to add a level of authority and trust to your website for your users. It's recommended for all sites regardless if you take payments or not.

Content Quality: Many of Google's penalties revolve directly around the quality of a website's content. It's a known technique to write poor quality content full of your chosen keywords in order to manipulate the algorithms to rank your pages higher in the search results. Well, Google has gotten so smart about this strategy that not only does it no longer work but also it's getting to the point where only the best content gets those top spots.

There are entire books about creating the right content for your audience, so we will just tell you that it's vital that your website is designed to help your customers solve a problem or answer a question. It needs to provide them with in-depth unique information on each and every one of the potential questions they may have to be successful.

As you can see, building a solid search-engine-friendly website is not something you can do overnight. However, the process is also not a secret process cloaked in mystery. There are a few trusted places to turn for up-to-date guidance on how exactly to approach SEO for your website. Here are a few experts in the SEO industry to explain it . . .

"Long term online success for 2017 and beyond is not about a secret tip, how much you spend or being sure you do that one thing exactly perfect," says Kristi

Hagen, president and senior editor of SearchEngineNews.com. "It's about getting all of the little things right because in today's competitive markets the race is won by inches. So find an SEO informational source you can trust and roll up your sleeves—that's when the magic happens."

"What's the current State of SEO? One focused entirely on User Experience. Google's push to Accelerated Mobile Pages (AMP), its recent war on mobile interstitials, its continual embracing of mobile-friendly content, HTTPS, and page speed are all about one thing: increasing User Experience. This means fast-loading pages designed around 1 MB in size that; eliminate interstitials, break up content into mobile-friendly chunks, and are designed for smaller screens," shares Casey Markee, founder, Media Wyse. "SEO isn't shortcuts and link schemes. It's a game of inches and it's constantly evolving. If you aren't testing and retesting your ranking hypotheses and marketing strategies constantly, you aren't innovating. Those that do all of this will rank higher now and well into 2017 and beyond."

As you can imagine, staying abreast of the changes within the search engines, as well as the trusted long-term ranking strategies, is a business in itself. That being said, here are some of the resources that we've worked with over the years and have leveraged for much of our own success. The top of the list is SearchEngineNews.com, a simple Internet-marketing-based membership site that is worth every penny. Travis has had an active membership for over a decade. Some others to consider are Search Engine Land, Moz, and Search Engine Journal.

The SMX, Mozcon, and Pubcon conferences are where you want to go to network with the brightest minds in the industry.

Finally, the oft-updated book by Eric Enge, Stephan Spencer, and Jessie Stricchiola, *The Art of SEO*—now in its third edition—is a must for anyone who wants complete digital sense.[11]

Enterprise Paid Search

If you've been in the enterprise search game for as long as we have, you've seen many of the same vendors dominate the ecosystem for the better part of a decade. Marin Software, Kenshoo, Adobe Media Optimizer/Efficient Frontier, Google DoubleClick, and others have been the major players, but many of these have yet to capitalize on the trend of using data science to automate the optimization of your pay per click (PPC).

Predictive Advertising Management

Predictive advertising management is supposed to improve advertising performance, but if that transition isn't smooth, chaos ensues—along with lost revenues and customers. Marketers who take advantage of all the data signals available have a competitive advantage over those who are using a more limited set of data. For example, what if you could target searchers based on keyword, device, time of day, zip code, weather conditions in two days and the current NASDAQ rates? Today, predictive advertising management platforms provide this level of granular targeting. When data science meets search advertising, you can improve advertising ROI dramatically (Figures 8.3 and 8.4). One of the reasons we personally think QuanticMind could have a leg up over its rivals is the sheer volume of data points it optimizes.

Data science, FTW! Digital Marketing Depot's *Enterprise Paid Media Campaign Management Platforms 2016: A Marketer's Guide* report by *MarketingLand,* discusses targeting and using data science on search marketing platforms, which is one of the cornerstone services that QuanticMind delivers.[12] This method ups the value of a customer for life, by mixing purchase intent with data.

At CCP Digital, we've found that QuanticMind is giving us a competitive advantage for our large clients, so much so that Travis is now advising for

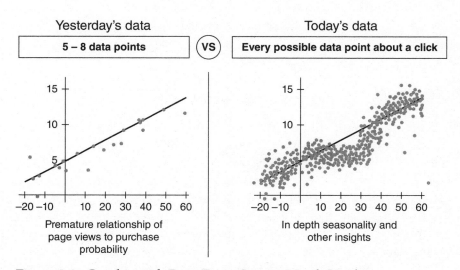

Figure 8.3 Graphic with Data From QuanticMind Graphic

PUBLISHER	PERFORMANCE	EXTERNAL DRIVERS	
Keyword	Impressions	Nasdaq	Airport status
Match-type	Clicks	NYSE	Sports calendar (US, UK)
Ads	Minimum bid	Fed interest rate	Football
Placement	Current bid	Weather.com	Soccer
Position	Location	Temperature	Baseball
Slot	Quality score	Rain	Basketball
Click-type	Competition	Humidity	Hollday calendar
	Landing page	Zip code—demographic	Events calendar
	Time of day	Tax	Starbucks index
	Day of week	Education level	Concerts (Live Nation)
	Device	Household income	Competitive search
		Marital status	SEM Rush
		Presence of children	Keyword spy
		Age	SpyFu
		Gender	Google

ADVERTISER	SEASONALITY	SCALING FACTORS	USER
Conversions	Time	Search engine	Search query
Revenue	Day of week	Campaigns	Device
LTV	Month	Keywords	Geo/location
Revenue parameters	Year	Ad copy	
Custom parameters	Holidays		
Business constraints			
Other business metrics			
Promotions			

Figure 8.4 Data Points to Optimize on Your SEM Campaigns

them. If you're spending more than $1 million a year on enterprise paid search, it may be worthwhile to your organization to consider moving onto a platform that uses smart data science to optimize your campaigns and ad spend.

GEO Targeting and IP-Based Advertising

Imagine if you were able to pick anyone's physical address, reverse-engineer it, and translate it into their IP address. You could then target company by injecting advertising into only that IP range. For example, a client of Travis's was hiring engineers. They wanted to target people who were engineers at Oracle. We figured out where the engineers in Oracle were located, and we injected advertising into their building only, so anyone using that Wi-Fi or the Internet in that IP range saw our ads. We were able to hire some great engineers with this simple yet somewhat expensive ad hack, using a technology by El Toro.[13]

DIGITAL BIT: We are both full of marketing hacks, case studies, and resources around social marketing. The thing is, they are always changing. To stay up to date with what's going on, check DigitalSen.se/marketinghacks for updated case studies, resources, and definitive guides.

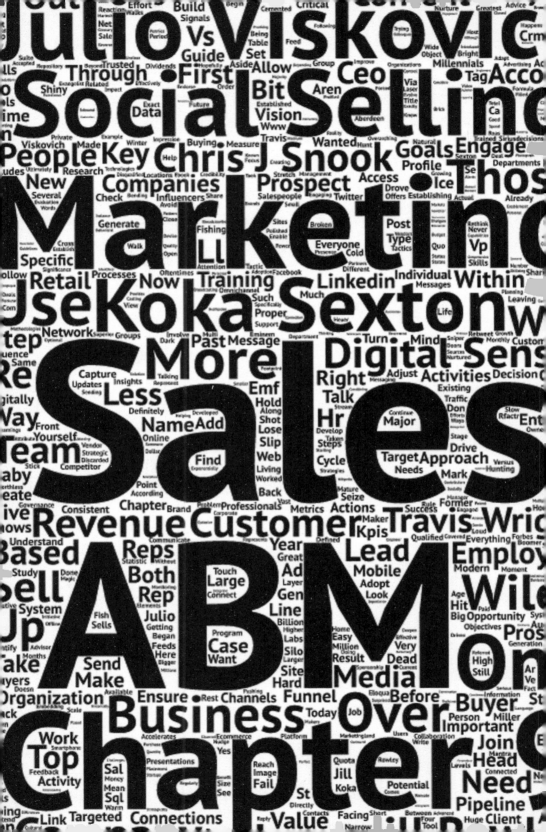

9 Social Business Strategy for Sales

"79 percent of sales professionals that used social selling over the past year achieved quota vs 43 percent of those who did not."

—Aberdeen Group[1]

Much like other departments in a social business/organization, a social sales team starts with establishing forecast objectives that line up to the major business goals and the vision. Then you build your road map, acquire staff, train the staff, and then define a set of department KPIs directly related to the overarching business goals of the company established and cemented in your EMF Vision Layer.

Along with marketing, customer support, and HR, sales is one of the first departments to adopt social media within a social organization. Since your sales team is customer facing, as well as revenue generating, having a well-trained team with digital sense is crucial. Your sales team oftentimes represents the first humans in your company, aside from your content marketing team, to actually touch and communicate with a potential customer or buyer. Since you can't change a first impression, it's critical to ensure salespeople represent a consistent company brand, use proper etiquette, and understand how social media both feeds into and accelerates the sales pipeline. This is where the effort made in going through all layers of the EMF pays dividends over and over as both a form of governance and repository of key learnings from your front line feedback that can improve future messaging.

What Is Social Selling?

Social selling is the layering of high-value social media activities over your existing sales communication process. Social selling was born from a need to adjust communication strategies with today's modern buyer, who happens to be mobile and digitally available 24 hours a day with their smartphone. In going with the mantra "be where your buyers are," sales reps have had to adjust the way they engage, interact with, and nurture their buyers as a result.

Julio Viskovich, VP of Marketing for rFactr, a B2B social selling platform, and one of *Forbes*'s top social-selling influencers, has this advice for sales teams: "Never use social media for the hard sell, it's for building relationships, value, trust, and credibility."

Our friend Jon Ferrara, CEO of Nimble, said this about social selling: "Social Selling is a natural evolution to the effects social media has had on the way customers make buying decisions and the way companies and salespeople need to sell. It has evolved the sales process so it's focused on buyers needs and leverages technology to put sales reps in front of the right prospect—at the right time—with the right message."

Why Is Social Selling Important?

Social selling is just selling with a shiny name, but the name has significance because it calls attention to a huge gap in skills that need to be developed within a company. Just as you would train your salespeople how to give presentations or guide a prospect through a sales cycle, you need to train your salespeople how to make use of the technologies that can generate pipeline.

"The natural reaction is to buy the bright shiny object; not do the hard work of strategy, planning, goals, and tactics," offers Jill Rowley, former Social Selling Evangelist at Eloqua. "It's all too easy to take a silo approach versus embedding Social Selling into existing processes, methodologies, systems, metrics. Culture and executive buy-in/sponsorship are critical."

Goals for Social Selling

There could be many different objectives for the sales team, but typically they are to generate more revenue, increase overall sales pipeline, increase contacts, and add more data on your leads and opportunities from social into the Customer Relationship Management platform (CRM).

"For any company building a social business strategy, it's important to stretch that to any customer facing employees, specifically sales professionals." Koka Sexton, former head of social for LinkedIn and founder of Social Selling Labs, says, "All research shows that employees sharing corporate messages get engaged higher and have an exponentially larger reach. If this is the case, then companies that fail to involve their sales team are effectively leaving actual money on the table."

Now that we are talking about leads and opportunities, here is a mind-bending statistic, from SiriusDecisions. Of qualified leads, 70 percent make it to sales get disqualified or discarded at some point. Up to 80 percent of those "dead end" prospects will ultimately go on to buy from you—or from a competitor—within 6–12 months.

Just because that lead or prospect isn't a sales-qualified lead—SQL—or a sales-accepted lead—SAL—doesn't mean that lead is worthless. It just needs to be nurtured before your competitor sells them. You have to keep the funnel growing and you have to engage those already in your funnel. If they aren't SQLs yet, and they are an important prospect, you'll definitely want to continue engaging them and adding value to them. Social selling can be broken down into two specific activities, fishing and hunting.

1. **Fishing** is what most people think social selling represents—simply pushing out content each day and leaving the breadcrumbs that leads hopefully find and follow. The problem is that this activity of broadcasting content as well as monitoring for new leads or buying signals only aligns with TOFU (top of funnel) elements of the sales process.

2. **Hunting** is the specific use of content and social channels to influence a specific person(s) within your pipeline. An example would be sending a private LinkedIn message to one of your prospects in the evaluation stage that includes a contextual message and link to a buyer's guide comparing you with your head-to-head competition.

Who Should Own Social Selling?

Social Selling is NOT a marketing campaign. The program should be owned by sales leadership. The formula for successful Social Selling: *Marketing + Sales Leadership + Sales Enablement & Training to align = SUCCESS!*

You also need HR to rethink the capabilities and competencies of the sales hires—at all levels—leadership, manager, and individual contributors. This will be covered in depth in the chapter on Social Business Strategies for HR.

The Social Selling System

Successful and advanced social selling teams that hit KPIs and measure success effective mature with the following system, based on the work of Julio Viskovich:[2]

1. **Presence**—it all starts with establishing which social channels you will be active on and creating a consistent and polished footprint on those channels.

2. **Adoption**—ensure sales reps have the right training and right tools to be successful. You will need a way for reps to quickly access sales-ready content, share, engage, and track their activities. A fool with a tool is still a fool—but a sniper without a gun is DEAD.

3. **Influence**—engage with each prospect according to their placement in your funnel and don't just use social media to stay top of mind . . . use it to strategically shape your buyer's needs and vision.

4. **Revenue**—track your sales activities to your CRM system to understand the exact impact on leads, opportunities, revenue, sales cycle time, and other key sales metrics

With proper tools, training, and implementation, sales reps who adopt social selling will be able to:

- turn cold calls into warm leads with superior prospect insights,
- go beyond just being a vendor and begin to establish yourself as their trusted advisor,
- build a bigger pipeline and drive more revenue,
- attribute social-selling actions to revenue through reporting,
- network and attend events remotely through various social interactions and hashtags, and
- identify buying signals that capture purchase intent from your prospect.

Social Selling Implementation

Step 1: Have each member of the sales team create or update a LinkedIn and Twitter profile.

Ensure that every rep's profile is 100 percent completed. This includes having a professionally done photograph. Marketing should give some guidelines on language used.

Step 2: Connect with everyone in your company.

This will allow each rep access to the rest of the organization's network and increase the number of second and third degree connections. Having these are crucial not only for network growth but also getting referred or introduced through trusted sources in your company.

Step 3: Join 10–15 LinkedIn groups

Groups allow you to send messages to those who aren't your first degree connections, and allow you to join in the conversation with your prospects. Follow the four-to-one rule: comment on four posts for every post that you write.

Step 4: Ask your past and current colleagues, customers, or vendors to recommend you. You'd be surprised at the importance a short recommendation can hold. Potential partners or prospects are likely to check out your profile when considering doing business with you.

Step 5: Interact at least once a day through your activity stream. Most of your home page is taken up with updates from your connections. There are several ways you can interact with these updates, depending on the type.

- **Send a message**—When your connections make new connections or take several actions on LinkedIn, this information shows up in your activity feed. You can send your connection a message to reengage them.

- **Retweet or Favorite**—Posts from other social media sites often enable you to favorite the posts. For Twitter posts, you can retweet or reply as well. This is a great tactic to do right before a call to nudge the prospect via a notification to their mobile.

- **Like/Comment/Endorse**—Jump in and engage with prospects regularly through these mini actions to stay relevant and avoid a dark period of the sales process to take hold. It also shows you as a value-add and someone who walks the social selling walk.

Social Selling Challenges

The greatest challenge for the individual is behavioral change, especially for salespeople, who are not historically digital savvy. The greatest challenge for the organization is culture change. Cross-functional collaboration is not optional. This is a change management initiative. (This is why chapter five and understanding the stick-person is so important.)

There are major cultural differences between the Baby Boomer generation and Millennials. Geoffrey Moore says it best: in his generation, collaboration was called "cheating and you got expelled for it"; whereas, the Millennials are used to living their lives out loud on the web, sharing everything with everyone. Although Millennials lack some of the business pattern recognition and experience of their Baby Boomer and Gen X peers, they are definitely more transparent, collaborative, connected, and digitally savvy. We're now living in the age of empowered customer, where buyers are digitally driven, socially connected, and mobile with multiple devices that give them nearly unlimited access to both information and people.

The modern buyer is proficient in utilizing their own device as a personal life-remote control, but many sales organizations have been slow to adapt and evolve their processes, training, and systems of selling to the way most people want to buy today. This is the BIG opportunity for those of you who take this serious and implement.

Account-Based Marketing (ABM)

"Account-based marketing: a strategic approach that coordinates personalized marketing and sales efforts to open doors and deepen engagement at specific accounts."

—*Jon Miller, Engagio*

According to Wikipedia, account-based marketing (ABM), also known as key account marketing, is a strategic approach to business marketing in which an organization considers and communicates with individual prospect or customer accounts as markets of one. Account-based marketing is typically employed in enterprise level sales organizations.

Forrester Research states that less than 1 percent of leads turn into revenue generating customers. Because of this, it's time to challenge the status quo and focus your time, budget, and resources on generating quality leads vs. quantity, especially in B2B.

In business-to-customer marketing and sales, B2C, it's more of a shotgun approach; you are casting a wide net from a large demographic of people. In B2B marketing and sales, it's a laser approach. You know EXACTLY the name and job title of your target.

Say, for instance, you're trying to sell to the CEO of Facebook, and you know that his name is Mark Zuckerberg. But Mark isn't the only one we have to talk to get the sale. We may have to talk with influencers, some members of middle management, and end users before we can get to the decision maker. In some enterprise businesses, there could be up to 17 people that you need to connect with before getting a yes from the decision maker. Now, how do you reverse-engineer a relationship with those people? That's where ABM comes in.

B2B companies are typically forced to "hunt and fish" to a narrow list of prospects. They use a combination of inbound, outbound, and account-based marketing techniques to make the magic happen.

Megan Heuer at SiriusDecisions has a great presentation on ABM where she goes over the "new reality" of B2B marketing. She profiled the companies already using ABM, as well as those thinking about starting this year.[3]

Company size:

- 45 percent less than $100 million are using ABM
- 18 percent between $101 million and $1 billion are using ABM
- 36 percent more than $1.1 billion are using ABM

It's interesting to see that nearly half of the companies that have $100m or less in revenue are using ABM to target decision makers on their narrow list of prospects. Over a third of companies with $1 billion or more in revenue use ABM, but less than 20 percent in the $101 million–$1 billion range use ABM.

Customer type:

- 75 percent enterprise (more than 1,000 employees)
- 21 percent medium (101 to 1,000 employees)
- 11 percent small (100 or fewer employees)

The vast majority of ABM-practicing companies are enterprise-level brands with more than 1,000 employees. Smaller companies can benefit from it, as well.

Five Steps to Develop an ABM Program

1. Identify target companies
2. Develop personas
3. Find or create the right content
4. Integrate your ABM into your multichannel strategy
5. Measure and optimize

 DIGITAL BIT: For deeper insights into ABM, check out Jon Miller's Engagio e-book at Engagio.com/guide.[4]

Case Study: #Closing $Millions for Pennies on the Dollar

We work with many well-funded startups that sell into large enterprises. Travis worked with one such company that provides an enterprise tag management solution (TMS). After identifying the top 100 targeted accounts, he began listening at scale for those companies to talk about omnichannel marketing, online/offline data, ecommerce, and so on. Words that were relevant to his clients' suite of solutions. One such company, a Fortune 100 retail company with locations all over the world, had their annual shareholder meeting and the CEO mentioned omnichannel and treating their online ecommerce customers the same as their brick-and-mortar locations. This was the perfect opportunity.

Travis took the news to the content team and worked with them to create a piece that talked about this retail company. The CEO of the MarTech company had an author account on MarketingLand, and we uploaded it as his monthly column. The next month, they did the same thing around a very large coffee company from Seattle.

Once that article was live, it was shared. The next day, we copied it and put it on their blog, with a link back to MarketingLand. Why? We wanted to drive traffic to their blog, not MarketingLand, for the sole reason of tagging them with our custom retargeting pixel. Everyone who came to that article from our ad campaign was placed in a custom audience. We could then advertise to that customer audience all over the web, like magic.

DIGITAL BIT: We've found that if you are advertising an article or news to a client of yours, it gets way more clicks if you use a picture of their CEO as the main image.

The result? We targeted 4,100 employees in San Bruno, CA, and Bentonville, AR, with a sponsored post of this article on Facebook, with an image of the CEO of the retail company. We drove all of the traffic back to the client's site, where our custom tracking pixel fired. In fact, we drove 1,108 people to site, all top employees of this retail company, due to our initial ad targeting. They were all added to a custom audience and we targeted them all over. Many key employees within that retail company filled out a lead-gen form, then marketing and sales began nurturing the relationship. The sales rep eventually closed a $700,000-plus deal, for less than $700 in total ad spend. Is that a good return on ad spend (ROAS)? The bottom line: B2B account-based marketing and advertising, with paid social amplification of relevant, targeted content to targeted prospects, can be a very potent combo in your social selling arsenal.

DIGITAL BIT: We host monthly webinars on case study how to's just like this, and if you would like alerts to upcoming video presentations, join our list at DigitalSen.se/webinars.

Advocacy
Employees
Influencers
Out
Make
Capabilities
Brands
Curate
Enterprise
Influential
Best
Agree
Reddit
Street
Profile
High
Biased
Everyone
Acquired
Try
Discovery
Five
Increase
Category
Tool
Covers
Video
Audien
Product
Grow
Trend
Data
Positive
Marketing
Pictures
Metrics
Hit
Pick
Six
See
View
Ya
Gx
Top
Awareness
Measure
Community
Definitely
Facebook
Danger
Engagement
Start
Media
Mia
Dand
Vendors
Topics
Survey
Amplify
Always
New
Ideal
Rise
Note
Cause
Employees
Hills
Inc
Peer
Building
Perspective
Published
Recently
Topic
Pinterest
Report
Mia
Www
Market
Industry
Quality
Different
Company
Brand
Global
Form
Sound
Tracking
Strong
Launched
Lot
Technologies
Years
Currently
Tweet
Picture
Reporting
Influencer
Mentioned
Use
Blockers
User
Offer
Email
Read
Bit
Pay
Talk
Others
Deloitte
Including
Nielsen
Stars
Online
Based
Much
Budget
Critical
Articles
Tools
Social
Together
Word
Each
October
Using
Stack
Marketers
Now
Unpaid
Spending
Agencies
Cmos
Solutions
Martech
Isn
Percent
Advocate
Through
Technology
Via
Resonates
Past
Art
Four
Wall
Advocate
Areas
Customers
People
Typically
Altimeter
Figure
Advertising
Clients
Trends
Chapter
Same
Dand
Doesn
10
Journal
Messages
Know
Yoy
Pdf
Vs
Format
Due
Wanna
Sales
Less
Look
Platforms
Digital
Internet
Important
Wiley
Docs
Quantity
Companies
Great
Engaged
Strategy
Spend
Allows
Categories
Cat
Million
Thing
Content
Videos
Time
Work
Life
End
Activity
Model
Credible
Efforts
Decline
Growth
Live
Service
Mess

10 Social Business Strategy for Influencers and Employee Advocates

nfluencer marketing is a hot topic in 2017 and it's also a "hot mess," according to *The Wall Street Journal*.[1] We tend to agree, as it's a challenge to build the ideal marketing technology stack. Currently, with influencer marketing technology, there isn't one solution that comprehensively covers all areas. From discovery to engagement to tracking and reporting, there are many different solutions, but they don't always fit together. Sound familiar? Welcome to MarTech Hell. (That should totally be an AC/DC song, by the way, with Axl Rose singing as their new front man when he isn't touring with the original G N' R crew.)

As Mia Dand, principal analyst at San Francisco-based market research and strategy consulting firm, Lighthouse3, says: "There isn't one version of truth out there around influencer marketing, so most of the information on this industry comes from influencers themselves or the vendors, which is biased. We needed an unbiased and objective perspective on the influencer space."[2]

Influencer Marketing Tech Is Fragmented

With more than 133 vendors across five categories, influencer marketing is a highly fragmented industry. There is no one-solution-fits-all. Lighthouse3's Influencer Marketing Technology research report found that three primary trends are behind the growth in the influencer marketing technology arena.[3]

Key Trend 1: Decline of Advertising Due to the Massive Increase in Ad Blockers Globally

According to Mary Meeker's 2016 Internet Trends report (slide 47),[4] there are nearly 640 million devices that are blocking online advertising. With iOS now allowing for ad blocking, there are currently over 420 million mobile devices alone that are blocking ads and that number will continue to grow. That being said, U.S. advertiser spending on digital advertising is expected to overtake TV in 2016 and hit $103 billion in 2019.[5]

However, not everyone is blocking ads. In fact, we are using Facebook, LinkedIn, Twitter, Pinterest, Reddit, and Google AdWords ads to help clients retarget and amplify influencer marketing efforts. They can definitely work together.

Key Trend 2: Rise of Influencer Programs Is Leading to Greater Need for Efficiencies and Proving ROI

More than 83 percent of global respondents in a Nielsen survey say they trust recommendations from people they know, vs. just 42 percent for online banner ads.[6]

People don't trust advertising, but they definitely trust people they know. This is why customers and employees are such strong advocates for your brand. Also, people trust the CEO much less than they trust employees. We know, big shocker there, as the gap between the 1 percent and 99 percent continues to widen and be an issue of tension across society. Lighthouse3 covers that more in-depth in their customer/employee advocacy technologies landscape report for October 2016 if you are interested in a deeper dive.

Key Trend 3: CMOs Are Driving the Budget Increase in Marketing Technology Spend

If you have seen Scott Brinker's MarTech landscape, you can tell that it's a crowded space.[7] And with good reason: CMOs are now outspending their IT counterparts in many organizations.

The Enterprise MarTech market size is projected to grow to $25 billion this year, with CMOs driving MarTech spending to $32.4 billion by 2018.[8] That's a lot of billions. More and more of enterprise marketing budgets are going to marketing technology, and the year over year (YOY) growth is substantial.

Key Trend 4: Four Critical Factors Are Fueling the Chaos in Influencer Marketing

Despite MarTech's incredible growth, influencer marketing technology is facing some key challenges:

- Lack of standard technical capabilities; service offerings and features keep changing.

- Unstructured, fragmented market with 133 vendors across five categories.

- With more than 60 percent of platforms launched within the past five years, this is still a nascent space.

- Lack of scalable enterprise solutions, as many vendors are startups and privately funded.

The Five Categories of Influencer Marketing Tech

As mentioned earlier this is a fragmented industry with 133 vendors across five related but distinct categories. Lighthouse3 broke down the number of tools in each category:

Influencer Marketing:

- Influencer Discovery—17 tools in this category
- Influencer Outreach—six tools in this category
- Influencer Marketing—38 tools in this category

Advocacy/Word of Mouth Tools:

- Customer Advocacy—66 tools in this category
- Employee Advocacy—14 tools in this category

  Note: Influencer Marketing is different from Employee Advocacy; see more at the end of this chapter. They are closely related cousins but with slightly different attributes.

An Advocate has a positive sentiment toward your brand, whereas an Influencer may have a negative, neutral, or positive view. Advocates are not typically compensated, although they may receive perks, such as new product trials or coupons. This differentiation impacts the features and capabilities of their respective technology platforms. For example: Influencer marketing technology platforms typically provide an Influencer rate-sheet, while Advocacy platforms offer gamification features to keep advocates engaged.

Influencer Marketing Platform "5 Capabilities" Model

Lighthouse3 created a "5 Capabilities" model to help marketers figure out whether or not a platform is an influencer technology platform.

These Five Capabilities Include:

1. **Discover**: Find Influencers based on user criteria including online/social metrics, audience, topics (e.g., Influencer profile).

2. **Connect**: Communicate with Influencers via the platform to discuss the engagement (e.g., e-mail integration).

3. **Engage (unpaid)**: Engage Influencer for an unpaid activity, such as writing a blog post (e.g., reporting dashboard).

4. **Recruit (paid)**: Engage Influencer for a paid activity, such as speaking at an event or creating content (e.g., budget planning).

5. **Measure**: Advanced metrics and analytics for performance management (e.g., ROI calculator).

   "Influencer Marketing" technologies typically have all five capabilities, while others only cover one area—such as "Influencer Discovery," which just covers Discover.

With the decline of online advertising due to ad blockers and lack of trust with big brands, now is a good time to begin looking into building an influencer marketing program at your company.

 DIGITAL BIT: This report on Influencer Marketing by Lighthouse3 should help guide you in the right direction. DigitalSen.se/influencermktg

The Influencer Marketing Manifesto

In the recently published *Influencer Marketing Manifesto* by the Altimeter Group, over 67 percent of marketers say their key challenge is influencer discovery.[9] Finding the right Influencer is both an art and a science. Here are some guidelines that marketers should use to select the right influencer for your campaign.

Community: Size and Type of Audience

Many "experts" try to justify lack of an audience by claiming that Influencer marketing is not about quantity of followers; it's about quality. Actually, successful Influencer marketing needs both—quantity *and* quality of influence. To be considered influential, the Influencer needs to have critical mass of the RIGHT type of followers, which is defined as the personas and look-alikes that the brand wants to reach. Start your Influencer selection by taking a close look at the Influencer's community and use the tools below to help.

> **Technology**: TapInfluence.com is an influencer marketing platform that allows marketers to influencers based on their profile data (reach, engagement, topics, etc.) as well as audience data (location, gender, age, etc.). Also Little Bird (GetLittleBird.com)is a great discovery tool for finding relevant influencers.

Content: Format and Type

Long-form (blog), short-form, videos, microvideos, pictures, livestreaming . . . the options for content format are endless. Product and Consumer Packaged

Goods (CPG) companies find visual formats work better, while service companies may find long-form or videos work better with their audience. Start by understanding which format resonates best with your audience and select the influencer that is great at the content type.

> **Technology:** Some influencer technology platforms, such as Hello Society (bought by *NYT*), focus on creator-influencers who create/curate beautiful images and have a large following on Pinterest, while others like *Roostr* (recently acquired by Chartboost) focus on YouTube gamer-influencers. Grapevine focuses on video content creators.[10]

Channel: Social Networks and Sites

Here's a key point that both marketers and their agencies often miss— Influencers do NOT have the same level of influence on all social networks. Marketers should select influencers based on the channel or social network where they are most likely to be active.

> **Technology:** Just like Influencers, the technology platforms also don't have the same reach across social networks. Platforms such as Niche (acquired by Twitter) focus on Viners and Instagrammers, and others, such as Cooperatize, focus on influential bloggers.

Credibility: Topical Relevancy

Please pay special attention here because this can make or break your influencer campaign. Topical relevancy and credibility is extremely important. This is usually measured through engagement—reshares, retweets, comments, and so on. Many influencers with large audiences talk about multiple topics. Some have lower engagement per post while others are focused on one to two specific topics but have much higher engagement. We've seen pitches from agencies for Influencers with high "average" engagement per post, but those numbers may be skewed because of their vacation pictures or cat memes.

> **Technology:** Little Bird uses social graph and peer validation to determine whether or not an Influencer has credibility on a certain topic. Lumanu is a newer Influencer technology platform that allows influencer discovery based on content that Influencers have created and/or shared.

Chemistry: Brand-Influencer Fit

Influencers are human beings, so make sure you work with professionals who follow through on their commitments. When things don't go per plan as they often do, you'll wish you hadn't picked an Influencer who is a prima donna and a pain to work with. Get to know them in advance. Make sure they are a good fit for your brand.

> **Technology:** No tool can help you figure out chemistry, yet, but Influencer technologies like Grapevine allow users to add notes based on their experience with the Influencer so you can make sure that history doesn't repeat itself with a bad influencer.

Controversy: Lack of Resonance and Transparency

Influencers can make headlines because of their controversial views and sometimes even a benign tweet can set off a firestorm. Brands need to realize that it's not about recruiting the most popular influencer but rather one that resonates with your audience.

Another issue we've run into is with Influencers who *don't disclose* they are being paid for their endorsements. And there are others who start pitching controversial or unrelated messages while still representing the brand. These are all red flags, and as of late 2016, the Federal Trade Commission (FTC) has created new guidelines for disclosing paid endorsements.[11]

As much as we want Influencers to be authentic, we also want them to be ethical and transparent so they are not misleading their audience.[12]

> **Technology:** Many platforms can track/measure impact of Influencer content but few can monitor/audit influencer content once published. Proofpoint is a security-as-a-service provider who recently started offering tools for marketers to scan influencer accounts and automatically flag any inappropriate content.

Employee Advocacy

According to the Deloitte Millennial Survey, millennials will constitute 75 percent of the global workforce by 2025.[13] And they are all on social media. But it's not just millennials. In fact, 50 percent of all employees already post messages on social media about their employers. Even though these employees are proud to share messages about their companies, it's almost impossible for brands to get their employees approved content efficiently to share externally.

Employees Are the Most Credible Voices in Your Organization

As mentioned in the *Edelman Trust Barometer* report, "Employees are the most credible voices on multiple topics, including the company's work environment, integrity, innovation and business practices." This means that no matter how often your PR team is out there sharing the gospel or the CEO is on television, *Inc. Magazine* or TechCrunch talking about your company, nothing is more effective than the voice of your employees.[14]

In addition to building brand awareness and improving company culture, employee advocacy has been proven to have a significant impact on revenue. From a lead generation perspective, employee advocacy is an "always on" marketing channel that results in five times more web traffic and 25 percent more leads.

Employee Advocacy Drives Sales

With some of our clients, we've personally engaged their employees to get the top tweet at over 50 different events, including competitor events! We've engaged employees to amplify content to gain mind share and influence, and where it's most important, helped them increase sales. Employee advocacy should be a vital part of any social business strategy.

Employee advocacy tools allow sales professionals to establish and extend relationships with prospects and customers via social media. In fact, 72.6 percent of salespeople using social selling as part of their sales process outperformed their sales peers and exceeded quotas 23 percent more often.[15]

"In today's social world, every person has an extended circle of personal influence and an opportunity to build their own personal 'brand.' By helping your employees build that brand rather than squelching individuality, you can build an army of very powerful advocates," says Ted Rubin, author of *Return on Relationship* #RonR and Dynamic Signal adviser.[16]

> *"Most people, when given the opportunity, will advocate for their brands, when they feel good about where they work. Two thousand employees, 2,000 followers each, you do the math."*
>
> —*Ted Rubin*

Who Is Doing Employee Advocacy Right?

One such company in the employee advocacy space is Dynamic Signal. It helps solve this disconnect by giving communications and marketing pros the ability to curate and upload company-approved content, so their employees can pick what interests them and share it in just a few clicks. This helps transform them into experts, advocates, and contributors. Employees can also submit their own content or industry content to be shared by others. Since people listen more to their social connections (those they trust) than to official marketing campaigns, brands can increase content engagement by as much as 700 times and brand awareness by as much as 24 times.

"One of the most underutilized and yet powerful things a company can do for itself is find a way to activate its employee base to socially tell its brand story," said Pavey Purewal, CMO, Dynamic Signal in a phone interview, who went on to say, "If employees are a company's best brand advocates, then why not let them share on behalf of the brand?"

Major global brands such as IBM, Humana, Pitney Bowes, GameStop, and SAP have all used employee advocacy tools to harness their employees' social reach to amplify company content. This type of tool keeps employees informed of company news and strengthens the brand. By extending their social media strategies, these companies ignite brand awareness, employee engagement, and revenue.

In a subsequent phone interview during the writing of this book, Tim Peacock, director of digital marketing, Ensighten said, "Everyone's busy, so tools like Dynamic Signal, Influitive, or GaggleAMP make it easy for employees to share coordinated content on a regular basis, boosting the impact of our social media efforts."

Keep in mind, there are many tools out there to choose from that can help engage your employees. The most important thing is to pick a solution and begin engaging your employees as soon as possible. The EMF has provided you the high level structure of Purpose, People, and Process. Now you have drilled deeper in these past few chapters to learn how to specifically evaluate some of these tools, and internal/external voice of customer listening paths to implement the proper data infrastructures and more human-centric tactics. In the final chapters we will bring it all home with the Social Business Strategy for human resources and a guide to building your ultimate marketing technology stack.

11 Social Business Strategy for HR

Social Recruiting

There are a few other areas where social media can have as tremendous an impact than in customer service and human resources. In this chapter we will briefly touch on some strategies, resources, and tactics for making those areas of your business socially savvy and filled with digital sense.

According to the Jobvite Recruiter Nation survey of 2015, relationships are the key to most hires at the organizations surveyed. Recruiters are facing an increasingly demanding and competitive talent market.[1] Consider the following statistics:

- 95 percent of recruiters anticipate the job market to remain or get more competitive.

- Over a quarter of companies anticipate hiring 100-plus people in the next 12 months.

- 30 percent of recruiters report an average employee tenure of just 1 to 3 years.

Today's dynamic recruiter uses every tool available to connect with job seekers.

- Only 4 percent of recruiters are not using social media in recruiting efforts (Figure 11.1).

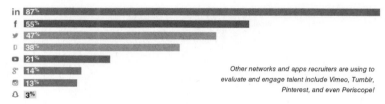

≪ SOCIAL

Only 4% of recruiters DON'T use social media in the recruiting process.
4% aren't sure, but the **92%** of recruiters that do use social media cast a wider net than ever:

in ▓87%
f ▓55%
y ▓47%
D ▓38%
▶ ▓21%
8+ ▓14%
◎ ▓13%
◊ **3%**

Other networks and apps recruiters are using to evaluate and engage talent include Vimeo, Tumblr, Pinterest, and even Periscope!

Figure 11.1 Social Media Recruiting by the Numbers[2]

- 72 percent of recruiters say data analytics is somewhat or very important in the hiring process.
- 19 percent of recruiters find quality hires via mobile career sites.

To recruit and retain the perfect fit, recruiters must prioritize relationships.

- After referrals (78 percent), recruiters find their best candidates through social and professional networks (56 percent) and intern-to-hire programs (55 percent).
- 69 percent of recruiters have increased their initial salary offers in the last year.
- 63 percent note that offering employees benefits like medical and dental care is the most attractive incentive for new candidates, over perks like free snacks or casual dress code.

It should come as no shock but it turns out that your business is all about relationships in recruiting, as well. Almost every part of your business deals with relationships which is why the EMF structure is held up and together by the three walls of Purpose, People, and Process. Isn't it crystal clear, by now, why we have invested such an ample amount of real estate in this book to improving your understanding of the archetypes of people in your organization, self, and the power of your mind to become a more effective communicator and leader? As Chris likes to say, "Stevie Wonder could see that."

Use Social Media to Evaluate Cultural Fit

Social media works both ways in social recruiting. If you are a job candidate and you are a total jackass online, guess what, you ain't getting the job at a reputable brand. Likewise, if you are curious whether a brand is a fit for you, you can do efficient research by following the brand and listening to the voice, tone, and message delivery and matching it up against your personal style and core values. Using your digital sense and these listening channels is a common sense way to sort through candidates and opportunities.

MILESTONE: Since most people statistically will not have reached this point in the book, we assume that you are in the top 10 percent of all purchasers of this book (i.e., "Amplifiers and Influencers," so congratulations and THANK YOU for your attention. Please Tweet #10percent to @teedubya @chrisjsnook, and we will celebrate your amazing accomplishment of getting to Chapter 11 with a surprise response to show our #gratitude.

The other reason that social media is a great tool to leverage in your hiring process is that you could be hiring Zombies into your organization unknowingly. Perusing their social media can give you a peek into their personality, their circle of influence (peers they hang around), lifestyle habits, and so on. There are also some sentiment analysis tools out there than can help you out.

BIG BOLD LEGAL DISCLAIMER: WE ARE BOTH AWARE THAT PLENTY OF ANTI-DISCRIMINATION LAWS AND POLICIES THAT NEED TO BE CONSIDERED IN THIS REGARD AND ARE IN NO WAY GIVING YOU ADVICE RELATED TO HOW TO USE THESE SOCIAL TOOLS WITHIN THE LETTER OF THOSE LAWS. YOU MUST CONSULT YOUR LAWYER BEFORE YOU PUT ANY OF THESE INTO PRACTICE. WE

(continued)

(continued)
ARE NOT EXPERTS NOR ARE WE QUALIFIED TO OFFER
YOU SOUND ADVICE RELATED TO STAYING COMPLIANT
WITH CURRENT LEGISLATION.

 DIGITAL BIT: We highly recommend using MercerMatch™ and Mercer Candidate Care™ for assessing fit to role. We also recommend using the Recruitics.com programmatic platform if you are running PPC campaigns for recruitment. Lastly, check out SocialTalent.co—a recruiting hub that teaches your team to become more socially savvy.

As you go about your talent hunt, focus on converting passive candidates to your brand. Most talented candidates already have jobs and anyone worth getting is typically not on the sideline for very long, but they may not be in the best vehicle for their goals or talents (remember the story about Amplifiers from Chapter 2). This means that they are passive in their job search. So you have to actively find ways (Figure 11.1) to get in front of them. Facebook ads work very well, which we will talk about in a bit.

The New Face of Social Recruitment

For many recruitment agencies, the days are gone when a well-placed ad in a newspaper was the go-to way to collect prospective employee information and build a pool of applicants. Social media has changed the way we recruit and the data that's available. This means more than posting a Facebook ad or letting a static job posting on LinkedIn do the work. HR recruiters now have more information about applicants than ever before. As it is with superheroes, with great power comes great responsibility.

It might seem like navigating endless information is akin to understanding biotech vapor compression. It turns out there is such a thing as too much data. Understanding when to collect social media data and when to go bare-bones is critical.

Are You Totally LinkedIn? Casting a job announcement to the LinkedIn world might get you flooded with responses. Some of the candidates might be appropriate fits and some are completely out of left field. If you have the time and staff, and if the position requires extensive knowledge or experience, take advantage of everything LinkedIn has to offer.

Many candidates will have references, sample projects, bibliographies, and photos. While it may not be acceptable in the United States to ask for photographs of applicants, if it's readily supplied on LinkedIn it's bound to make an impression. This kind of data is highly subjective. However, if there is a photo, try to stick to gauging the professionalism of the photo. Does the person have a professional headshot or is it a blurry self-portrait?

Play Sherlock

When you're charged with filling an important position, you're free to use whatever means are at your disposal (reminder to see our legal disclaimer from earlier that we are not offering you direct advice). This might mean Googling shortlisted candidates' full names or finding them on Facebook. Playing fair here is also subjective, but try to give everyone a fair shot by conducting the same level of investigation for every candidate. It's common knowledge nowadays that people should either keep their Facebook profiles private or make sure nothing "inappropriate" is on the page. "Inappropriate" can mean anything from the Mardi Gras profile pic to a page riddled with poor grammar and spelling. Is it fair to use this kind of social media data when filling a position? That's up to HR (and your legal team) to decide.

Another great resource on the subject is the blog Recruiting Daily. The editor in chief, Matt Charney, published an e-book called *Structure Hiring: The Advantage of the New People Team.* He has been at the forefront of the social recruiting space, and his book lays out the structure and processes necessary to lead a social business initiative in the human resources dept.

> *"Without structure and training, even the most strategic or innovative of recruiting processes fall apart."*
>
> —MATT CHARNEY, EDITOR OF RECRUITING DAILY.[3]

Case Study: #Hirecarlos:
How to Get Your Dream Gig with Social Media

In early January 2015, Carlos Gil lost his job with the Save-A-Lot grocery chain out of St. Louis, MO. At the time, Carlos was video-blogging and reaching out to his network to see if anyone had a connection for a social media leader position. Since he and Travis were connected on LinkedIn, he had TW's e-mail address, as he downloaded his LinkedIn connections. Carlos began reaching out to his connections who he felt had some influence or who might be able to help him, and then he set up phone meetings to chat.

Travis shot him a response and they scheduled a call through his scheduler tool, Calendly.com. This allowed him to pick a block of 15 minutes that Travis had free on his calendar. On the phone call, Travis mentioned that he had this idea that he'd like to test. "Let's create a Facebook page called, 'Hire Carlos'. We can run Facebook ads targeting only HR and talent acquisition specialists at the companies that you most want to work for."[4] (Figure 11.2)

People Who Match the Following Job titles:

Staffing specialist, ManPower, IT training and staffing firm, human resources, recruiter admin, talent manager, HR recruiter, talent acquisition-HR, chief human resources officer, recruiter, talent acquisition, or HR-resource management group

Travis had Carlos go to Indeed.com, LinkedIn, and Angel.co Jobs pages to pick out the top jobs that he thought he would most enjoy. Travis then set up Facebook ads targeting HR and talent acquisition titles at the companies he was interested in pursuing. Carlos came back with a segmented list of his top companies (Figure 11.3).

They both thought it would be an interesting case study to test. They agreed that after Carlos got a job, he would write about the experience of using paid ads for helping him find a job. Travis ran the "Hire Carlos" ad for almost 9 days, at $20 per day. Travis covered the cost of nearly $180 dollars; the ad was seen by 1,053 people and clicked on 53 times. More important, it got Carlos 25–30 phone interviews and face-to-face interviews.

Figure 11.2 Carlos Gil for Hire Post

At around this same time, Travis was interviewing for a specific role at LinkedIn, head of Social Media Strategy–Sales. Travis wasn't actually looking for a job, as he was building an agency, but thought his business partners and team could handle it if he got the LinkedIn gig. And quite frankly, it appealed to Travis's ego to be the head of Social Media Strategy for one of the social media networks! Travis flew out to LinkedIn to their downtown San Francisco offices and just killed the interviews. The head recruiter informed him that it was down to him and a woman from Twitter, and that he'd be hearing back early the next week, as they wanted to move fast on this role.

(*continued*)

(continued)

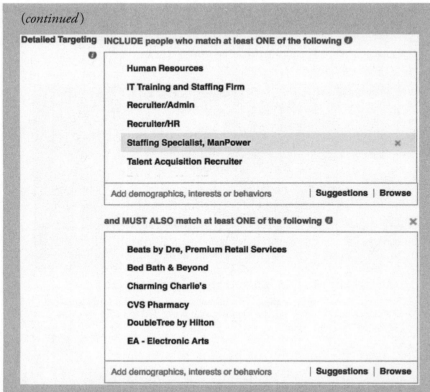

Figure 11.3 Carlos Gil Detailed Targeting Screenshot

That same day, Carlos Gil was in the Bay Area on a face-to-face interview with Clorox out somewhere near Oakland. They had seen his "Hire Carlos" page and flew him out to interview with them. He tweeted at Travis that he was in town, and Travis recommended a bar to come hang out and meet. They hung out and actually met for the first time. Social media has a way of creating friendships without requiring meetings in person, at times.

Travis asked how Carlos's interview at Clorox went. He then mentioned that he was a finalist for a LinkedIn Social Media Strategist role. They hung out for about an hour, drinking beer and bull-shitting. After the bar, they left in different Uber rides. Carlos was in an Uber Pool, where you can share rides with other random Uber customers. Tonight, as luck would have it, Carlos was in the Uber with a recruiter from LinkedIn.

Carlos then remembered that Travis was in town for a LinkedIn role, and works his mojo on the recruiter. He sat in an Uber with the very recruiter who had told Travis that he was a finalist for the role. Of all of the people in San Francisco to get an Uber with Carlos Gil that night, what were the odds?

As a result of their in-Uber conversation, Carlos ended up getting an interview at LinkedIn for the very same role. He mentioned that he used to curate jobs in a job group on LinkedIn called JobsDirectUSA, and had a community of over 35,000 job seekers. Bottom line? Carlos, not Travis or the gal from Twitter, got the job at LinkedIn. LinkedIn said the tipping point for them choosing Carlos was the innovative use of Facebook ads to target the HR professionals at jobs he was interested in. The idea that Travis had around the "Hire Carlos" Facebook page helped Carlos get the job at LinkedIn over Travis.[5]

Then Travis had to see this stuff in his newsfeed (Figure 11.4).

Figure 11.4 Carlos Gil Welcome to LinkedIn Post

(continued)

(*continued*)

The irony is thick on this one. Carlos was at LinkedIn for around three months before he moved over to BMC as their global head of Social Media. To hear this story from Travis and Carlos directly, here's their Snapchat Story of "The Secret Job Interview" from February 2016 at Social Media Strategies Summit.[6]

Guess what? Travis never heard back from LinkedIn. Of all companies, LinkedIn should know better than to ignore their declined applicants. LinkedIn needs to call Mercer and implement Mercer Candidate Care.[7] **Note:** *Travis was also a finalist for jobs at Facebook in 2010 as an SEO director. Travis was a finalist for a role in digital at Amazon in 2011. Travis was a finalist for a role with Google Local/Maps and had 14 interviews. Turns out he was only 13/14ths Googley, as one person didn't quite like him. Symantec did hire him. Of all of those companies, only Google actually got back to Travis to tell him the bad news. Travis has yet to apply to Twitter or Snapchat. Travis is always passively looking to level up (hint, hint).*

Case Study: Finding 500,000 Worth of Talent for $250 in Ads

Using social media advertising in clever ways is what makes Travis a true marketing hacker. He is always coming up with unique ways to get visibility for your project or product, including using FB ads to target specific types of people to their job postings.

When you are building ads, think of different images to capture their attention. Videos work very well on Faceboook, as long as you caption the words on the video. The vast majority of people on Facebook don't turn on the sound for the videos, so you need to display the words. Testing different types of images and targeting can help make or break your campaign (Figure 11.5 and 11.6).

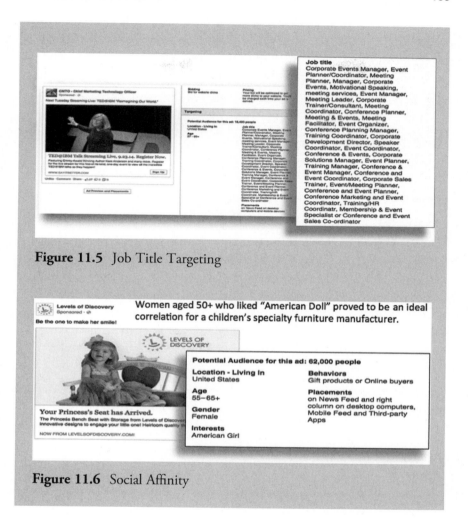

Figure 11.5 Job Title Targeting

Figure 11.6 Social Affinity

Themes for Your Advertising

An analytics client that needed to hire 100 data scientists in one year came to CCP Digital to have them find some data scientists around certain parts of the world. We used a hero image (Figure 11.7), an image showcasing culture, a woman engineer, and various other pictures and themes to test them out to different demographics and see what worked.

Another client, Ensighten (Figure 11.8), wanted to hire an operation manager, a UI developer, and a director of Product Marketing Management.

Figure 11.7   Data Scientists Hire Ad

These represent roughly a $90K–$100K role, a $145K–$175K role, and a $115K–$140K role. In total, it added up to roughly $400K–$450K in sala-ries. *It's crazy how quick half a million dollars goes in Silicon Valley.* Sad thing is all four of these folks probably ended up sharing a two-bedroom apartment since they couldn't afford to live alone on such paltry incomes in the Valley. Yes, that was a not-so-subtle recruiting plug by both of us for talent that wants to build something great in Phoenix and KC (Chris and Travis's respective markets).

So we targeted ads for people that were the right kind of candidates. And to top it off, Travis and his team narrowed it down to only these types of persona characteristics: "PLUS they like Star Wars." The CEO of Ensighten,

Figure 11.8   Operations Manager Hire Ad

Josh Manion, is a huge Star Wars fan. The Ensighten HQ conference rooms are all named after places in the Star Wars universe. One room is the Death Star, one is Dagobah, one is Tatooine, and so on. It's part of the culture fit and was able to be part of the targeting effort.

On this particular campaign, we reached 14,576 people, got 456 clicks, and 17 resumes. Total ad spend: $209.15. Imagine if Ensighten would have used a headhunter to find you those employees, and took 20–30 percent of their annual salary for helping them? That would have cost around $100,000 in fees alone. That's another person's salary that they could be using! Ensighten actually filled all of those roles on just $209.15 and they remain employed today.

Having digital sense and creativity allows you to come up with different ideas to help utilize social media in your business as it relates to the most important foundational aspect of your EMF structure, your people.

12 Social Business Strategy for Customer Service

Eighty-six percent of consumers will pay more for a better customer experience.[1]

Customer service is a specific touch point in the overall customer experience. It is oftentimes where the lofty and effective front end marketing promises, made through your digital tactics, get fumbled through nonhuman interfaces. It is also where you can shine!

For example, think of your favorite robotic phone tree that has you pounding the zero key repeatedly or yelling "representative, representative . . . OPERATOR!!" to get into a place where you can actually have a conversation. Companies that have mastered customer service invest heavily in the training and infrastructure and culture to ensure continued success.

One of our favorite and most recommended experiences the next time you are in Las Vegas is the Zappos Cultural Tour. When you want to understand what a commitment it takes to nail the customer-centric service side of your operation, there is no better or more inspiring 2-hour tour in this country. Those who want to take it a step further may want to look into the Zappos Insights culture camps offering at ZapposInsights.com.

The nuances of how your customers want to be served depends on limitless factors including their past experiences (positive and negative), their personality type, their mood (which can be influenced by something like the weather that day), or as minor as whether they got their morning coffee. Their cultural background also plays a role. Fortunately today there are endless amounts of tools from IBM's Watson and the weather.com application program interface (API) that can provide you technologically efficient ways to personalize at scale, but before you can put the tools to work you have to begin with the same assets you uncovered at the Insights Layer around your customer needs and persona.

Providing great customer service really just means providing a variety of service approaches and doing your best to intuit what each customer wants. Some customers aren't even sure what they want themselves! We will discuss how to build your marketing technology and customer experience stack in the following chapter, but several great tools exist to consider depending on the size of your enterprise and budget. For call-center heavy businesses, such as health care, insurance, financial services, and so on, we strongly recommend you look into a solution such as the software offered by Aspect.com to provide you with a strategic and technical partner with enterprise level infrastructure designed to secure and personalize the channels of your customer success teams.

However, regardless of your size, there are some standard "best practices" that offer a great starting point. Begin here, gauge the reaction of your customer, and if possible personalize the next interaction based on each customer's reaction to the last one.

We All Want the Same Simple Pleasures

"Customers who engage with companies over social media spend 20 to 40 percent more money with those companies than other customers."[2]

Ready to put the "customer" back into the customer service touch point? The following fundamentals are a great place to start.

1. **Transparency:** Customers want price and support transparency in their shopping experience (at least that's true of Western customers—

customers from countries such as South Korea and India may prefer negotiating). Make prices fair and readily available, and honor sales that may take place immediately after a big purchase. Don't make everything your customers' fault on the support side. Train and empower your agents to empathize and be empowered to solve problems. Transparency is akin to honesty. It is authentic unscripted communication that stays within the boundaries of your brand guidelines but doesn't feel robotic or generic.

2. **Genuine hospitality:** A customer can instantly see through a sales pitch or a forced greeting. Hire customer service reps who actually enjoy interacting with customers, and who don't bring their personal problems to work. Everyone will have off days, including sales reps, but they should be minimal. A warm welcome and genuine relationship building is what creates loyal customers.

3. **Zero pressure:** The day of pushy sales tactics are over. The "I am sorry, I can't help you, I just work here," response is no longer a sufficient reason to end the call either, regardless of your metrics around call processing time. Zappos has succeeded because they literally removed any constraints that cause service reps to pressure someone off of the call or into a cross sale script that is unnatural or unwarranted. Your products or services should speak for themselves. Pressure will make a client never want to come back. Speed doesn't require pressure.

4. **Easy secure transactions:** This is true in brick-and-mortar shops as well as online shops, but especially the latter. The virtual shopping cart should be easy to manage, customize, and check out. Take as many forms of payment as you can, including new online services such as Venmo. You should make it as easy as possible to accept money. After all, no sale is final until that happens. Remember that the Ubers and Amazons of the world have changed all of our expectations and that anything harder than checking out on those platforms feels like a dinosaur. Life isn't fair, we know, but if you want to compete you have to invest in updating your UX/UI across all transactional platforms.

You may think it is too expensive now, but a failure to do so will be catastrophically expensive later. The customer is not going to go back in time with their expectations. They will judge you harshly and deal with your archaic interface only until they discover an alternative means to solve that problem and be gone to you forever.

5. **A comfortable shopping experience:** A great visual merchandiser and/ or web designer can make or break your business. In a physical store, customers should be able to intuit where to find what they need. Online, the website should have easy navigate, be user friendly, and boast mobile readiness and responsive design. The more comfortable a shopping experience is, the longer a person will stay. Empowering in-store personnel with the same technology tools as your customer so that they can provide on-the-floor checkout or accurate in-store inventory numbers leveraging beacons and tablets is a must.

6. **Empathy:** Training your staff across the board on the lost art of situational awareness and emotional intelligence will be a worthy investment. Understand where you customer is coming from and try to defuse situations. Train your people to remember that everyone is right from their own perspective and that the easiest way to get someone to potentially see something your way is to first invest the energy into trying to see it from the perspective they are looking through. However, don't put up with abuse. There's a thin line here, and one that should be considered on a case by case basis. Zombies buy stuff too. Have protocols in place that keep your employee health as a priority and have clearly established core values that allow your brand to take an effective stand that strengthens its bond with core customers and employees alike.

Relevant Goals for Customer Service with Social Media

1. Increase customer satisfaction
2. Lower customer service costs
3. Improve efficiency
4. Increase NPS (Net Promoter Score)
5. Reduce call volume by increased social care

Social Media Triage

It has been noted that in European countries, customer service is akin to courtship, whereas in North America we tend to think of it more as triage. What is "triage?" Typically, it's a medical term, defined by Wikipedia as "a process of prioritizing patients based on the severity of their condition so as to treat as many as possible when resources are insufficient for all to be treated immediately."[2]

Sounds like an inspiring place to start, right? So how does the concept of "triage" apply to social media monitoring?

The number of social posts that mention brands continually increases. In 2012, 53 percent of social media users complimented brands at least once a month.[3] In addition, 50-plus percent of social media users expressed concerns or complaints about brands at least once a month. That was 5 years ago. The amount of noise coming through social channels is now at an all-time high.

If your organization has a social media monitoring program, you are likely becoming overwhelmed with incoming mentions. How is a smart social business to deal with all of the growing volume?

One solution is to use Social Monitoring Automation Triage to separate incoming signal from the staggering amount of Internet noise. Travis worked closely with Tristan Bishop at Symantec. He is now the head of Social Media for Informatica.

Tristan set up and managed the triage for Norton customer support. Can you imagine how many complaints and comments came through each day? It was off the charts. Tristan and team chose Radian6 for social listening, customer support, and triage.

Once this initial triage phase is complete, you can use manual triage to sort the signal, separating posts that require immediate company response from those that simply require research. Finally, a third level of triage can help you connect the optimal employee to the customer, based on the content of the social mention.

> *"Failure to respond via social channels can lead to up to a 15 percent increase in churn rate for existing customers."*
>
> —*Gartner*[4]

What you are looking for are the messages that come through that you can act on. You can direct these to the employee in your organization who can best solve your customer's issue.

We chose to segment actionable posts into seven data classes:

1. **Case:** Request for help resolving real-time issue
2. **Query:** Question that doesn't require support resource
3. **Rant:** Insult that merits brand management consideration
4. **Rave:** Praise from your brand advocate
5. **Lead:** Pronouncement of near-term purchase decision
6. **RFE:** Request to enhance a product with a new feature
7. **Fraud:** Communication from an unauthorized provider of your products

Tristan helped set up the Symantec Global Triage team (Figure 12.1). They were like the British Empire, as the sun never set on them.[5]

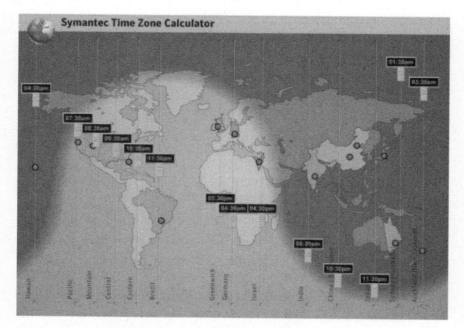

Figure 12.1 Symantic Timezone Calculator

We had people around the world helping sort, manage, and route posts of each class of customer message to a different business function for response, as follows:

1. **Case:** Routed to Technical Support for immediate interaction

2. **Query:** Routed to Information Developers and Technical Writers

3. **Rant:** Routed to PR for brand protection assessment

4. **Rave:** Routed to Marketing for proactive engagement with advocates

5. **Lead:** Routed to Sales for pipeline consideration

6. **RFE:** Routed to Product Management for road map consideration

7. **Fraud:** Routed to Legal for follow-up and official action

"By using Social Media Monitoring Triage, wise brands can reach customers on their channel of choice, connecting them to the employees best equipped to meet their needs. This attentive strategy improves customer experience and builds customer loyalty," says Tristan Bishop.

Audit Your CX Center of Excellence

The definition of a Center of Excellence (COE) is a team, a shared facility, or an entity that provides leadership, best practices, research, support and/or training for the customer experience and social business domain within your organization.[6]

As you have already done with your earlier efforts in the Vision Layer of the EMF, we suggest you start with a clear list of goals, and the list below are the most common found across our client base. We hope they give you a good starting point or secondary source of external validation if you are auditing your current COE.

Goals of the Social/CX Center of Excellence

1. Provide best practices

2. Education and training

3. Administration control

4. Governance and compliance

5. Policy adherence

6. Executive visibility and buy-in

Where to Begin?

1. Start creating a social business COE by gathering a team of leaders from the various lines of business as well as representation from corporate communications and legal.

2. Next, define an operating model for the COE. This will include defining the mission and vision of the COE, tools, content strategy, staffing, training, education, and measures of success.

3. There is one thing that all COEs have in common: namely, assuming the role of change agent.

"I look at my role more as an enabler than anything else. The only way you're going to get true scale is by allowing people to have accountability for their efforts and ownership of their own programs, where they benefit," said Don Bulmer, VP of Communication Strategy at Shell.

"We're able to then have a dialogue where they [business] see the benefits of working with our Center of Excellence because we give them data and information and context that allows them to be able to run with their programs benefiting from this platform that we've established. It's one company, right? It's one brand."[7]

One of the core social business functions for your organization is community management. The community manager is the social face to your customers. The community manager role may fall under the COE or more frequently in the marketing department, although subject matter-specific community managers do tend to remain distributed across the company.

Executives are also key stakeholders of the Center of Excellence. Their participation in the COE can be instrumental in making your organization a true social business. They can use the COE to better exert oversight and social media governance directives, set goals, and monitor the transformation of the organization into a social business.[8] Michael

Brito wrote a great book called *Your Brand* that walks through this in depth.

Your brand's business pulse doesn't stop at 5 PM; why should you? Don't miss a beat. Having a COE helps keep your key players plugged in on-the-go, engaged with your community, and monitoring your brand in real-time 24/7/365.

Section IV
Data and Automation

13 Designing Your Ultimate Marketing Stack

Now that you have clearly stated goals, objectives, a vision, executive buy-in, and a strategy in place, it's time to looks at some tools and technologies to make your life easier and more efficient.

Marketing technology—MarTech—is a hot topic, but actually adopting these tech items can be intimidating for most business owners and executive leaders. The intimidation makes sense. New technology can be scary, and you don't want to struggle with a tool that has a steep learning curve. Unfortunately, this means companies are missing out on some great products that can make life and business so much easier.

Consider this: What if you created your own MarTech starter kit with several key solutions (Figure 13.1) that you could use to optimize your marketing and tech departments? You could grow revenue, give your employees a break, and optimize your time, money, and efforts. If you apply it correctly, you create the magic bullet.

Here's how you might begin to build your own MarTech stack so that you can make data-fed iterations to optimize reliability within your customer experience and uncover new insights for ongoing innovation. We've included some potential software products in each category to point you in the right direction. Keep in mind, no two tech stacks are the same.

Figure 13.1 The Data Node of the EMF Success Layer

How to Build a Solid MarTech Stack

Just as you can't build a solid, long-lasting edifice on a foundation of mucky soil, the foundation of the marketing technology stack is critical to its efficacy and long-term benefit to the organization. You need to build on bedrock, and for MarTech,[1] that means customer relationship management (CRM), marketing automation, and tag management.

"The stack"[2] at any given company was likely conceived by the chief marketing officer (CMO) and chief technology officer (CTO), but in many businesses—from startups to enterprises—it now stands alone in a marketing technology department. And given recent rapid changes in marketing technology, it may have been built on shaky ground (by today's standards). That's where you come in.

Ideally, the various tools in your stack take your data and turn it into customized marketing programs that are (1) automated and (2) measurable. Ultimately, this means happier customers because they're getting exactly what they want at exactly the right time. Plus, the CEO is happy, which means *you're* happy. Everyone wins.

To achieve that goal, however, you need to ensure you're building on a rock-solid technological foundation.

Bottoms Up

A foundational principle of this book and the EMF is that you need to focus on customers first. As it relates to your MarTech stack, enter CRM, the place where you keep your customer information organized.

CRM

You should be able to import data that you find, create, or buy so that it can be marketed—automatically. This ties into customer management, which can overlap with CRM but is also part of the stack in its own right. You can use an enterprise-level CRM, like Salesforce, or an SMB-level CRM like Nimble, and there are many others to choose from. The key is to start collecting your customer data so that your sales and marketing efforts will work more effectively.

Remember that it's more of an approach than a specific technology—there are oodles of great, specific options out there. There's tech to automate, sync, and/or organize everything from actual customer service to sales or tech support. CRM should be customer-oriented and usually features sales force automation, data warehouse technology to aggregate data, and opportunity management.

Marketing Automation

Marketing automation is designed for marketing departments and organizations to more effectively market on multiple channels online (such as e-mail, social media, and websites) and automate repetitive tasks.[3] It's what gets you there, and it's made up of all kinds of campaigns, activities, and other goodies that help you follow leads while relying on the criteria you need. Lead nurturing via sales funnels, all ending with an automatic CRM update? Yes, please.

We've worked with Eloqua, Marketo, Pardot, Silverpop, and many other marketing automation platforms. Pick one that you feel works best for your organization.

Tag Management

Finally, tag management[4] rounds out the MarTech stack foundation trifecta. Did you know there are well over *2,000 marketing technologies*[5] out there and counting? If you can nail these three, you are well on your way. How is that for taking away some overwhelm?

Tag management helps you deploy tags on your websites with ease. If you're not tagging, you're not providing a link between your customers and your online presence. You want to be agile, quick, and nimble. Deploying marketing technologies through a tag management system (TMS) makes it quick and painless. This also allows you to test multiple competitive tools at the same time and get real data to show you which is the best.

Analytics and Tracking: You Need to Track Your Performance, Ads, Technology, and Everything Else

How else will you know what's working—and what isn't? You need to be data-driven, so you need to have your analytics in place to track everything. By far, Google Analytics is your best weapon, which is why more than 80 percent of smaller businesses use it. They've also released Google Analytics 360, which is a comprehensive suite of tools. You might also want to check out Adobe Analytics, especially if you're an enterprise or headed in that direction.

Invest in Keeping Your Stack Open

While the large Frankenstein marketing clouds (Figure 13.2) being built through acquisition are getting great mind share, their promise of supposedly fulfilling everything an advertiser needs within one company/cloud seems to be more and more disjointed (from what the market wants), rather than connected.

For instance, advertisers who want to use Adobe's Experience Manager and Site Catalyst—but also try Oracle's new Maxymiser acquisition,[6] IBM's Silverpop, Salesforce's Radian6, or any other number of marketing technologies from the MarTech landscape—are able to do so when they're deployed through an independently owned premium tag management tool like Ensighten, Tealium, or Signal.

New automation and marketing capabilities are being added all the time, and agile marketers need to be able to deploy whatever they want, wherever they want, and to remove it if it's not delivering. They also need to collect, own, and act on all of their marketing data. To do that, they must use tools that work well with others, rather than those that lock them into a certain "system."

Figure 13.2 The Marketing Cloud That Travis Created

As the Chief Marketing Technology Officer at a technology consulting firm and digital ad agency, CCP Digital, Travis always suggests to his clients that they build their own custom, scalable marketing cloud, starting with the foundational tools of CRM, marketing automation and tag management. Sometimes, they don't have the resources for that; however, that is the aspirational goal. Once you have a solid MarTech stack foundation, it's time to start building up the rest of your marketing structure in earnest.

Your marketing technology stack will likely depend on your business model, size of your company, if you're ecommerce versus media or B2B, for example. Here are some other key areas of focus for your marketing technology stack aside from analytics, tag management, CRM, and marketing automation.

Data Management Platform (DMP)

In lay terms, a data management platform is a data warehouse. It's software that grabs, sorts, and stores information—and then spits it out in a way that's useful for marketers, publishers, advertisers, and other businesses.

Vendors that sell DMP technology to the digital media world currently include Adobe, Krux, Lotame, Aggregate Knowledge, BlueKai, and others.

Content Delivery Network (CDN)

A CDN works by providing alternate server nodes for users to download resources (usually content like images and JavaScript). These nodes are spread throughout the globe and are therefore physically closer to the end users, which ensures a faster response and content download time. While CDNs are a great solution for websites looking for speed improvements, not every site needs a CDN. Akamai is a popular CDN, but there are many CDN vendors from which to choose.

Conversion Optimization

Getting someone to your website is just the beginning of the battle. You can lose your prospect with an unattractive layout, long forms, or a slow site. Conversion optimization can easily double how many people fill out online forms, getting you that invaluable big data. Try out Optimizely or Conversioner for A/B testing of your pages, the complimentary Landing Page Grader from WordStream, or Ion Interactive to easily craft marketing apps with absolutely no tech background required.

Enterprise businesses should consider Maxymiser, which was recently acquired by Oracle, Monetate, or the original Adobe Target. With the right conversion optimization tool, such as Adobe Target, you can change the content of a site based on the content of the visitor coming to your site. This is huge. For example, look at Figure 13.3. This is a layered look at Facebook; on a typical ecommerce site, you can switch out any of those areas for other content based on what you know about the visitor. Facebook is a complex site, as everyone has a completely unique, personalized experience. All of these areas are different based on your user profile.

Campaign Management

Campaign management applications help organizations segment, target, and manage multichannel marketing messages. Elements of functionality include attribution, data mining, customer segmentation, customer-event triggering, next-best-action recommendation engines, and campaign optimization.

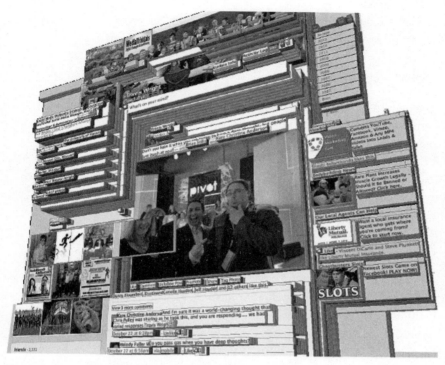

Figure 13.3 The Many Layers of a Website

Many of these components may be in your marketing automation platform, but not necessarily. Some of the better campaign management platforms are Integrate, Ensighten, Pardot, and Adobe Campaign.

E-mail Marketing

E-mail marketing isn't going anywhere, but most people aren't using it as well as they could be. One of the most important opportunities in delivering great customer experience is how you strategically utilize and craft your nurture streams and e-mail. This isn't about spam, but about genuine e-mails sent to people who have opted in because they are interested in your offerings. Only send valuable materials—period. Content should be personalized and sent in just the right doses. Some fantastic tools include Constant Contact, ExactTarget/Salesforce Marketing Cloud, Emfluence, and MailChimp, all pillars in the world of e-mail marketing. Infusionsoft is the king of the solutions for businesses with fewer than 20 employees. Keep in mind that most marketing automation tools already have great e-mail marketing tools within them, so you might already be sitting on a goldmine!

Mobile Optimization

The majority of people now use their smartphones or other mobile devices to do just about everything. This means your site has to be easy to navigate and view on mobile devices. Deploy responsive design from a designer who knows the importance of mobile readiness. You can also create a mobile site that's totally different from your "desktop site" and/or an app to help with mobile access. Mobile tag management is also a thing to manage aggressively.

Advertising Networks

There are many types of advertising tracking codes that you may want to use on your site, as there are tons of ways to advertise. If you're a smaller business, you probably use Google AdWords, or maybe Google Retargeting or DoubleClick. You probably use Facebook for ads, as well. If you don't, you should. Who knows more about your potential customers than Google and Facebook? You want to optimize your Facebook ad campaigns using a variety of tools and retargeting platforms. It works incredibly well for B2C and B2B.

Remarketing

You may not think you know it, but you already know firsthand what remarketing is. If you visit a website and then later see an ad for that website somewhere else, it's most likely no coincidence. Remarketing helps you reach people who have already searched for your offering—or something very similar. You pay for these connections via a CPM approach, snagging a bundle of impressions. You can use Google AdWords, AdRoll, or Perfect Audience to get started.

Search Engine Marketing

Search engine optimization (SEO) is optimizing your site for good rankings in Google and other search engines. Of course, SEO demands regular, original, valuable content. Many companies depend on WordStream, gShiftLabs, or BrightEdge to complement Google's tools—and don't forget that Bing and YouTube are search engines that deserve a little SEO too.

Search Engine Advertising

You have to be where people are searching for products or services like yours. Search ads let you test and improve copy, forms, and keywords, then track potential customers via Google AdWords and Analytics. Bing Ads is a great platform, as well. You can use the internal ad management platform within Google or Bing, but it's much more effective to use a third party. Many search advertising platforms have popped up over the past couple of decades. One that is really standing out is QuanticMind, based out of Redwood City. QuanticMind been instrumental in finding efficiencies in our client's paid search campaigns. Sometimes as much as 40 percent lift in results and efficiencies, by using data science with your search marketing. We are big fans of QuanticMind.

Monitoring the MarTech Stack

Looking at other sites' MarTech stacks can help you imagine your own. Here is a great example of a MarTech stack that is organized well, according to data pulled by Ghostery. Figure 13.4 refers to HomeDepot.com. They have many of the right pieces in place.

Here is another example: FoxNews.com (Figure 13.5) You can see that they don't have a tag management solution serving as a centralized hub for managing vendors and customer data, so many of their tags are all over the place.

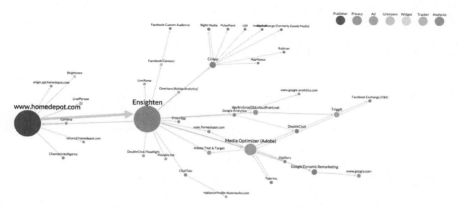

Figure 13.4 HomeDepot Technologies as of September 2015

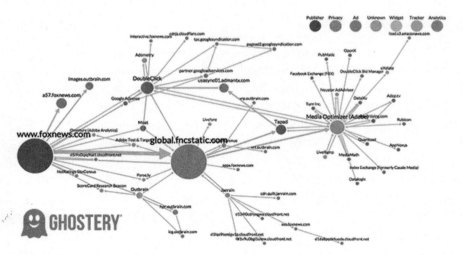

Figure 13.5 Fox News

These Ghostery graphics can also be fascinating for competitive analysis as you work through the competitor research node of the Insights Layer. One more example (Figure 13.6) is the worst marketing technology stack that we've seen so far and it may come as somewhat of a shock given the nature of their business. Whoever is managing TMZ.com is clearly a fan of duct tape, Band-Aids, hope, and prayers, because it sure doesn't look like there is a solid plan behind their stack. They have Google Tag Manager, but nothing is deployed through it. This stack is cringe-worthy.

Another great tool for competitive analysis is BuiltWith. It allows you to see all of the technologies on any site, which sites have those technologies, and which other technologies are present on those sites.

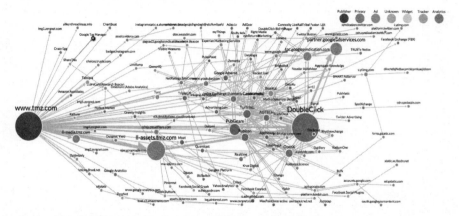

Figure 13.6 The Worst MarTech Stack Ever?! TMZ

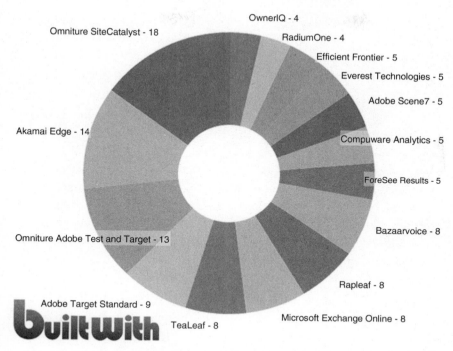

OwnerIQ - 4
Omniture SiteCatalyst - 18
RadiumOne - 4
Efficient Frontier - 5
Everest Technologies - 5
Adobe Scene7 - 5
Akamai Edge - 14
Compuware Analytics - 5
ForeSee Results - 5
Bazaarvoice - 8
Omniture Adobe Test and Target - 13
Rapleaf - 8
Adobe Target Standard - 9
Microsoft Exchange Online - 8
TeaLeaf - 8

Figure 13.7 BuiltWith Graph of Which Technologies Are Also on Sites That Also Use Ensighten

Figure 13.7 shows which technologies are present on sites that are also using Ensighten technology.

> *DIGITAL BIT: If you want to discover all of the marketing technologies in the landscape, check out our full MarTech Glossary: DigitalSen.se/martechglossary.*[7] *We have mapped out more than 300 categories of tools with the help of CabinetM, a MarTech stack configuration tool. Or if you like something a bit more interactive, explore GrowthVerse.com, as it has a dynamic visualization mapping the whole marketing technology ecosystem.*

There is no doubt about the exponential growth in the marketing technology landscape. It is very obvious both in terms of the sheer breadth of the types of marketing as well as the number of marketing technology vendors. It just continues to explode (Figure 13.8).

From 150 marketing technology vendors in 2011 to 5,500-plus in 2017 and counting. Just 5 short years ago we were still striving to define the role of a marketing technologist, where marketing technology should sit within an organization, and who owned the budget (the CMO or the CIO)? Look at where we are now: most Fortune 500 companies and beyond have either a chief marketing technologist or at least a marketing technology function within their respective models. Several have implemented a chief customer officer to ensure that all of the silos are aligned with the same end game in mind and yet there is still plenty of progress to make. We have come a long way in a short time, however, and we hope that your efforts to raise the digital sense of your organization continue that trend.

Despite that exponential growth of MarTech, the response from brands and marketers has been rather slow and algorithmic. Technology has overshadowed the fundamental promise and has made us technology obsessed. There has been a rush to adopt a high number of these marketing technologies, putting a tick on most areas. Yet in the rush to go after these shiny objects, we are missing three key aspects of marketing and customer

Figure 13.8 The March 2016 Marketing Technology Landscape by Scott Brinker[8]

experiences and genuine relationships. Two glaring needs remain for further focus and integration:

- The need to deliver human experiences that will change behaviors and lives and inspire participation
- The need to "apply" these technologies to drive tangible business growth

Needless to say, the whole landscape has been so *overwhelming*, that marketers don't know where to start, how to plan, prioritize, budget, and scale especially if the technologies themselves change and evolve every few months. They either diversify or consolidate.

MarTech That Drives Business Growth

While the solution may be easier said than done, here are keys to pierce through the clutter and focus on the "application" of these technologies to drive business growth and transformation (see Figure 13.9).

Find the "human" within your marketing technology landscape. We need to flip the equation, shift from a technology-led approach to a human- and consumer-obsessed mindset. The opportunity is in the "application" of these marketing technologies to solve business challenges like:

- Increase market share
- Maximize lifetime value

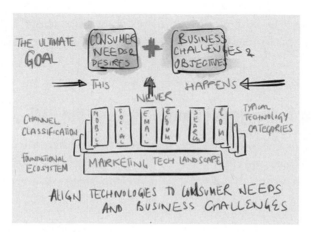

Figure 13.9 The Ultimate Goal by Mayur Gupta

- Increase share of wallet
- Drive household penetration

  Or drive behavioral change for instance:

- Drive trial
- Increase loyalty
- Build trust
- Or resolve for issues such as stigma as a behavioral problem, related to adoption and usage for certain type of products

Design a stack that will address these needs. The KPIs should center on the customer need and the business challenge. Instead, most times we focus on delivering a personalized experience to an underdefined persona or adopting programmatic media buying capability because it seems more efficient. That needs to change.

Agile Is Your Savior

There is no such thing as a static road map. With an ever-changing landscape that diversifies faster than it converges, does anything like a road map exist anymore? How do you plan, prioritize, and budget for these technologies? The competitive ecosystem gets more fragmented each day, and smaller players are able to move faster as they have no historical baggage. So how do you compete and stay ahead of the curve? These are very real challenges that require a fundamental shift across a few aspects:

Marketing Technology Frameworks and the EMF

Within your overarching EMF you must establish an internal framework that allows you to map and prioritize the marketing technology landscape against your needs. A process to execute a current state assessment across different dimensions:

- Mapped against consumer journeys—the most efficient process

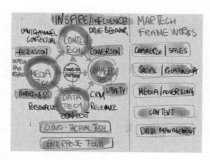

Figure 13.10 MarTech Framework

- Mapped against key technology categories and buckets—you could summarize the entire landscape within these categories; data, media, content and commerce
- Mapped against horizontal layers

Relying on a MarTech framework like the one in Figure 13.10, you identify the high-, medium-, and low-focus areas based on business priorities and consumer needs. No more "business or functional requirements"—move away from a technologist waiting for requirements, the traditional specifications and needs. The marketing technologist needs to think and operate like a product owner, a product evangelist who understands the only requirement—the most optimized, secure, and reliable customer experience.

Always-On Assessment, Evaluation, and Adoption

There cannot be an end date to your road map. You need to be always assessing and evaluating new capabilities, technologies, and partnerships. Dedicate a small percentage of your resources to scouting, industry analysis, thought leadership, and building external partnerships.

No Single Platform Winner aka "Marketing Operating System"

Many had hoped the big four—IBM, Adobe, Salesforce, and Oracle—would do to marketing what Apple and iPhone did to the smartphone industry; provide a marketing operating system (mOS) that could provide a development kit to marketers and technologists to build on. It would provide all the fundamental pieces including the universal view of the consumer, the necessary connection points across different components. The marketer could extend and build more creative applications on top of it. That did not happen. The landscape exploded at a faster rate than these players could build, acquire, and integrate. So how do you survive in all this fragmentation until there is a consolidation in the future?

Answer: make APIs and service-oriented architecture your best friend. Invest in and establish an API service layer in a loosely coupled architecture giving you extendibility and flexibility to plug in and plug out technologies as necessary. Believe in "data is the new oil," the only lynchpin that can wire your ecosystem, and tie the customer journey together with your customized MarTech stack. We recommend using a service layer such as Cloud-Elements.com to connect your entire app ecosystem.

Build, Buy, or Rent?

It's fascinating to see how many organizations still invest in building commoditized capabilities that are available outside at probably half the cost, while containing more advanced feature sets and that could be adopted and scaled at 10 times the speed. It's the traditional false notion of "control" and "ownership." Unless:

- it's something you will sell in the market at scale,
- it's your core competency and it represents who you are,
- it makes you unique and differentiated, or
- no one else can solve it for you

> "DO NOT build it; just rent it or buy it. The price for commodity capability in market is cheap. Your strategic headcount is priceless. Apply that in your core competency. You may not find the perfect match but by the time you build perfection on your own, the world would have changed another 10 times. In marketing today, the need for speed is much higher than the desire for perfection."
>
> —MAYUR GUPTA

Mobile Marketing Technology Stacks

VB Insight recently did some new research about mobile marketers about mobile marketing in general. Hundreds of respondents told us that more than half of their significantly sized budgets are going into mobile.

Where Are Marketers Spending Their Mobile Dollars?

43 percent are spending their budgets on user acquisition.

20 percent on branding and awareness

12 percent customer retention

5 percent customer advocacy

It is surprisingly bad that companies are pouring so much into acquisition when customer retention and advocacy are what drive the long-term value of your company. You want to build great long-term relationships with your customers. Keep them. Loyal customers are gold. And listen to this shocking stat: Sixty percent of the mobile marketers who responded to the VB Insights questionnaire shared that mobile was a complete silo as a channel strategy in their organization. "Many organizations miss mobile and lack mobile expertise in-house," Stewart Rogers said.[9]

During a recent VB Engage podcast, Roland Smart, VP of Social and Community at Oracle, said, "Marketers, in general, are overwhelmed by the sheer volume of marketing technologies that are coming into the market. A significant share of that relates to mobile. And because of that, there is not enough maturity within their organizations. Many people at the organization have no idea on how to maximize these mobile marketing technologies. Many marketers are still thinking solely about campaigns, which is incomplete and suboptimal."[10]

He was alluding to the fact that even a lot of marketers lack digital sense. Roland Smart is a smart man (pun not intended). He is a fellow Wiley author of the book *The Agile Marketer*. Get it, if you want to have your mind blown.

Drive Internal Buy-In and Stakeholder Influence by Measured ROI

Just like marketing and sales, marketing technology needs to be measurable and accountable to deliver the major business objectives within your EMF. Quantify the impact of your marketing technology investment. This is the proof point of tying marketing technologies to business objectives and consumer behavioral change. The only way you drive influence internally within the leadership is by measuring, analyzing, and continuously optimizing the ROI.

Within the S-Curve of innovation for marketing technology, we are only through the early stage of adoption. We have overcome reasonable technology obstacles and have seen early returns and efficiencies. The real application and exponential "business growth and progress" is yet to come, but well underway. In the coming years with a clear alignment around the customer as the number one asset and the EMF as a model to build on, we believe marketing technology leaders will continue to innovate and shape the future of marketing with their cross-departmental peers in unprecedented ways. We hope to learn and tell your stories of brilliance in future editions and podcasts.

Section V
Future-Proofing

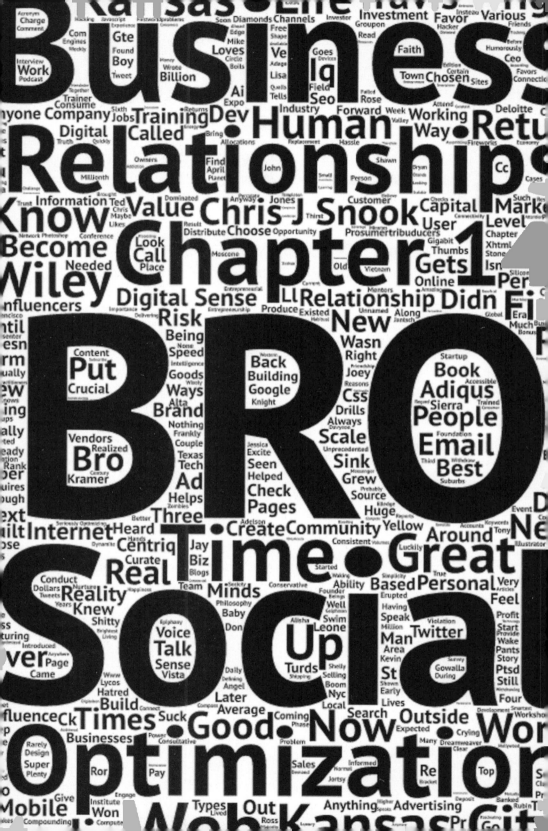

14 Building a Personal Brand, BRO

Like all great loves in your life, when you look at your career and your company as a relationship, it won't feel like work to put the effort in. If you have ever seen Travis speak or conduct a workshop, he drills his point home humorously with his philosophy of Business Relationship Optimization. You need to optimize the relationships in your life.

Business Relationship Optimization

You become who you hang around. Travis realized while working on a couple of startups that he didn't have enough connections and business relationships outside of Kansas City. In 2007, Travis was working on a startup called AdiQus. The inspiration for the company was to create Advertising Intelligence. Ad IQ, get it?

Quite frankly, most ads suck. Both of us have a deep hatred for shitty advertising and marketing but Travis and his partners at the time decided to do something about it.

What about ads that could be targeted on hundreds of various parameters and geo-based? AdiQus was to be a cross between Gowalla and Groupon, neither of which existed yet. Partners Gary Jones, Joey Knight, and Travis had built quite a team in Kansas City. Kansas City has been historically conservative with its capital allocations. The Kauffman Entrepreneurial Foundation in Kansas City wasn't as accessible to the community then, as it is now. When Kansas City was chosen as Google Fiber's first Gigabit City in 2012, the town erupted with entrepreneurship. Having superfast Internet connectivity has been great for the area.

In the 2007 version of Kansas City there were few investors, but through mentors, AdiQus was introduced to an unnamed angel capital firm in Texas. AdiQus was to get a check for $500,000 in four days, when the FBI came to the office.

What?????

1. The principal of the capital firm gets arrested by the FBI for a Financial Industry Regulatory Authority (FINRA) stock market violation.

2. AdiQus doesn't get the funding and

3. Travis had already trained his replacement at Centriq Training.

4. **Travis gets really f#%king drunk that night.**

5. Travis wakes up next day and hustles on to what's next.

6. Travis starts doing freelance web-dev and marketing.

7. ???

8. Profit!

Instead of crying about his First World problem, Travis got up, put on his big-boy pants, and found a way to not sink. Economy be damned. Travis was able to choose one conference to go to, and he chose the Web 2.0 Expo, an O'Reilly event April 2007, at Moscone Center in

San Francisco. Biz Stone was a presenter and that's when Travis first heard about Twitter. Also during the week, Travis got a ticket to attend the Digg 1 Millionth User Party with founder Kevin Rose and Jay Adelson.

Travis had an epiphany at the Digg 1 Million User Party. "It's all about who you know, what you know, and who knows that you know what you know."

Travis needed to know people who knew people, because he didn't know anyone outside of Kansas City.

Travis needed to optimize his business relationships. *Business Relationship Optimization. Boom goes the dynamite.* Building, growing, and nurturing relationships with influencers is genius. Social media helps you build the hell out of online relationships. Who knew? Well, once he did there was no going back.

Ass Kiss it Forward

As a standard rule of thumb, you need more and better relationships with experts, thought leaders, practitioners, and influencers in your chosen field. It's real life PR hacking for your personal brand. Who do you want to know? First, find ways to add value to them. Add lots and lots of value. Optimize the relationships. Engage with them on social media. Tweet or retweet them, comment on their blogs, maybe interview them for a pod-cast. Give them some publicity. Do favors for your customers, partners, vendors, friends, and so on. Ass kiss it forward; do a favor for them first. As Chris says, #GiveFirst, #GiveOften, #GiveTilItHurts, and then #GiveSomeMore.

Both us will rarely ask anyone for anything up front, but we'll provide all types of value. This is a great habit because when you actually do need a favor, you're withdrawing from a bank account that has plenty of good will already banked.

Relationships are like a bank account. You can deposit into it, or withdraw from it. If you overdraw on your account, you will probably lose that friendship. You need to optimize your business relationships, not just around social media, but in all mediums. Spend time with people, not just on e-mail or messenger, but on video call or human to human (H2H), in person at events.

It's one more reason that Zappos is such a great company. They kiss their customers' asses. They have hassle-free shipping and returns. The CEO, Tony Hsieh, wrote a book called *Delivering Happiness*. That's all about customer experience. Business in the twenty-first century requires that you nurture relationships with your customers, employees, partners, vendors, and industry influencers. It's crucial, bro. Seriously though, isn't BRO a great acronym?

After he started his post-apocalyptic rebuild in 2008, Travis began connecting with the top thought leaders in the marketing industry, following them on various social media sites. Twitter was huge as a tool and just gaining real traction so he rode that wave of attention. The ability to read what the smartest minds in Silicon Valley, NYC, and Hollywood had to say was fascinating.

In Kansas City, a great community of like minds were also assembling via social media. The community grew rapidly. Amazing entrepreneurs and marketing minds like John Jantsch, Shelly Kramer, Shawn Elledge, Davyeon Ross, Mike "Jortsy" Gelphman, Lisa Qualls, Alisha Templeton, and Jessica Best began to percolate in the city.

You've heard the adage, "You become who you hang around." Your circle of influence is crucial to defining your moral compass, and helps shape who you become. So, choose wisely. We both tell are kids that in life, you should flush the turds. Don't let the turds or—Zombies—bring you into the toilet with them.

Social media has helped connect the world with the best and the brightest. Web 2.0 and social media has brought the world together. You can communicate with almost anyone, almost anywhere, at almost any time of day. Over time and over 35,000 tweets later, Travis grew this huge network, optimized the relationships, and has grown and helped several businesses as a direct result of those relationships. As a matter of fact, to show the power of these platforms, this entire book was written using Google Docs and Facebook Messenger; Travis and

Chris never sat face to face in the same city once during the entire process. The final day before submitting this manuscript to Wiley, Chris was online for 15 straight hours editing and formatting away in the Google Doc while Travis was 37,000 feet in the air on a flight to Shanghai connected to the in-flight Wi-Fi. What an amazing time to be alive!

The Internet today is social. Proximity is now possible from anywhere in the world. It is because of this new reality that there are three types of ROI you must measure. They have an interrelated relationship over time to your personal and enterprise value.

- ROI=Return on Investment
- ROI=Return on Influence (aka, "ROR"=Return on Relationships fans of Ted Rubin)
- ROI=Risk of Inactivity

According to Deloitte, the average human being alive today (age 18–74) with a smartphone checks it an average of 46 times per day.[1] Those in the 18–24 age bracket check it an average of 74 times per day. Other reports have shown even higher volumes of more than 150 times a day, but the point is every 6 to 15 minutes of a normal waking day, human beings are interacting with their mobile devices.

This unprecedented and ever-compounding habitual thirst for engagement is the current state of the Internet. It is not a fad or a phase, but a new reality. An always-on demand level that is ubiquitously available to the majority of western society. By 2018, 3 billion more people that have lived on this planet outside of the commercial market will come online via the mobile web. In the new reality none of us are actually just employees or consumers.

ProSumerTribuDucers

With the power and processing speed in our hands and the addiction we all have to this digital sixth sense, we are now all what Chris likes to call

"ProSumerTribuDucers" living in an age of opportunity. Say that three times quickly. Every human now has the ability to produce, consume, distribute data, curate information, and create content, goods, and services, in real time with nothing more than a mobile web connection and their voice or thumbs.

 DIGITAL BIT: This would be a great time to subscribe to the Digital Sense e-mail: DigitalSen.se/email. The e-mail newsletter is where we produce, consume, and distribute data, curate information, and create content, goods, and services, in real time with nothing more than our mobile web connection and our voice or thumbs weekly! After all we are ProSumerTribuDucers just like you.

With an additional 3 billion people joining this new truth in the coming few years, we have an unprecedented challenge and opportunity to build or lose our relationships value at scale at the speed of trust.

H2H was an old-school yet unscalable way of doing business in the pre-Internet era. As we are firmly embedded in the third decade of a World Wide Web, it is now not only scalable but imperative for brands that wish to succeed. Bryan Kramer speaks about human-to-human at scale in his book, *There is no B2B or B2C: It's Human to Human #H2H.*

Where big data has failed, small data has become more relevant than ever. Personalization is an expected commodity because of machine learning, search, AI, cookies, pixel tracking, etc. This all boils back down to the fact that your business is a relationship before it is anything else. Like all relationships that last, there must be a consistent and mutually beneficial return on the investment of time, energy, and money put into the maintenance of that endeavor. It requires constant, consistent, and clear communication in good times and bad.

Return on investment is now completely dictated by how great you are at engagement at the right time with the right information to generate a return on influence. You have spent the bulk of this book learning how to apply these social business strategies to your business, but you must apply it to your personal brand of relationship building as well.

15 Avoiding Obsolescence and the Road Ahead

Congratulations on making it through the entire book and to the final chapter. By now you probably feel as though you just drank water at point blank range from a fire hose. We appreciate your participation more than you know. As you can tell we had a lot to say. But anyone who knows the two of us won't be surprised.

We thought the best way to wrap up this book was to finish up with a few thoughts on the future that highlight the amazing opportunity and ethical challenges we face as we all endeavor to elevate the digital sense of humanity.

Dead Ideas

Let's start with a chart in Figure 15.1 that shows the newest paradigm shifts of what Chris called "the Opportunity Age" in a blog post back in 2013. These are important shifts to noodle on as a business leader and marketer, as they will influence and shape your thinking around everything from where the gaps in your market will be in the years ahead and

R.I.P. 1989–2013	2013–circa 2020
Information Is Valuable	Information Is Noise
Marketing Gathers Data	Data Defines Marketing (Viva La Growth Hacker)
Marketing Adjacent to Content	Marketing IS Content
Wisdom from the Crowd	Wisdom from Trusted Curators
Monopolized Distribution	Democratized Distribution
Consumer Driven Economy	ProSumerDucerTributor Driven
Currency=Money	Currency=Attention/Trust—then Money
Advertising Builds Brand	Relevant Engagement/Content Builds Brand
ROI=Return on Investment	ROI=Return on Influence + Risk of Inactivity=Return on Investment
G7/G20 World	GZero World with Global Co-Dependence
Western Centric World	Southern Hemisphere Tilted (The O3B)

Figure 15.1   Chart from Chris J Snook's Blog R.I.P. Information Age . . . Welcome the Opportunity Age[1]

where your organization must mentally move on to broken "x" type ideas that no longer hold value or merit.

It's estimated by Forrester Research in their "Death of a B2B Salesman" report that 1 million B2B salespeople in the United States will be obsolete in the next four years. The report says that buyers in this market "overwhelmingly prefer" a DIY approach.[2] After all, they're one of the *B*s in that equation, and marketing automation is delivering increasingly personalized and relevant value without the annoyance of the dreaded salesperson follow-up voice mails and inbox notes with "just touching base" in the subject line.

With online research readily available, it's often not necessary to talk to a salesperson anymore. You can manage the entire sales process by yourself, at home, and never with the awkwardness of "dealing" with a human who is worried about the end of month number. It's said that websites, not people, are what's keeping the B2B sales process ticking now.

Experts Evolve into Sensemakers!

Okay, buyers might not need "salespeople," but they will always need experts in the form of sensemakers. Sensemakers are able to rapidly learn, assimilate, leverage their network, and customize a solution to the buyer's problem and architecture. The role of trusted advisor/sensemaker is your goal to avoiding obsolescence.

There's another study from SiriusDecisions in 2015 that argues against Forrester's research, stating that "Buyers interact with sales representatives at every stage of the buyer's journey."[3] It's a false perception that salespeople are "declining due to disintermediation by digital buying behaviors."

Instead, this research encourages the B2B community to remember human interaction can and will happen no matter what. Digital marketing doesn't equate to human interactions leaving entirely, according to Senior Research Director Jennifer Ross. She says, "It just means that buyers and providers are interacting in new digital ways. Just because buying behavior is done digitally does not mean that sales representatives are no longer required to instigate or facilitate a buying process."

The business world is moving forward faster and faster, and as a marketer or sales leaders you need to position yourself as the person who can help organizations make sense of it all and to keep pace.

Lifelong Learning as a Habit

Good leaders all have at least one thing in common: you need to develop the childlike curiosity of your youth again and see learning as a daily habit. The other area you must invest in developing more of is your emotional intelligence, because at least for the next several decades, it will be the only advantage and form of intelligence humans will have in exclusivity from the machines and deep learning protocols.

If you consider the idea that 70 percent of learning happens at work, 20 percent via mentoring, and 10 percent in classroom settings, the message is clear: we need to be learning more at work since it's prime time to do so. To try and appease this formula, we've embraced the concept of incremental learning at work. Basically, we get an idea, practice it (maybe with some feedback), and eventually "master" it. This kind of learning is easy, obvious, can be addictive, and is a culture worth cultivating in your office.

5G, IOT, AI, VR, and Drones, Oh My!

Are you feeling excited and ready? 5G is coming soon! Get ready to feel like that Colonial soldier we spoke of at the outset of this book. In many ways, the world will become more open, transparent, and amazing. It will also be filled with more examples of chaos, polarization, and violence as humanity adjusts and deals with the terror barrier en masse. Some will be well equipped emotionally and intellectually and many will not. Leadership will be needed at all levels across society. We all face an amazing opportunity to move beyond the cyclical norms of violence and war, and in other ways, if we aren't careful, it could become a bit dystopian. The extra effort we need to make now as you have upgraded your digital sense is truly "thinking" about what Humarithms said: we need to embed in our methodology as much as we have obsessed over our proprietary algorithms.[4] The ethics and moral center will be tested and are uniquely ours as humans to keep at the heart of all we design moving forward. Technology, like money, is a great tool, but can be a horribly dangerous God/master.

On the positive side of near-term technology upgrades, as 5G rolls out to everyone with 10Gbits/sec connections, information will flow to us faster than ever. We will be able to stream gigantic files at impeccable quality. Factor in virtual and augmented reality, and we'll be able to stream virtual worlds that are virtually indistinguishable from our true reality (no pun intended). Dominique Bonte, VP of ABI Research, recently produced a report on 5G that envisions three versions of 5G:

- Enhanced mobile broadband for higher-bandwidth mobile applications
- Low-bandwidth, high-latency connections designed for supporting hundreds of millions of devices on the Internet of Things
- Ultrareliable, low-latency connections, which is best for automotive applications

In October 2015, Huawei and NTT DOCOMO partnered to test 5G wireless data at a large scale, using sub-6GHz bands. Unlike previous lab experiments, the entire test was conducted in a public place. Huawei and NTT DOCOMO were able to reach data speeds of 3.6Gbps! The International Telecommunication Union recently standardized that 5G data speeds should reach up to 20Gbps speeds.[5] However, Nokia believes that 5G can be as fast as 30Gbps. This is like having Internet speeds of a faucet drip and moving to a firehose!

In late June 2016, U.S. FCC Chairman Tom Wheeler circulated a proposal to kick off 5G wireless for the United States. "If the Commission approves my proposal next month, the United States will be the first country in the world to open up high-band spectrum for 5G networks and applications," Wheeler stated in prepared remarks. "And that's damn important because it means U.S. companies will be first out of the gate."

Lightning-fast Internet. Everything connected to the cloud. Mixed reality headsets and 360 cameras becoming a commoditized norm. Connected autonomous cars driving in unison. Everything with a battery linking to 5G. Wow. This is your next decade in real time.

The Fourth Industrial Revolution

With all of these technologies rolling out, there will be a mass elimination of jobs performed by actual human beings. Gerd Leonhard has predicted that 50 percent of the jobs that exist in 2017 will be eliminated within 5 years, never to return, while 50 percent of the jobs needed in 5 years have not even been conceived of yet. Take restaurants for example: we are already seeing kiosks eliminating order takers. Manufacturing jobs, truck drivers, repetitive tasks from accounting to tax preparation and paralegal reviews will all be replaced by machine learning AI.

In fact, look to the survey date from the 2016 World Economic Forum in Davos, Switzerland. At this gathering of world political and economic leaders, the Fourth Industrial Revolution was a central topic.[6] The forum surveyed senior executives from over 350 of the world's largest companies and found that as many as 7.1 million jobs in the world's richest countries could be lost through technology advancements, redundancy, and automation. These losses could be partially offset by the creation of 2.1 million new opportunities in various sectors, but current estimates show that in the short term there will be a gap of 5 million jobs until we come through the other side of the curve and figure out the true need there.

There is a large chance that even the concept of money will need to be rethought or will face a forced disruption as 7 billion-plus people try to navigate continued survival in a world where crony capitalism and central banking theory has become completely inequitable and unsustainable as a faux free-market ideology that creates far too many losers and far too few winners. Innovation can be stifled but it is highly unlikely at this point, since we are officially in the knee bend of the technology curve, and the dark side of the Force has fewer and fewer places to hide as hackers for humanity begin to appear in deeper density around the globe.

Virtual Reality Mini-VRcations

It seems unlikely for many who have not seen how powerful VR simulations have become, but we could take minivacations in the middle of the afternoon, while our robots work! We call them "VRcations." You can put on your virtual reality headset, sit on a hammock in your office, put on your headphones, spray some coconut scent, turn on a fan, and relax for 15 minutes (okay, 30) or so before getting back to work.

Our actual reality may be a bit polluted with smog, and many humans may lack the financial health to take a real vacation, but in virtual reality we would be sitting in a lovely location somewhere in the world. With 4K and 8K video resolution streaming via 5G download speeds, we will be able to "teleport" to any destination on Earth at a moment's notice. As we perfect the scale of suborbital flights it will also be very likely that transcontinental air flight in the future will be reduced to hours or minutes versus half of your day. Once affordable you could hop in a Virgin Galactic ship in Los Angeles (or similar) and head straight up into suborbital space to allow the world to spin below you and then reinsert right back down in an hour or two to Dubai.

No need to worry about translation, either, because according to Baidu Research voice recognition will jump to 99 percent accuracy from 95 percent within the next few years, and that will mean that language translation and dialect interpretation will be as good as our normal language processing, making cross-cultural communication a breeze and replacing the need for typing forever. We can't wait and have agreed not to write another book until that is a reality LOL.

Virtual Reality Masterminds and Uploadable Consciousness

One area where we are particularly excited about the potential of VR and 5G is the prospect for a new type of mastermind meeting area. If you've ever seen Travis's business card, on the back of it he has a group of about 50 people who have inspired him throughout time. Ray Kurzweil has discussed the possibility of digital immortality within the coming two decades. There will come a day when each member in the mastermind group is fully integrated with artificial intelligence and we are all able to interact with each other and legends of the past (Figure 15.2). Their audio, writings, books, and videos from the past will detail their personalities. You could eventually have conversations with them—or at least their AI twins. Who do you wish you had the chance to meet? Soon you will be able to have virtual coffee with anyone in the history of humanity. Imagine what happens to disease when your medical doctor can download the totality of the world's best surgeons in that practice area from around the world before they operate on your loved one.

Do you remember the scene from *The Matrix* where Trinity downloads the knowledge of how to fly a helicopter in seconds? The singularity is predicted to occur somewhere around 2023. This will all become real in the next 6 or 7 years and it will all become widely affordable shortly thereafter.

Figure 15.2 Travis Wright's Personally Customized Virtual Mastermind

5G Allows Minimal Latency

Another thing that fascinates us is the prospect for vehicles in the future being interlocked in an autonomous grid. The minimal latency of 5G will allow fleets of cars to communicate with each other on a massive scale. With only a 1-millisecond latency, your car can adjust slightly and all of the cars nearby will be able to react in almost real time. This could potentially eliminate many car accidents. It also comes with a major opportunity to secure the gaps in security to prevent a large terror hack that can be executed from a remote location with catastrophic consequences. There are two sides to every coin but solving some of the more humanistic aspects of these scenarios first for the benefit of all humanity and not just for profit will also provide us an unprecedented shot at peace on a large scale.

"5G could also open up other commercial applications, including lifecycle management, enabling car manufacturers to update vehicle firmware wirelessly, in the not so distant future," said Dominique Bonte of ABI Research.

A "Hilton hotel car" with no driver will pick you up at the airport and take you to the hotel. As of the writing of this manuscript Uber had already launched its driverless pilot project in Pittsburgh, Pennsylvania. Your vacation or business trip will begin with minimal transportation stress.

The Dark Side of Drones

Drones will unfortunately begin to litter the sky. You may actually need to put on virtual reality goggles just to see a peaceful blue sky with scattered clouds if we aren't careful. Google has a top secret project called "Project Skybender," and it aims to deliver 5G Internet from solar drones; it is also experimenting with millimeter-wave radio transmissions.

One concern for many civilians is drones becoming so connected. Israeli startup Airobotics recently launched their autonomous industrial drones and announced $28.5 million in funding. It makes drones that fly, with very little human involvement, thanks to a series of breakthroughs in robotics, sensors, and navigation systems.

Why is this important? Well, these aren't consumer drones that are retro-fitted; these are fully redesigned autonomous drones that fly in squadrons. They can handle much larger payloads than consumer drones, allowing them to become weaponized. And if you think you could escape them by jumping into a body of water, well, enter the Hydroswarm: the drone that can swim in water. For some reason humans have always designed technology to create more efficient and better ways to eliminate our existence before we move to more productive uses. With nanobot technology becoming more prevalent as well, we could have swarms of mosquito-sized nanobots flying around on various military missions.

OpenAI is a nonprofit artificial intelligence (AI) research company, associated with business magnate Elon Musk, that aims to carefully promote and develop open-source friendly AI in such a way as to benefit, rather than harm, humanity as a whole. The organization aims to "freely collaborate" with other institutions and researchers by making its patents and research open to the public. The company is supported by over US$1 billion in commitments; however, only a tiny fraction of the $1 billion pledged is expected to be spent in the first few years. Many of the employees and board members are motivated by concerns about existential risk from artificial general intelligence.[7]

This is an area where we could take a wrong turn in the future. As marketers and business leaders, we are only sharing these potential dark futures so that you are not marketing or developing paths to profitability today that will have an unlikely chance of being benign in the future. One of the most important open source projects out there right now is OPENAI and we encourage you to follow the blog at OpenAI.org/blog.

We should always strive to use technology for the betterment of humanity, not for killing or controlling people. That would openly lead to our extinction as machines reach superintelligence in three decades.

5G Possibilities

5G wireless networks will connect 50 billion people and things by 2020. Only the next generation of networks optimized for 5G will able to meet the speed, latency, and energy efficiency required to deliver the Internet of Things (IoT) experiences of the future. "5G will give birth to the next phase of human possibilities, bringing about the automation of every-thing," said Marcus Weldon, chief technology officer at Nokia. "This automation, driven by a smart, invisible network, will create new busi-nesses, give rise to new services and, ultimately, free up more time for people."[8]

The future is set up to be one helluva ride for all of us. There are some dangerous roads that civilization could go down, but personally, we are hopeful that digital sense will continue to spread as you solve the short term needs of your business sustainability and focus on putting the human touch back into every interaction and decision point using the EMF.

You may look around and feel as though we are living a real world version of that movie *Idiocracy,* but we see much more progress in the opposite direction. Youth have always held humanity's future promise. The next 9 to 10 years will be filled with evidence that can be interpreted as the end of the world, but if you read *The Fourth Turning* by Neil Howe and William Strauss and *The Watchman's Rattle* by Rebecca Costa, you will be gifted with more knowledge on what dynamics are at play as humans navigate our evolutionary biology within times of quantum technology.

We have enjoyed giving you a thorough and practical model for upgrading your human software layer with more digital sense, and thank you for joining us on the journey to bring more light to humanity and commerce with each action we take as a collective from this day forward.

The End (and The Beginning)

NOTES

Preface

1. Travis Wright's tweet to the Chiefs, "The Tweet Hear 'Round the World," https://twitter.com/teedubya/status/245324813265145857.

2. Jay Baer, *Hug Your Haters* (Penguin Publishing Group, 2016), www.jaybaer.com/hug-haters.

3. Joel Thorman, "Chiefs Have Plenty of Salary Cap Space Entering 2012 Season," *SB Nation*, September 4, 2012, http://www.arrowheadpride.com/2012/9/4/3290986/chiefs-salary-cap-space.

4. Jason La Canfora, "Updated Cap Space for All 32 Teams," *NFL.com*, August 16, 2011, http://blogs.nfl.com/2011/08/16/updated-cap-space-for-all-32-teams.

5. Sam Laird, "Dissed Fan Teaches NFL Team a Social Media Lesson on Twitter," *Mashable*, September 12, 2012, http://mashable.com/2012/09/12/nfl-fan-chiefs.

6. Save Our Chiefs Facebook Fan Page, https://www.facebook.com/SaveOurChiefs/Chiefs.

7. Joel Thorman, "Kansas City Chiefs Break Guinness World Record against Patriots with 142.2 Decibels: A New Record for Arrowhead Stadium and Chiefs Fans." *SB Nation*, September 29, 2014, http://www.arrowheadpride.com/2014/9/29/6870283/kansas-city-chiefs-guinness-world-record-crowd-noise-decibels-patriots-mnf.

8. Travis Wright, "Data Strategy Symposium," *Ashton Media*, YouTube video, 59:24, from Data Strategy Symposium, February 9, 2015, https://www.youtube.com/watch?v=xosapBvUeQ4.

9. Optus Twitter page and Travis Wright's Twitter feed, accessed May 14 2015, https://twitter.com/search?q=%40teedubya%20%40optus&src=typd.

10. Klaus Schwab, "The Fourth Industrial Revolution: What It Means, How to Respond," *World Economic Forum*, January 14, 2016, www.weforum.org/agenda/2016/01/the-fourth-industrial-revolution-what-it-means-and-how-to-respond.

Chapter One

1. Greg Ferenstein, "Futuristic Simulation Finds Self-Driving 'Taxibots' Will Eliminate 90% of Cars, Open Acres of Public Space," *Medium.com*, April 24, 2015,

https://medium.com/the-ferenstein-wire/futuristic-simulation-finds-self-driving-taxibots-will-eliminate-90-of-cars-open-acres-of-618a8aeff01#.oma4n6sbf.

Chapter Two

1. Customer Experience Professionals Association, www.cxpa.org.

2. Lizette Borreli, "Human Attention Span Shortens to 8 Seconds Due to Digital Technology: Three Ways to Stay Focused," *Medical Daily*, May 14, 2015, www.medicaldaily.com/human-attention-span-shortens-8-seconds-due-digital-technology-3-ways-stay-focused-333474.

Chapter Three

1. "16 Famous Songs Written in 30 Minutes or Less," *Tone Deaf*, June 26, 2015, http://www.tonedeaf.com.au/346979/16-famous-songs-written-in-30-minutes-or-less.htm.

2. Jeanne Bliss, *Chief Customer Officer 2.0* (Hoboken, NJ: John Wiley & Sons, 2015).

Chapter Four

1. Fletch, "It's All Ball-Bearings," *Ditto Greetings*, December 2, 2014, https://www.youtube.com/watch?v=pbWWxGmbS9s.

2. "Driving Marketing Performance with Multi-Channel Content, Communications and Analytics," *CEB*, accessed October 4, 2016, https://www.cebglobal.com/marketing-communications/digital-evolution.html.

3. The Economist Intelligence Unit, "The Future of Marketing: Six Visionaries Speak," *Marketo*, accessed October 26, 2016, https://www.marketo.com/articles/the-future-of-marketing-six-visionaries-speak.

4. "Screenshot," accessed July 31, 2016, www.aa.com/newamerican.

5. Brian Solis, *X: The Experience Where Business Meets Design* (Hoboken, NJ: John Wiley & Sons, 2015).

6. Gartner Research Methodologies, "Gartner Magic Quadrant," accessed October 26, 2016, http://www.gartner.com/technology/research/methodologies/research_mq.jsp.

7. G. Kofi Annan, "Reaching 50 Million Users," accessed October 4, 2016, www.gkofiannan.com.

8. "50 Million Users: The Making of an 'Angry Birds' Internet Meme," *Real Time Economics* (blog), *The Wall Street Journal*, March 20, 2015, http://blogs.wsj.com/economics/2015/03/20/50-million-users-the-making-of-an-angry-birds-internet-meme.

9. Geoff Fripp, "Limitations of the BCG Matrix, accessed October 4, 2016, http://www.thebcgmatrix.com/bcg-matrix-theory/limitations-of-the-bcg-matrix.

10. Marc Andreessen, "Why Software Is Eating the World," *The Wall Street Journal*, August 20, 2011, http://www.wsj.com/articles/SB10001424053111903480904 576512250915629460.

11. "24 Things Made Obsolete by Smartphones," *ET Bureau*, April 21, 2015, http://telecom.economictimes.indiatimes.com/news/internet/24-things-made-obsolete-by-smartphones/46995729.

Chapter Five

1. "Elon Musk, Full Interview, Code Conference 2016," YouTube video, 1:24:14, June 2 2016, 1:24:14, https://youtu.be/wsixsRI-Sz4.

2. Dogs of the Dow, "Largest Companies by Market Cap Today" accessed October 4, 2016, http://dogsofthedow.com/largest-companies-by-market-cap.htm.

3. Chris J. Snook, *The 7 Universal Laws*, www.digitalsen.se/the7laws.

4. Maxwell Maltz, *Psycho-Cybernetics* (New York, Simon & Schuster, 1989).

5. Joseph Murphy, *The Power of Your Subconscious Mind* (Courier Corporation, 2012).

6. "Bell Telephone v Western Union (1879)," *The Guardian*, August 6, 2007, accessed October 4, 2016, https://www.theguardian.com/technology/2007/aug/06/bellvwestern.

7. David A. Vise, *The Google Story* (Dell Publishing, 2005).

8. Napoleon Hill, *Think and Grow Rich* (BN Publishing, 2007).

9. Malcolm Gladwell, *The Tipping Point* (Back Bay Books, 2002); Malcolm Gladwell, *Outliers* (Back Bay Books, 2011); Malcolm Gladwell, *Blink: The Power of Thinking without Thinking* (Back Bay Books, 2007).

10. Russell Conwell and John Wanamaker, *Acres of Diamonds* (Tremendous Life Books, 2004).

11. Charles F Haanel, *The Master Key System* (SoHo Books, 2013).

12. Maltz, *Psycho-Cybernetics*.

Chapter Six

1. "Business," *Wikipedia*, accessed October 4, 2016, https://en.wikipedia.org/wiki/Business.

2. Dan Poynter, "Book Publishing Statistics," http://www.textetc.com/resources/book-publishing-statistics.html.

3. Mike Negami, "Lean Six Sigma Has to Start from Voice of Customer: VOC," June 17, 2016, www.linkedin.com/pulse/lean-six-sigma-has-start-from-voice-customer-voc-excel-mike-negami.

4. Brian Solis, *X: The Experience Where Business Meets Design* (Hoboken, NJ: John Wiley & Sons, 2015).

5. Saga Briggs, "45 Design Thinking Resources for Educators," July 29, 2016, http://www.opencolleges.edu.au/informed/features/45-design-thinking-resources-for-educators.

Chapter Seven

1. "The Digital Continuum: The Digital Organization in Its Ideal State," www.digitalcontinuum.com.

2. "The Social Business Strategy Map by Leader Networks," http://www.leadernetworks.com/resources.

3. "Market Drivers: Why 'the Economy' Is Better Than You Think," http://rollyson.net/social-business-strategy-use-cases.

4. Brian Solis, "The Race against Digital Darwinism: Six Stages of Digital Transformation," *Principal Analyst*, last accessed on October 4, 2016, http://www2.prophet.com/sixstagesofdigitaltransformation.

5. Charlene Li and Brian Solis, "The 7 Success Factors of Social Business Strategy," Altimeter Group, April 5, 2015, https://www.flickr.com/photos/briansolis/17044011632/sizes/l.

6. Jeremy Hudgens, "Programmatic Marketing Slideshare," Genius Monkey, 46 slides, February 2015, www.digitalsen.se/geniusmonkey.

7. Joe Pulizzi and Ann Handley, "B2B Content Marketing: 2016 Benchmarks, Budgets, and Trends—North America," *The Content Marketing Institute (CMI)*, accessed October 4, 2016, http://contentmarketinginstitute.com/wp-content/uploads/2015/09/2016_B2B_Report_Final.pdf.

8. Anna Hrach's ROT Content Worksheet template at Ethology, www.etho.me/rot.

9. Dean Montandon, "Don't Get Social Media? Here's Each Network Explained with Beer," June 2015, https://blog.red-website-design.co.uk/2015/06/19/dont-get-social-media-heres-each-network-explained-with-beer.

10. Gary Vaynerchuk, *Jab, Jab, Jab, Right Hook* (New York: HarperBusiness, 2013).

11. Sujan Patel and Rob Wormley, *Content Marketing Playbook* (ebook), 2015, accessed October 4, 2016, http://sujanpatel.com/content-marketing-ebook.

12. Azmat Batool, "How and Why You Should Conduct a Brand Audit," *Kissmetrics*, December 13, 2013, https://blog.kissmetrics.com/conducting-a-brand-audit.

Chapter Eight

1. Symantec Wikipedia page, accessed October 4, 2016, https://en.wikipedia.org/wiki/Symantec#cite_note-15.

2. Symantec Wikipedia page, accessed October 4, 2016, https://en.wikipedia.org/wiki/Symantec#cite_note-16.

3. Quicksprout, "Advanced Content Marketing Guide," accessed October 4, 2016, www.quicksprout.com/the-advanced-guide-to-content-marketing.

4. Grace Caffyn, "How KFC Gets the Media to Do Their Marketing for Them," August 23, 2016, http://digiday.com/brands/kfc-gets-media-marketing.

5. Audrey Bruno, "Dairy Queen Has Something Special for Singles This Valentine's Day," *Delish*, February 10, 2016, http://www.delish.com/food-news/a45719/dairy-queen-valentines-day-specials.

6. Travis Wright, "8 Top Tech Conferences You Can't Miss This Fall," *Inc.* magazine, August 16, 2016, http://www.inc.com/travis-wright/8-can-t-miss-tech-conferences-remaining-in-2016.html.

7. Chris J. Snook, "15 Lessons for Success from the Organizers of Fort Collins Startup Week," *LinkedIn SlideShare*, May 29, 2014, http://www.slideshare.net/chrisjsnook/15-lessons-for-successfrom-the-organizers-of-fort-collins-startup-week-fcsw14.

8. Chris J. Snook and Brianne Snook, "The Definitive Guide to Fort Collins Startup Scene," *LinkedIn SlideShare*, September 23, 2013, http://www.slideshare.net/chrisjsnook/pdf-definitiveguidetofortcollinsstartupscene.

9. Chris J. Snook and Brianne Snook, "The Definitive Guide to Fort Collins Startup Scene," *LinkedIn SlideShare*, September 23, 2013, http://www.slideshare.net/BrianneSnook/the-definitive-guide-to-the-fort-collins-startup-scene?qid=ea410b2d-0ca4–459d-8a7a-d22efca7ffc3&v=&b=&from_search=1.

10. Eric Schurenberg, "How They Do It in Flyover Country," *Inc.* magazine, July/August 2015, http://www.inc.com/magazine/201507/eric-schurenberg/how-they-do-it-in-flyover-country.html.

11. Eric Enge, Stephan Spencer, and Jessie Stricchiola, *The Art of SEO* (O'Reilly Media, 2015).

12. MarketingLand, *Enterprise Paid Media Campaign Management Platforms: A Marketer's Guide, Sixth Edition*, 2016, accessed October 4, 2016, http://downloads.digitalmarketingdepot.com/MIR_1602_PaidMediaR_landingpagebuersguide.html.

13. "Welcome to El Toro, the Only One-to-One 100% Cookie Free IP Targeting Solution," accessed October 26, 2016, http://Eltoro.com.

Chapter Nine

1. Aberdeen Group, "Social Selling: Leveraging the Power of User-Generated Content to Optimize Sales Results," February 2013, accessed October 4, 2016, https://business.linkedin.com/content/dam/business/sales-solutions/global/en_US/site/pdf/ti/linkedin_social_selling_impact_aberdeen_report_us_en_130702.pdf.

2. Julio Viskovich home page, accessed October 26, 2016, http://www.julioviskovich.com.

3. Megan Heur, "Account-Based Marketing: Welcome to the New Reality," *LinkedIn SlideShare*, April 30, 2015, http://www.slideshare.net/Demandbase/siriusdecisions-account-based-marketing-welcome-to-the-new-reality-inb2b.

4. Engagio, "The Clear and Complete Guide to Account Based Marketing," accessed October 4, 2016, www.Engagio.com/guide.

Chapter Ten

1. Mike Shields, "The Danger of Automating Social Influencer Marketing," *The Wall Street Journal*, June 16, 2016, http://www.wsj.com/articles/the-danger-of-automating-social-influencer-marketing-1466071200.

2. Mia Dand quote via in-person interview by Travis Wright, June 9, 2016, http://digitalsen.se/influencermktg.

3. Mia Dand, "Everything You Need to Know about the Influencer Tech Market," *Lighthouse3.com*, accessed October 4, 2016, https://lighthouse3.com/influencertech.

4. Mary Meeker, "Internet Trends 2016–Code Conference," KPCB, June 1, 2016, slide 47, http://www.kpcb.com/blog/2016-internet-trends-report.

5. "Digital AD Spend to Reach $103B by 2019," *Forrester Research*, press release, November 4, 2014, https://www.forrester.com/digital+ad+spend+to+reach+103b+by+2019/-/e-pre7448.

6. "Global Trust in Advertising: Winning Strategies for an Evolving Media Landscape," *Nielsen*, September 2015, https://www.nielsen.com/content/dam/nielsenglobal/apac/docs/reports/2015/nielsen-global-trust-in-advertising-report-september-2015.pdf.

7. Scott Brinker, "Marketing Technology Landscape Supergraphic (2016)," accessed October 4, 2016, http://chiefmartec.com/2016/03/marketing-technology-landscape-supergraphic-2016.

8. Rich Vancil, Kathleen Schaub, and Gerry Murray, "IDC's Worldwide Marketing Technology 2014–2018 Forecast: $20 Billion and Growing Fast," October 17, 2014, http://techmarketingblog.blogspot.com/2014/10/idcs-worldwide-marketing-technology.html.

9. Brian Solis and Altimeter Group, "Free Industry Report: The Influencer Marketing Manifesto," accessed October 4, 2016, http://pages.tapinfluence.com/altimeter-report-influencer-marketing-manifesto.

10. Anthony Ha, "The New York Times Acquires Influencer Marketing Agency HelloSociety," *TechCrunch*, March 11, 2016, https://techcrunch.com/2016/03/11/new-york-times-acquires-hellosociety.

11. "The FTC's Endorsement Guides: What People Are Asking: Influencer marketing FAQs update," *Federal Trade Commission*, accessed October 4, 2016, https://www.ftc.gov/tips-advice/business-center/guidance/ftcs-endorsement-guides-what-people-are-asking.

12. Jeff John Roberts, "This Hollywood Studio Got Busted for Social Media Marketing," *Fortune*, July 11, 2016, http://fortune.com/2016/07/11/warner-bros-social-media.

13. Deloitte, "The Millennial Survey 2014: Big Demands and High Expectations," accessed October 4, 2016, http://www2.deloitte.com/al/en/pages/about-deloitte/articles/2014-millennial-survey-positive-impact.html.

14. Edelman, "Credibility from Within: Harnessing Trust in Employees to Strengthen Business's License to Lead," *LinkedIn SlideShare*, January 2014, http://www.edelman.com/insights/intellectual-property/2014-edelman-trust-barometer/trust-in-business/trust-employee-engagement.

15. Aberdeen Group, "Crossing the Chaos: Managing Content Marketing Transformation," *LinkedIn SlideShare*, August 2013, https://www.slideshare.net/secret/kFdU767zyWS30G.

16. Kathryn Rose and Ted Rubin, *Return on Relationship* (New York: Tate, 2013).

Chapter Eleven

1. *The Jobvite Recruiter Nation Survey 2015,* Jobvite, January 2015, https://www.jobvite.com/wp-content/uploads/2015/09/jobvite_recruiter_nation_2015.pdf.

2. Social Talent home page, www.socialtalent.co.

3. Matt Charney, *Structured Hiring: The Advantage of the New People Team* (RecruitingDaily, 2015), http://recruitingdaily.com/structured-hiring.

4. The Hire Carlos Facebook Fanpage, accessed October 4, 2016, www.fb.com/hirecarlos.

5. LinkedIn, JobsDirectUSA Linkedin Group Admin Carlos Gil, https://www.linkedin.com/groups/1880575.

6. Case Study, www.digitalsen.se/hirecarlos.

7. Mercer Candidate Care™, http://mercercandidatecare.com.

Chapter Twelve

1. Oracle, *2011 Customer Experience Impact Report*, 2012, http://www.oracle.com/us/products/applications/cust-exp-impact-report-epss-1560493.pdf.

2. "Triage (disambiguation)," *Wikipedia*, last modified October 13, 2016, https://en.wikipedia.org/wiki/Triage_(disambiguation).

3. Chris Barry, Rob Markey, Eric Almquist, and Chris Brahm, "Putting Social Media to Work," *Bain Brief*, Bain & Company, September 12, 2011, http://www.bain.com/publications/articles/putting-social-media-to-work.aspx.

4. Jasmine Jaume, "How We Use Social: Highlights from the Social Media Report 2012," *Brandwatch Blog*, December 19, 2012, http://www.brandwatch.com/2012/12/how-we-use-social-highlights-from-the-social-media-report-2012.

5. Gartner, "Gartner Predicts That Refusing to Communicate by Social Media Will Be as Harmful to Companies as Ignoring Phone Calls or Emails Is Today," press release, August 1, 2012, http://www.gartner.com/newsroom/id/2101515.

6. Tristan Bishop, "Loyalty and Social CRM," Symantec, *LinkedIn SlideShare*, February 5, 2012, www
.slideshare.net/KnowledgeBishop/nps-13-loyaltyandsocialcrmatsymantec.

7. "Center of Excellence," *Wikipedia*, last modified October 26, 2016, https://en
.wikipedia.org/wiki/Center_of_excellence.

8. Oracle, "White Paper: The Socially Driven Collaboration in Enterprise," 2013, https://go.oracle.com/LP=2970?elqCampaignId=6074.

Chapter Thirteen

1. Scott Brinker, "Martech and the Marketing Technology Landscape," Marketing-Land, September 21, 2016, http://MarketingLand.com/library/martech-news.

2. Bill Peatman, "What Is a Marketing Technology Stack and Why Should You Care?" *Ensighten*, April 29, 2014, www.ensighten.com/blog/what-marketing-technology-stack-and-why-should-you-care.

3. Paul Roetzer, "The Missing Piece of Marketing Automation That Could Change Everything," March 4, 2015, http://martechtoday.com/missing-piece-marketing-automation-change-everything-120143.

4. MarketingLand, "What Is Tag Management," May 11, 2016, http://Marketing Land.com/library/analytics-news/tag-management.

5. MarketingLand, "Infographic: The 2016 Marketing Technology Landscape," March 21, 2016, http://MarketingLand.com/infographic-marketing-technology-landscape-113956.

6. "Oracle and Maxymiser," Oracle Acquisitions feed, August 20, 2015, https://www
.oracle.com/corporate/acquisitions/maxymiser/index.html.

7. Travis Wright and Chris J. Snook, *The Marketing Technology Glossary* (ebook), www
.digitalsen.se/martechglossary.

8. Scott Brinker, "Marketing Technology? Digital? It Should Be #HumanFirst," *Chiefmartec.com*, September 15, 2015, http://chiefmartec.com/2015/09/marketing-technology-digital-humanfirst.

9. Stewart Rogers, "Mobile Marketing: What's Wrong, What's at Stake, and How to Build a Strategy for Success," *VentureBeat*, May 19, 2016, http://insight
.venturebeat.com/report/mobile-marketing-whats-wrong-whats-stake-and-how-build-strategy-success.

10. Roland Smart, *The Agile Marketer* (Hoboken, NJ: John Wiley & Sons, 2016).

Chapter Fourteen

1. Deloitte, *2015 Global Mobile Consumer Survey: US Edition*, 2015, https://www2
.deloitte.com/content/dam/Deloitte/us/Documents/technology-media-telecommunications/us-tmt-global-mobile-executive-summary-2015.pdf.

Chapter Fifteen

1. Chris J. Snook's Blog Post, February 12, 2016, http://www.chrisjsnook.com/my-rants/2015/2/12/rip-information-age-1989-2013welcome-the-opportunity-age.

2. Andy Hoar et al., "Death of a (B2B) Salesman: One Million US B2B Salespeople Will Lose Their Jobs to Self-Service eCommerce by 2020," *Forrester Research*, April 13, 2015, https://www.forrester.com/report/Death+Of+A+B2B+Salesman/-/E-RES122288.

3. Ibid.

4. Gerd Leonhard, "Algorithms and Humarithms: Futurist Speaker Gerd Leonhard Digital Transformation (Short)" YouTube video 1:13, excerpt from his speech at the KPMG 2015 Executive Symposium on Robotics and Automation, September 16, 2015, https://www.youtube.com/watch?v=kbsfc1MvOS0.

5. Dominique Bonte, VP of ABI Research, recently produced a report on 5G that envisions three versions of 5G.

6. Klaus Schwab, "The Fourth Industrial Revolution: What It Means, How to Respond," *World Economic Forum*, January 14, 2016, www.weforum.org/agenda/2016/01/the-fourth-industrial-revolution-what-it-means-and-how-to-respond.

7. "Open AI," *Wikipedia*, October 25, 2016, https://en.wikipedia.org/wiki/OpenAI.

8. Marcus Weldon, chief technology officer at Nokia.

ABOUT THE AUTHORS

Travis Wright is a marketing technologist, digital marketing strategist and consultant, keynote speaker, entrepreneur, data and analytics geek, tech journalist, startup growth hacker, podcast host, and standup comic. He is the former global digital and social strategist at Symantec for the Norton brand. Over the past 20 years, Wright has helped hundreds of B2B and B2C companies, from well-funded startups and SMBs to Fortune 10.

Travis has given more than 100 keynote presentations, webinars, and workshops since 2012, in the United States and internationally. Wright works globally with company executives and company influencers on digital media ad spend, social business strategies for marketing, sales, and HR, as well as marketing technology consulting. When Travis isn't working, he is thinking about working, traveling, or taking one of his two kids, Jharek and Liliana, to some school event.

Chris J. Snook is an award-winning entrepreneur, venture catalyst, and the executive brand humanizer at large Ethology heading up corporate development for his agency. He is also cofounder at Launch Haus whose purpose is "to solve problems in sustainable ways for the betterment of all humanity through entrepreneurship and technology."

He has been decaffeinated since March 2016 but still runs Mach 5 with his hair on fire. Chris racks up A-List preferred status on Southwest Airlines speaking at dozens of events each year and produces and curates the invite-only loopthinkCXO (for marketers, CX, and technology leaders) and Offshorepreneur (for digital nomads) events in Phoenix, Arizona and Grand Cayman.

Outside of working voraciously on any projects that involve future technologies, content strategy, digital marketing, customer-centric organizational design, venture capital finance, M&A, IoT, and publishing, his hobbies are mentoring startups and teaching entrepreneurship around the world. He is an active mentor supporting HacksForHumanity at ASU and Founder Institute, traveling with his two favorite people (Brianne and Beckett), and being an avid foodie.

On Sundays in the fall he indulges in his only true pop culture vice for three hours as a die-hard Dallas Cowboys fan.

INDEX

Note: Page references in *italics* refer to figures.